FIXING HELL

FIXING HELL

AN ARMY PSYCHOLOGIST CONFRONTS ABU GHRAIB

Col. (ret.) Larry C. James, Ph.D.
with Gregory A. Freeman

Foreword by Dr. Philip Zimbardo

GRAND CENTRAL
PUBLISHING

NEW YORK   BOSTON

Grand Central Publishing
Hachette Book Group USA
237 Park Avenue
New York, NY 10017

Visit our Web site at www.HachetteBookGroupUSA.com.

Printed in the United States of America

First Edition: September 2008
10 9 8 7 6 5 4 3 2 1

Grand Central Publishing is a division of Hachette Book Group USA, Inc.
The Grand Central Publishing name and logo is a trademark of Hachette
Book Group USA, Inc.

Library of Congress Control Number: 2008927428
ISBN-10: 0-446-50928-0
ISBN-13: 978-0-446-50928-2

Book design by SD Designs

This book is dedicated to the soldiers we've lost in the global war on terrorism.

Note to the reader: Due to the sensitivities of the subject matter of this book, I have changed the names and identifying characteristics of some of the people in this story, including that of my wife and some of the military individuals involved. I have also altered names, locations, and military unit numbers to provide confidentiality to service members while telling this story. However, the names of several military personnel, including Colonel Morgan Banks and General Geoffrey Miller, have not been changed, as the public is already aware of their roles in the events that follow.

Contents

Foreword

I was asked to write the foreword to this remarkable book for two reasons: first, Colonel Larry C. James is a respected colleague and personal friend; and second, we have both witnessed how deeply the human mind can descend into depravity.

In 1971, I served as a superintendent of a prison with situations remarkably similar to those witnessed in the prison at Abu Ghraib in Iraq: guards repeatedly stripping prisoners naked, bagging their heads, verbally abusing them, and finally, sexually degrading them. Only my prison was a relatively benign simulation in which guards and prisoners were all normal, healthy college students randomly assigned the roles of guards and prisoners. The Stanford Prison Experiment was projected to last two weeks but had to be terminated after only six days because it was running out of control. My efforts to identify the factors that can lead to prison abuse worked all too well, as my subjects and I all succumbed to circumstances that encouraged degeneracy. The experiment has been studied extensively ever since, considered a key to understanding how circumstances can drive normal people to acts of evil.

The parallels between these two prison settings so removed

in time, place, and culture were highlighted in one of the Abu Ghraib investigations by a committee headed by James Schlesinger, former secretary of defense. It concluded that the "Landmark Stanford study provides a cautionary tale for all military detention operations." But it was not heeded, and the abuses at Abu Ghraib followed. The parallels have not been adequately explored until now; Larry James reframes the essential comparative question: "How did Zimbardo fuck it up?"

Answering that question helped my friend understand what went wrong in Abu Ghraib and that, in turn, helps us understand the bigger question about this war. In reflecting on what went wrong in America's war against Iraq, *Newsweek* magazine's Baghdad bureau chief highlighted one event. "What went wrong? A lot, but the biggest turning point was the Abu Ghraib scandal. Since April 2004, the liberation of Iraq has become a desperate exercise in damage control. The abuse of prisoners at Abu Ghraib alienated a broad swath of the Iraqi public. On top of that it didn't work. There is no evidence that all the mistreatment and humiliation saved a single American life or led to the capture of any major terrorist, despite claims by the military that the prison produced 'actionable intelligence.'"

The damning photos of American soldiers, men and women of the Military Police, seemingly enjoying their creatively sadistic abuse and torture of Iraqi prisoners, mark a low point in our history as a nation, as well as an enduring shame for the military command and the Bush administration. Where were the safeguards against such cruelty that we expect from following the guidelines of the Geneva Conventions? How could it happen, particularly as enacted by supposed protectorates of the Leader of the Free World? Who is responsible for such outrageous behavior? Was it an isolated incident? Imagine our outrage at the reverse scenario, if Americans were depicted at the bottom of a pyramid of naked prisoners! Such vital moral, psychological, and political issues are why we all must care about the reasons for the digitally documented depravity that erupted in that strange prison in 2003.

While it is convenient to discharge our moral outrage by blaming it all on the random, impulsive actions of a few "rogue soldiers"—a few "bad apples," as the military rushed to assert—it is not sufficient to merely acknowledge the Abu Ghraib abuses as yet another thing that somehow went wrong, as we do with media-exposed scandals in the nation's police stations or of politicians. In this insightful book, Colonel James shows us how he came to terms with the complex questions of how American soldiers could commit such vile acts, and he shows us that there is not one simple answer. We all need to go on this quest for the deeper understanding of the whys and hows of such inhumane human behavior. If these were merely a few "bad apples," then the solution would be simple: identify, prosecute, court martial, and imprison the culprits; voilà, problem is solved. However, suppose that these Army Reserve MPs were "good apples" when they were assigned to play their role as prison guards. Then something bad happened to them at that time, in that place, causing major character transformations. But what could make people who set out with noble intentions commit such depraved actions? What could make good people turn so evil so quickly? We want answers not only to satisfy our intellectual curiosity, but also to find out how to change such "bad barrels" so they do not continue to corrupt good people. Punishing the evil doers—when situational and system forces are responsible for creating and maintaining those bad barrels—is like the Inquisition's witch hunts as a cure for evil during the Middle Ages. Instead, we need to seek a public health model to discover the vectors of disease that induced suffering and moral affliction, so that it can be prevented in the future. Colonel James's work provides a major step forward in this effort.

But why should we follow the path that our guide, Colonel James, has laid out for us? Why should we follow along on his quest to understand how such outrageous behavior could erupt in a military compound? Because he is in a unique position to guide us. Larry James is a colonel in the Army, with a long and distinguished career as an officer, but more importantly to me, as an innovative researcher and dedicated practicing psychologist. He not only understands individual mental problems that can be treated with psychotherapy and medication, but also social-situational problems that call for different kinds of intervention in modifying behavioral contexts. I have known Colonel James for many years as a colleague, meeting regularly at our profession's conventions, reading his research, and corresponding with him about various issues, and I know that as one of the Army's most seasoned psychologists and behavioral scientists, Colonel James has a particular appreciation of how external forces acting on individuals within groups can shape their behavior. Colonel James was the man we sent to fix hell, and we can learn from his experience.

As I read through his amazing book, I was fascinated by the depth of his personal involvement not only with understanding the causes and forces responsible for the Abu Ghraib abuses, but equally with his earlier efforts to change for the better the conditions of prisoner interrogation at the military's Guantanamo Bay,

"Gitmo," facility. It was distressing to discover the psychic toll that these personal ventures into hellholes of human experience had on him. Within these pages, his PTSD symptoms are vividly depicted—without any macho minimizing of their impact on his sense of personal identity nor on his loving family. In reading his account, I couldn't help but try to put myself in his shoes; after all, I too was close to experiencing these events up close. Larry had invited me to join him on his trip to Baghdad to establish new procedures designed to prevent any reoccurrence of such assaults on human dignity by U.S. soldiers in charge of inmates. Unlike Colonel James, I had a choice in the matter, and family pressures against going to such a dangerous war zone without adequate preparation made me decline. I still wish I had been there to learn firsthand about the conditions in that place, and I imagine my close social support might have lightened his mental toll. Not only did Colonel James put into place a set of explicit operational procedures that are a model for all correctional facilities, but before leaving the facility he insured that staff learned and practiced them faithfully. For that special service to his nation, Larry James was awarded the Bronze Star Medal.

In one chapter, Colonel James describes the meeting we had in Hawaii just before he jetted to Baghdad. We discussed in detail the psychological forces that had been operating in my little basement prison, which transformed a bunch of kids, selected because they were really good apples, into very bad ones. On his way overseas, he then repeatedly viewed the video I had made of the study (*Quiet Rage: The Stanford Prison Experiment*), and found the answers he sought. Those answers helped establish the necessary precautionary conditions to fix the hell of that horrific place. In Abu Ghraib, as in the Stanford Experiment, there was no detached observer and no systematic oversight, and there were no clear rules of engagement for prohibited and permitted behaviors. Not incidentally, the worst abuses in both prisons broke out on the night shift. It was then that the big cats were away, and so the mice could play at what one of the MP female guards described as "fun and games."

As I tagged along with Larry James on his very personal, insight-filled journey relayed in this book, what I found most important was the revelation that none of those abuses need have occurred. Had the military system cared enough to create in advance the conditions that Colonel James outlined for them during his work at Guantanamo Bay, it is likely nothing sinister would have happened in Abu Ghraib. As Colonel James so ably relates, the importance of understanding situational and systemic forces that shape our thoughts, feelings, and actions must be at the core of a new appreciation of the dynamics of the human condition. Through the efforts and actions Colonel James describes in this book he helped resolve evil at this diabolical place—and hopefully in all U.S. military detention facilities.

Dr. Philip Zimbardo, author of *The Lucifer Effect*:
Understanding How Good People Turn Evil
and creator of the Stanford Prison Experiment

FIXING HELL

Treat a man the way you want to be treated.
—REVEREND JOHNSON

1
Entering Hell

June 2004: Abu Ghraib prison in Iraq

For weeks I'd been unable to think about hardly anything but Abu Ghraib, a prison in Iraq that was rapidly becoming known for abuse and torture, with tales of American soldiers running amok. Since the moment my command told me I would be sent to this faraway prison to make things right, to bring some sanity back to an insane situation that was embarrassing the United States and crippling our efforts in the global war on terrorism, images from Abu Ghraib filled my mind during the day and haunted my dreams at night. The same images that were splashed all over the media back home—the Iraqi prisoners with hoods over their heads, stacked in a human pyramid, standing in stress positions with electrodes attached, or being taunted by military dogs—ran through my mind in an endless loop. And there were the classified details that didn't make the evening news.

As I sat in the helicopter ferrying me right to the doorstep of this snake pit, the deafening rumble drowned out the rest of the world and I sat wondering if I was truly ready for what I was about to face. I'd seen plenty of challenges already in my career as an Army psychologist, some of it pretty ugly, but what was happening at Abu Ghraib was in a different class altogether. I closed my eyes and tried to relax amid the vibration and noise in the Black Hawk, but the horrors of Abu Ghraib played through my mind like a movie I couldn't switch off. And this was only from reading the reports and seeing the pictures. I was about to step into this for real. I felt challenged but also heartened that I would be able to make this situation better, to bring the skills of both an Army officer and an experienced psychologist to bear on this crisis. My goal was to correct the abuses at this prison while preserving the U.S. military's ability to hold and interrogate terrorists and Iraqi combatants. As an Army officer I supported the global war on terrorism and knew that military prisons and interrogations were necessary components of warfare, but as a psychologist I was compelled to prevent the abuse of prisoners in our custody. Drawing the line between aggressive interrogation and abuse was not always easy, and the task was deeply intertwined with my own internal conflicts about whether my first duty lay with being a soldier or a doctor. It was clear, however, that the line had been crossed in Abu Ghraib.

I was steeled for a bad situation, but as I stepped off the helicopter, I still wasn't quite prepared for what I saw. Abu Ghraib could be charitably described as a set of damaged buildings that had been built on a garbage dump. The whole compound was in disrepair. Trash was everywhere. Within my first five steps after disembarking from the helicopter, the smell of raw sewage overwhelmed my senses and nearly made me retch. This was a barren wasteland interrupted only by garbage and filth.

My God. I've never seen anything like this. I can't believe our people have to work in this.

As I walked from one side of the compound to the other, I tried to maintain my composure, but I was growing increasingly lightheaded and nauseated. I found my way to my room, actually an old prison cell with bars, about thirty square feet in size. It smelled of mold, dirt, and body odor. Its only furnishing was a green Army cot, onto which I collapsed, and passed out. After a brief, restless nap, the clamminess of my sweat-drenched shirt and pants awakened me. It was 11 p.m. I was feeling ill, probably dehydrated from the now 130-degree heat.

The physical battering had caught me off guard. I was so focused on steeling myself mentally for what I would find with the prisoners that the heat and the overall level of hardship in the camp had blindsided me. But I had work to do and the Army didn't send me here to lie around on a cot and grouse about the heat. I hauled myself from the bed, found the chow hall and visited with a few soldiers on the night shift, and asked them for directions to the intel center—the building where prisoners were interrogated. I had to see what was going on here, and the intel center was the heart of it all. Because it is surrounded by the enemy, it is more psychologically demanding to work there. Whatever was wrong at Abu Ghraib was coming out of that building.

During my five-month tour at the military prison in Guantanamo Bay, Cuba, if I had learned one thing above all others, it was that good leaders need to be present at all hours of the day and night. That had proved to be key to correcting some of the problems at that prison, and as bad as those problems were, Abu Ghraib promised to be much worse. In Cuba I found that when good leaders were missing, bad things happened. So how better to see the level of supervision at Abu Ghraib than to arrive at the intel center, unannounced, at about 1 a.m.? As I walked to the center, I didn't realize how pivotal a role my first thirty minutes of observations would play in my understanding of how and why everything went so wrong at Abu Ghraib. I approached the guard shack, but instead of an alert soldier asking to see my badges, I saw a very young female military police officer, an MP, maybe nineteen or twenty years old, who couldn't have weighed a hundred pounds with all of her gear on—with her head down, sound asleep. Falling asleep on guard duty is a grave failing, a huge infraction that should result in immediate reprimand and formal discipline, but I didn't wake her. A tiny little MP sleeping soundly at the door to a prison full of POWs and terrorists was a disconcerting sight, and it took some self-control to calm this Army officer's natural urge to explode with an angry tirade that would sure as hell wake the guard up. My goal on this first night was to simply observe, to see the situation before I started trying to fix it.

I walked unnoticed right past the sleeping guard, my loaded 9mm pistol hanging from my belt, and directly into the interrogation section of the facility.

Beyond the guard station I walked down the long hall, encountering no one else. For a moment there was no sound but that of my boots on the concrete floor. But soon I could hear angry screams, cursing, and yelling, in both English and something else. I immediately surmised that an interrogation was in process and realized I was about to see the infamous interrogation process at Abu Ghraib.

Here we go. Let's see what's really going on in this place. Sure sounds like some awful shit going down in there.

I headed for the terrible sounds, fearing I would see an example of the abuses I had heard so much about already. As I continued toward the source of the screaming, I passed by empty interrogation booths, each roughly the size of a college dorm room, with cheap furniture, usually a table and three chairs. When I reached the occupied room the screaming became clearer to my ears and I began to make out the sounds of an Iraqi screaming in his own language and then a male voice I assumed was the interrogator, screaming equally loudly and viciously. I had seen plenty of interrogations before, but I wondered what I would see on the other side of that door. The images of abuse and prisoner degradation raced through my mind again, and I braced myself for the scene that might accompany the screaming.

I took a deep breath and opened the door slowly, peeking in without the occupants noticing. Inside the interrogation booth was a twenty-two-year-old female soldier trying to conduct an interrogation. Sitting across the table from her was a shackled forty-year-old male prisoner, who had been brought into the prison for being a hardcore, killer terrorist, and he looked every bit the part. Alongside the prisoner was a male Arabic interpreter.

The American soldier was slumped in her chair and had tears in her eyes as the prisoner yelled at her ferociously in Arabic. The translator interpreted the prisoner's words effectively, repeating them in English with a harsh yell and fast pace consistent with the prisoner's voice. It all made for a strange combination: the screaming vitriol from the prisoner, followed quickly by the translation of the harsh words from a kind-looking Iraqi translator.

"I'll kill you, bitch! When I get out of here, I'll sodomize you before I cut your throat! You American women are nothing but whores! After I rape your mother I will set fire to that bitch's body. In my country a bitch like you would be beheaded for looking in the eyes of a man like me!"

Clearly the tables had turned in that room and the interrogator was in trouble. No supervisors were around, this violent prisoner was clearly out of control, threatening the life of a young soldier, and the lone MP guard was asleep. I chose to remain quiet and observe the wrongness of this awful place at that time — a young soldier abandoned by her superiors, practically on her own at night with a vicious terrorist, struggling to do her job in a horrible place, under wretched conditions. She was so young and innocent-seeming that she immediately reminded me of my niece, whom I pictured in the same situation. I felt sorry for this young soldier. As I watched her, I realized the reports of prisoner abuse, as bad as they were, did not tell the full story of Abu Ghraib.

This, too, was Abu Ghraib.

2
Journey to Gitmo

May 2002

When I was sixteen, I attended an all-black, all-male Catholic high school that was strict about rules and heavy on the discipline. For me, that meant constantly getting in trouble for running my mouth too much. A buddy named Tyrone and I were talking about what our parents did for a living one day, and he said his old man was a psychologist. I didn't really have any idea what a psychologist did, so Tyrone explained that his father talked to people for a living. I didn't think much more about it until I visited Tyrone's house one evening and had a chat with his dad. I asked Tyrone's father exactly what he did at work.

"Well," he said, "I get paid a lot of money for talking to people."

This sounded interesting, but I was still trying to fit the concept into the world I knew at my strict school. "Do you ever get sent to detention for talking too much?" I asked.

Tyrone's father laughed long and hard before catching his breath and answering my question. "No, son, I don't go to detention," he said. "I talk as long as I want, and the longer I talk, the more I get paid."

I was sold on the idea. Many more conversations followed with Tyrone's father in the next few years, and by the time I went to college in 1975 I had my plan all laid out: an undergraduate degree in four years and on to a PhD and a career in psychology. I left my beloved New Orleans, where I felt truly at home as a light-skinned black man of Creole heritage, to attend the University of Dubuque in Iowa, where I feared I would stand out like a palm tree in a cornfield. The folks in Iowa welcomed me warmly, though, and my full football and track scholarship paid for nearly everything I needed. I was an intensely focused student athlete, spending every minute on my studies or on the practice field, so much so that my roommate insisted on setting me up on a blind date because he figured I would never make the effort myself. The blind date turned out to be a lovely, petite Iowa girl named Janet who had fourteen brothers and sisters, all of them raised by their father to be fiercely independent and capable. When he was repairing the roof and needed someone else up there with a hammer, he didn't give a damn if the closest offspring's name was Jack or Jane, the kid better scramble up on the roof.

On our first date, we were riding around in Janet's little white Gremlin when a tire went flat. Already liking this gal enough that I wanted to impress her with my gallantry, I hopped out and went right to changing the tire. What I had forgotten, and what I could never tell this girl I'd just met, was that being raised in a house full of women had left me with absolutely zero mechanical skills. I looked into the trunk of that car and had no idea how to even get the spare tire out. After I fumbled with it for a while, Janet finally came around and, with a look of consternation, showed me how to do it. At least she wasn't strong enough to actually lift the tire out by herself.

Once we got the tire around to the side of the car, I began fumbling with the jack, getting more embarrassed and ham-handed as I realized I didn't know how to work it. Janet watched for a few minutes and finally had had enough. With a heavy sigh and a roll of the eyes, she said, "Stand back and get out of the way." I did as I was told and watched this beautiful little gal change that tire like she'd done it a hundred times before and didn't need any man to come to her rescue.

Ten minutes later, we were back on the road and I was in love. Later, I called my mother back in New Orleans and told her I'd met the woman I was going to marry. She expressed skepticism, to say the least, but I kept going on and on about how capable Janet was and how I'd never seen a woman take charge like that before, a woman who could be so delicate and gentle but also so independent. By the end of the phone call, my mother knew I was serious.

I married Janet while still in school and we had our son soon after. While obtaining my doctorate, I wrote my dissertation on child molesters. That required working twenty to thirty hours a week in a prison, interviewing prisoners. Still facing several more years of training as a psychology resident in a hospital, I looked at the different opportunities and my attention kept going to the military option. Medical residents were, and still are to some degree, treated like indentured servants, working extremely long hours under stressful conditions for very little pay. Of all the places you could train, the military provided the best pay, and it also offered excellent benefits for my family. And on top of that, I liked the idea that I could serve my country while seeing the world. I joined the Navy and trained at Bethesda Naval Hospital in Washington, D.C., and then my first assignment right out of training was the naval hospital at Pearl Harbor in Hawaii, where my years of experience working with prisoners for my dissertation prompted my boss to immediately assign me as the brig psychologist.

Temporary assignments followed in Guam, Japan, and the Philippines. Though the experience was largely positive, I didn't reenlist in the Navy when the time came. Instead I became an assistant professor at Louisiana State University in Baton Rouge, not far from New Orleans where I always felt at home. While teaching at LSU, I also worked as a consultant at the local prison. The work was satisfying, but I soon felt out of place in the almost entirely white suburb where I lived with other professionals from the university. This was Louisiana, but it wasn't New Orleans. My wife and son also didn't feel at home in Baton Rouge, but none of us wanted to complain. The final straw for me came in 1991 when the white supremacist and Ku Klux Klan leader David Duke came in second in the Republican primary for governor. I was dismayed to see that 85 percent of voters in my district had voted for this former Grand Wizard of the KKK. How could I raise my biracial son in this community?

I was miserable but I didn't want to uproot my family again after only eighteen months in Louisiana. With great hesitation, I broached the topic of moving from Baton Rouge and was relieved when my wife and son revealed that they, too, hated this place and wanted to go. Was there any chance of moving back to Hawaii? we wondered. I was still a Navy reservist so I looked into going active duty with the Navy again, and found they would be glad to have me back. But the most likely assignment would be Beaufort, South Carolina, or Cherry Point, North Carolina, and I didn't think that would be much of an improvement for my multiracial family. I was having a drink in a bar one evening, mulling over what to do next, when good fortune walked in wearing an Army uniform and sat down next to me. I was wearing my Navy reserves uniform, so we struck up a conversation and I soon learned he was the chief psychologist for the Army. As we talked and compared notes on our previous tours in Hawaii, he mentioned that he was having a hard time finding qualified psychologists in the Army who were willing to pick up and move to Pearl Harbor. I could hardly believe what I was hearing.

"Sir, don't jerk my chain," I said. "If I could do it, I'd join the Army and take that assignment in Hawaii myself."

My new friend made a few calls and soon I was in the Army, headed to Hawaii. I spent eight good years there and then in August 1999 I was reassigned from Tripler Army Medical Center in Honolulu to Walter Reed Army Medical Center in Washington, D.C. By then I had established myself as a leading military psychologist and an expert on the psychology of prisoners.

In the spring of 2002, I had already had a long, interesting career as a military psychologist. A colonel with plenty of experience in the field, I was not going to be at a loss for stories to tell after dinner or having a beer with other veterans and psychologists. I still had several years before retiring from the Army, but my three-year assignment at Walter Reed was winding down. I had about six to eight months left on this tour before my wife and I returned to our quiet life in Hawaii, where I would return to working at Tripler Army Medical Center.

Until then, the global war on terrorism was ensuring that,

as for most people in the military, there was always something to keep me busy. I always loved it when people asked me about my position on the war. Some assumed that because I was an Army colonel, I would be a gung-ho, conservative Republican, over the top in support of the war, praising President Bush at every opportunity. Others assumed that because I was a psychologist, a medical professional dedicated to caring for people's mental well-being, I would be a liberal Democrat opposed to the war and the president, only begrudgingly following my orders as an Army officer. Plus, I am a black man and everyone knows that black Republicans are about as rare as white running backs in the National Football League. The truth was I didn't fit any of those templates and many people who knew me well considered me something of a paradox.

My political orientation is best described as conservative Democrat. I carry a gun at all times, even in civilian clothing with a concealed weapon permit, and I believe very strongly in the right to bear arms. But I also believe in a woman's right to choose. I believe in less government but also that all Americans should have health insurance. Those positions made it hard to align myself simply with one political party or the other, but politics didn't come into play when my country launched the global war on terrorism. As an Army colonel I followed orders and did as my commander in chief instructed, and I was largely supportive of the growing calls to invade Iraq. In 2002 it was becoming clear that Saddam Hussein was a modern-day Hitler, killing hundreds of thousands of his own people and committing unspeakable atrocities on men, women, and children. Humanity, in the form of the United States military, had to stop him, and if the president decided to abandon the sanctions, inspections, and talking, I was glad to be part of the effort to go in and stop this dictator. I just wanted President Bush to do a better job of explaining why we might have to go. The oft-cited explanation that Iraq had weapons of mass destruction was pure nonsense; a group of angry Girl Scouts could have posed more of a threat to our national security than Iraq did. There was a perfectly valid reason to send in U.S. troops, but I cringed every time I heard my commander in chief tell the world that it was weapons of mass destruction.

By May 2002, the U.S. military and our allies had been fighting the Taliban in Afghanistan for eight months and we were treating many casualties from that operation at Walter Reed, where I was chair of the Department of Psychology. One day in May there was a knock on my door. It was my deputy department chief, Lieutenant Colonel Denise Dobson. Denise wore two hats as my deputy and also as the director of training for the Department of Psychology. I had enjoyed working with her for nearly three years. It had been a long haul and we had been through a lot, notably the tragedy of 9/11, in which Lieutenant Colonel Dobson and I relocated most of our clinical services to the Pentagon to provide mental health services to those who survived the attack and responded during the rescue efforts. I had worked sixteen hours a day for three months, from September 12, 2001, to December. Managing the Department of Psychology also had put Lieutenant Colonel Dobson and me through the wringer with the usual administrative hassles, a hospital-wide power failure, tremendous staff shortages, facilities in disrepair, and even a mold problem that threatened your health when you were merely sitting at your desk.

Dobson had proven herself a tough officer and a valued colleague, but I was worried about her. In spite of her desire and energy to keep up with me, which sometimes is a tall order, she had had a scare with a life-threatening disease and at times didn't look well. She responded by always taking on more duties, as if trying to prove to herself that she was not weakening. On top of this, the invasion of Afghanistan had produced a type of patient we had never seen before—the Islamic extremist terrorists. Treating them, even understanding their mental health issues, was proving to be exceptionally challenging. Dobson came to my office with a specific intent and a special purpose on this day. She was winding down in her capacity as the director of training for the clinical psychology training program and we needed to select a new director. Lieutenant Colonel Dobson requested permission to assign these new duties to Major (Dr.) John Leso, a slender, good-looking fellow who was about five feet eleven inches tall and gave the appearance of spending a great deal of his off time in the gym. John was a very capable military officer who had the confidence of everyone in the department, and in particular the young Army captains who were interns in my department.

As much as I respected Major Leso's performance, I was not convinced that he was the appropriate choice to replace Lieutenant Colonel Dobson, because a few weeks earlier he had requested a Professional Filler System (PROFIS) position, a temporary assignment for a medical professional to a field hospital outside of their primary hospital. A PROFIS assignment provides the physician with unique experience outside the walls of Walter Reed, and in this case Major Leso wanted some time with the 85th Combat Stress Control Company (CSC), located in Fort Hood, Texas. A CSC is made up of a psychologist, a psychiatrist, a social worker, psychiatric nurses, and enlisted psychiatric technicians. Their mission is to provide mental health services to soldiers in the field—sort of a mental health MASH unit. His request was reasonable, and I was inclined to approve it, but letting him go to the field unit might create a problem if that unit deployed. It would be a real shit mess if I appointed him director of training at Walter Reed, on the assumption that he would be away in Texas for only a couple weeks, and then he ended up on a long deployment with the PROFIS unit. It was more than just a matter of needing someone qualified to fill the position here at the hospital. The American Psychological Association has strict standards for accredited training programs like ours that require we maintain continuity in the director of training position, so appointing him and then having him away on deployment could cascade into other problems for us.

I balked at appointing Major Leso, but he and Dobson convinced me that my worries were unfounded because there were no deployments on the horizon. Lieutenant Colonel Dobson was enthusiastic about Major Leso's qualifications for the position, and I had no argument with her on that point, but she had limited experience in thinking out strategically what was about to happen in the Army world around her. She did not see the buildup in the war that was about to occur and how this would affect not only her life, her world, but Major Leso's and mine as well. She and Major Leso were both hard-charging, highly motivated officers with the best intentions, but they didn't have enough years in the Army to fully appreciate how the system can kick you in the butt when you least expect it. I was just like them twenty years earlier.

But really, Lieutenant Colonel Dobson argued, how likely was it that the CSC unit would be deployed in the two weeks that

Major Leso was assigned to it? I had to agree that would take some colossal bad luck for him to be there when the unit deployed. So finally I relented, but I restated my concern to them both that the war on terror was cranking up and warned that Major Leso might get deployed. Perhaps, just maybe, my nearly twenty years of experience in both the Army and Navy was off base and I was worrying over nothing.

After we gave Major Leso the good news, Lieutenant Colonel Dobson and I returned from lunch and were soon joined by the major, who was ecstatic about the opportunities he would be afforded and wanted to thank me. He was very excited that he was going to be able to go to Fort Hood for a two-week field training exercise and then be allowed to return to Walter Reed and assume duties as the director of training. I again expressed my concern to him, still worried even after granting permission.

"Sir, don't worry. It's not a problem," the major told me. "I spoke to the commanding officer of the 85th CSC down there in Texas and she assured me that it is not a problem at all. I'll be gone for two weeks, sir, and then I'll be back in time to greet the new incoming intern class."

Even though I had some regrets about letting him go, I needed to express confidence in this young officer, so I said, "John, I know you'll do a great job in Texas with the 85th. I'll see you in a couple of weeks."

Almost in a sprint, Major Leso left my office and busied himself with getting to Texas. After he left my office, my phone rang. It was Colonel Ed Cooper, the chief psychologist of the Army. Chief psychologists were known for how they could sell snow to Eskimos, and on this occasion, I was the Eskimo. Colonel Cooper was encouraging me to remain at Walter Reed and replace him because he was ready to retire. I was quite flattered, but I had to laugh.

"Ed, there's no way in hell I'm going to stay at Walter Reed and be psychologist of the Army," I said. "I'm tired, my wife is tired, and we just want to go home to Hawaii and be with our granddaughter. I'm supposed to head home in about six months."

Colonel Cooper laughed and said he couldn't blame me, that he just had to try to make his exit smoother by finding a good replacement. "Hell, I'd get myself reassigned to Hawaii if I could," he said.

Major Leso soon left for his brief training assignment with the 85th CSC in Texas. He hadn't even been gone for four days when I received a call from the commanding officer of the 85th informing me that the unit had received its orders to deploy to Cuba. The unit would be providing mental health services to the soldiers and enemy combatants being held at the prison on the American base at Guantanamo Bay in Cuba. Known as "Gitmo" from its military abbreviation GTMO, this Cuban base was a strategic stronghold in one of the last Communist dictatorships still on earth, and in recent years it had been used to house terrorist prisoners captured in Afghanistan and elsewhere.

Located in the southeastern part of Cuba, Gitmo had an interesting history. Beginning in 1903 the U.S. military leased it from the Cuban government. Prior to the global war on terror most Americans had never even heard of it. Those who did know of this faraway place recalled that it was used as the transient facility for the Cuban and Haitian flotillas in the 1980s and 1990s. Until we began bringing in the Afghan terrorists most high-ranking officials wanted the base at Gitmo closed because it had no real purpose. Then we needed a place in a real hurry to put the detainees from the war with Afghanistan. Suddenly Gitmo became the epicenter for the growing debate over the human rights of detainees in the war on terror.

Although apologetic about the bind she was putting me in, the commander of the 85th nonetheless requested that Major Leso be allowed to deploy to Cuba as part of her unit. Not surprisingly, she saw him as an outstanding young officer and thought he would be a significant asset for their unit in Cuba. I hesitated before replying, because I knew the 85th's reputation included many problems that are common to combat stress control companies. The biggest problem was that CSC units had psychiatrists or psychologists as their commanding officers, and most psychologists, social workers, nurses, and psychiatrists didn't make good field commanders. They had an unrelenting need to be liked, which often got in the way of a successful military command. Most mental health military officers had no real formal training to be military unit field commanders, and they were usually very bad at this endeavor. So she needed Major Leso not just for his capabilities as a psychologist but also for what he could bring to the unit as a capable military officer. Saying yes would create problems on my end, but there was only one right answer. This unit was going into the field and they needed my officer, so I had to allow Major Leso to deploy. I could hear the relief in the commanding officer's voice when I said yes.

Major Leso was given some leave from his temporary duties at Fort Hood and he returned to my office at Walter Reed posthaste to pack up his furniture and belongings. He was very apologetic.

"Colonel James, sir, you were correct," he told me. "It looks like I'm going to deploy and I won't be able to be the director of training this coming year."

I told him not to worry. "We'll figure out a way to get it all done," I said. "Go on down to Cuba and perform your duties like I know you will, soldier. I'll see you in about six months or so."

Major Leso had no idea, nor did I at that time, that his future, my future, and the shape and direction of the profession of psychology would never be the same.

Major Leso assumed, given the typical clinical mission of the 85th, that he would work as a clinical psychologist for the next six months down in Cuba—much longer than he had planned to be with the unit, but not all that long for a deployment. He did not know that by the time he departed for Cuba, hell had already begun to engulf the Joint Task Force in Gitmo, and it was waiting to swallow the life and soul of this young, brilliant Army psychologist. His world would be irrevocably altered.

The problems at Gitmo all related to the unusual command structure. Gitmo had a two-star general and a one-star general who did not see eye to eye. In a typical military command, the senior ranking officer, in this case the two-star general, would be in charge of everything. Not at Gitmo. In the haste to prepare for war after 9/11, the command there was thrown together with the already existing Navy personnel at the base, a blend of some active-duty Army staff, and many Army reservists and National Guard troops. At this very early stage in the war, many of these reservists had never deployed and had little experience. Their inexperience was compounded by the two-star general not being in charge of all the staff at Gitmo. The one-star general felt that he did not work for the two-star general and that the two-star couldn't tell him what to do. This divisiveness hurt morale and got in the way of the troops accomplishing the mission. It would be like the CEO of any American company not having control over all of his or her employees. In any well-functioning military command, one person and only one person has complete control and veto authority over everything—the commanding general. The lack of a clear chain of command at Gitmo left most soldiers asking, "Who's in charge here?" This sentiment would not be found on any other active-duty Army post anywhere else in the world. Problems between these two generals flowed downhill to affect the mission and every soldier in the whole task force.

Unknown to Leso while he was en route to Joint Task Force Guantanamo, the pressures were mounting on the military to collect "actionable" intelligence that could yield quick results. The top brass wanted intel that would save lives on the battlefield, and units from halfway around the world were delivering plenty of prisoners to Gitmo that looked like hot prospects. But so far, efforts at interrogating these terrorists were not going well. The Army did not have many seasoned old crusty warrant-officer interrogators left. Most of the interrogators from the Vietnam era, those with enough experience to produce good results, were either retired or dead. The majority of interrogators were very young, inexperienced, and did not have the ability to extract accurate and reliable actionable intelligence from the prisoners. Seeing little results from the inexperienced interrogators, the commanding general, Major General John McKipperman, brought a group of former CIA contract psychologists to Cuba—a few months before Major Leso's assignment—to teach the interrogators harsh and abusive interrogation tactics. The goal was to get the detainees to talk—quickly. Results were marginal, but by the time Leso arrived a culture of severe tactics had taken hold as the norm for much of the Joint Intelligence Group at Gitmo. The bar for what might be considered abusive was raised higher and higher, and the leaders at the base turned their backs on conduct that was, at a minimum, questionable. The interrogators learned that they could try pretty much whatever they wanted to get the prisoner to talk, and a lack of good information often just spurred them to attempt something more extreme.

Major Leso jumped right into his role as a clinical psychologist with the 85th CSC in Cuba, seeing patients immediately and maintaining optimism about his deployment. In less than a month, though, his assignment changed drastically. He was removed from his clinical duties and reassigned to work with the Intelligence Control Element section of the Joint Intelligence Group. The commanding general realized that there were problems with the intel unit's productivity, cohesion, and focus, so he directed Major Leso to assist with improving the unit's interrogations. Major Leso's concern was that he had never been trained to perform these duties, had no real strong in-depth forensic background, and had never consulted or received extensive training with police detectives in his doctoral work. The task force surgeon, the chief doctor of the task force and Leso's superior at the time, expressed concern about putting him in this position, but the general insisted. This was the moment when a bright, promising young officer's future was stolen. Within a matter of days, he was reassigned from his clinical duties as a doctor, helping soldiers cope with the stresses of working at Gitmo and being away from home, to advising interrogators on how to interrogate prisoners.

In August 2002, I got a phone call from John Leso. I knew immediately that something was wrong and this was not the same eager young man I had last seen in my office. I was shocked at the voice I heard on the line. I could hear and almost feel the anxiety, hopelessness, uncertainty, and terror in his voice. He briefed me on what had transpired and his new mission and told me how uncomfortable he was in his new role. I told him that I would consult Colonel Morgan Banks down at the Fort Bragg Special Operations Command to see if Major Leso could be reassigned. Colonel Banks oversaw all psychologists working in the special operations community, and now Major Leso had become a part of that community, involuntarily, overnight, and without the proper training.

When I spoke with Colonel Banks, we agreed that we had grave concerns about Leso's lack of preparation for his new role, but we also saw this as an opportunity for psychologists to do the right thing and influence the interrogation process, assuming we could get Major Leso the appropriate training. Colonel Banks and I agreed that the right thing to do was to bring Leso to Fort Bragg as soon as possible and provide him training so that he could help what was rapidly starting to look like a sinking ship at Cuba. During the week of September 16, 2002, Leso was sent to Fort Bragg for briefing on the appropriate and inappropriate behaviors, the rules of engagement, what was legal and not legal, and, most importantly, the Geneva Conventions. Colonel Banks emphasized to Major Leso that it was imperative for him to teach interrogators how to treat all prisoners with decency and respect and how to use incentive-based interviews rather than harsh interrogation tactics. This was the first training of its kind in the country, to teach psychologists how to ethically work with interrogators, and I hoped it would give Major Leso more confidence in his ability to contribute in a meaningful way as a psychologist, rather than feeling that he had been thrown into a role wholly inconsistent with his background.

Meanwhile I still had to run my department. With Leso deployed to Cuba for a six-month assignment, he would be away from Walter Reed from approximately June to December 2002. Given that Cuba was in the Atlantic region of the country, this new deployment would be an ongoing responsibility of my psychology department at Walter Reed. So in addition to getting by without Major Leso while he was in Cuba, I also had to begin searching for a suitable replacement, most likely from within my department, for when Leso returned from Cuba. And I had to get moving on it because Leso's six-month tour of duty was going to go by fast, at least for me.

Indeed, it seemed as though September and October 2002 passed in a flash. My wife and I began the exciting process of planning our return to Hawaii around September 2003. Thinking about the freshness of Hawaii, the joy of being around our granddaughter, and the pleasantries of visiting with old friends served as a respite from the tragedy of Joint Task Force Guantanamo, any leftover problems from 9/11, and the daily grind at Walter Reed Army Medical Center. In the first week of October my phone rang, and it was Colonel Cooper. He began emphasizing the importance of coming up with a suitable replacement for Major Leso, whom, it was clear, would be another psychologist from my department.

I told Ed I would make it happen, confident because I had a hard-charging young officer who was at my door every day eager to take the assignment. I had complete trust and faith in him. But then he found out that he had a serious medical condition that would prevent his deployment. There were two more

officers I might send, but neither was a promising choice. One
was a young female captain who had a six-month-old baby at
home. The other was the oldest psychologist in the Army and
his wife had just completed a round of chemotherapy. I considered every possible solution, but in the end it was clear that there
was only one right answer. I would have to deploy to Cuba and
replace Major Leso myself. Colonel Cooper and Colonel Banks
agreed that this was the right course of action, particularly because things were getting worse down there. Gitmo needed an
experienced senior Army psychologist with a significant background in correctional and forensic psychology. Once the matter was settled, I started making arrangements to go down to Fort
Bragg, North Carolina, and receive many classified briefings and
review relevant documents.

I was less than thrilled about going to Cuba instead of Hawaii, and I knew my wife wouldn't be happy either. But when I
informed her of my pending deployment she was undaunted.
With approximately six years in the Navy prior to transferring
over to the Army, we were veterans of many deployments. We
both felt that a six-month deployment was a long weekend as
deployments go. No sweat, we thought. Six months in Cuba and
then back to our plan to go home to Hawaii.

The remainder of October and November 2002 continued
to fly by like a runaway freight train going downhill. I occupied
myself with making sure that I was in the best physical shape
of my life and reading everything that I could read about the new
mission at Joint Task Force Guantanamo.

In the first week of January 2003 I boarded a civilian plane
out of Baltimore-Washington International Airport and headed
south for the Combat Redeployment Center, which was a train-

ing and mobilization center down at Fort Benning, Georgia. My civilian plane from Baltimore arrived at 7 p.m. at the Columbus, Georgia, airport. I got my bags, then sat on a huge bus with what seemed like three hundred soldiers. *Why do soldiers need so many goddamn bags*, I thought as I sat crammed on this unheated bus on a cold Georgia night. It seemed that these soldiers had a thousand suitcases and duffel bags on a bus that was designed to seat thirty or forty people. We waited for three hours until every seat on the bus was filled because the contract driver, Mr. Pete, was getting paid by the head and did not want to go back to Fort Benning with seats unfilled. Finally, Mr. Pete started the bus and we arrived at Fort Benning, about two hours south of Atlanta, late on a Sunday night. It was dark, cold, raining, and we were met by a first sergeant who seemed angry at the world but toned down the vitriol when he saw a colonel standing in front of him. He showed me to my barracks, wanting to provide me with a finer touch because of my rank. He thought that somehow, if he assigned me to a single room that night, I would overlook this dump of a barracks. It didn't work.

My barracks room had holes in the walls, broken windows, and water dripping from the ceiling. The shower facilities were filthy. I was simply appalled that we had young soldiers going to—and more importantly, returning from—a combat zone living in these barracks. I looked around and thought I wouldn't want to let a cat or dog live in this building for fear of it being eaten by a rat. I called the concierge over and told him so.

"First Sergeant, these berths are unfit for human habitation!" I barked at him.

He was unimpressed with my opinion and my attitude on this late Sunday night in Georgia. "It's what we got, sir." And with that he went away to yell some more at the other soldiers grousing about their accommodations.

I stayed in the barracks for about three of the ten days I was scheduled to be at Fort Benning. After that, I just couldn't take it anymore. The mixture of alcohol, women, and young soldiers filled with testosterone at this remote part of the post was a bad combination. I would be awakened in the night by brawls, women screaming, and the sound of beer bottles breaking. On the third night of my stay I was given a roommate, a lieutenant colonel who farted louder than the detonation of any hand grenade I had ever heard. His snoring could have competed with the sound of an Amtrak train struggling to make up time in the snow. That next morning, I found my way to the first sergeant's office and saw that his mood was still as foul as mine.

"First Sergeant, I'll be back in formation at 0500, but I'm not going to spend another night in this roach motel," I told him. He mumbled a "yes sir" without hardly looking at me, but I suspect he said more to my back as I walked out. I spent the remaining nights basking in the luxury of the local Motel 6. I could at least get to sleep.

The next morning, I was in formation at 5 a.m. with about five hundred other soldiers who were all freezing their asses off. I, on the other hand, was not. I had learned nearly twenty years ago never to deploy anywhere in the world without long underwear. It doesn't matter if they tell you you're going to Hot As Hell, Texas, or an expedition to the sun, take some long underwear because it's going to be cold at night. The first sergeant barked out instructions and told us the plan of the day, adding comments that indicated to this experienced psychologist that he was either seriously delusional or just enjoyed messing with us.

"And to anyone who wants to come to me with some bullshit complaints about your barracks, just do yourself a favor and keep it to yourself," he yelled. "The accommodations here at Fort Benning are top-notch, five-star housing and damn near luxurious. So I'm not interested in your complaining."

We crammed on the bus and spent the rest of our six days getting equipment, shots, and disrobing in a room filled with thirty of my closest friends who I had just met. Of course, a variety of more medical exams, more shots, getting more equipment, going to more meetings and more briefings were to follow. On the tenth day, I was scheduled to fly out of Fort Benning, down to the naval air station in Jacksonville, Florida. There, I would board a military-chartered Continental Airlines 737 to Cuba.

About two hundred or so passengers boarded the 737 that morning for Guantanamo Bay, Cuba. As we reached Cuba and flew over the Caribbean island, I couldn't help but notice the beauty of the place. The coral reefs were mesmerizing, with a bluish, turquoise water similar to Maui, Hawaii. Upon landing I was quickly escorted through the in-processing—my rank usually got me the fast-lane treatment in these situations—and given my badge. I was officially part of the staff at Gitmo.

Major Leso met me at the airport when I was finished with all the arrival processing. As I looked at him coming across the terminal, I knew something was wrong. I had hoped that he was coping better in the new position after his training, but my first look at him erased that idea. Major Leso did not look like himself. He had lost the innocent, naïve look that I remembered seeing in my office so often. The insatiable energy and optimism that had surrounded him every moment were gone. He no longer had a brightness in his eyes. He was worn physically and, I suspected, tattered emotionally as a person and human being. After chatting with him for half an hour, I began to feel a loss for the young John Leso I once knew. Major Leso welcomed me to Cuba, but it was a formality. He spoke softly, with no energy, in the voice of the deeply depressed.

What in the hell is so wrong? I asked myself. *This isn't just a stressed-out soldier or someone who's tired from being in the field. My God . . . This man has been traumatized.*

I didn't let on right away that I was concerned about Major Leso and just allowed him to go through the motions of showing me around the base. The post at Cuba consists of two almost completely separate sections separated by a huge bay spread across approximately forty-five miles. One of the ironies about this base in a Communist country, home to the military prison that housed some of the worst terrorists in the world, was that it had many familiar touches from home. A McDonald's restaurant offered the same Big Macs and fries that any soldier knew from home, and the post exchange (PX) carried everyone's favorite magazines and snacks. There was a movie theater, good roads, beautiful beaches, some limited Internet access and e-mail. The air terminal that soldiers flew into was on the leeward side of Guantanamo Bay across the water from the main part of the post, on the windward side of the island. This required all personnel to ferry from the airport to the main post. While we were in our SUV on the ferry, Major Leso began to share with me some of the horrors and tragedies he was neither trained to deal with nor had emotionally expected. There was something different about him when he talked about those issues. He seemed angry, depressed, exhausted, disappointed, and afraid all at once. He was also goddamned glad to see me, partly because my arrival marked his imminent departure.

We disembarked the ferry in the SUV and headed for my quarters. When we arrived at my barracks room John and I unloaded my gear into my hooch. Every passing moment made it more clear to me that this once vibrant, young, hard-charging, almost naïve officer and psychologist was not himself.

Don't force the conversation, Larry, I told myself as we hauled my gear inside. *Remember to let it happen when he's ready. Just follow where this takes you.*

I did. Leso obviously welcomed me as a familiar face, a fellow medical professional, and a superior he trusted. I could tell he needed to talk, and once we started to relax at my new home, it was only a matter of time. Within the first thirty minutes in my hooch, his eyes began to tear up. He told me he felt that he had received increasing pressure to teach interrogators procedures and tactics that were a challenge to his ethics as a psychologist and moral fiber as a human being. He was devastated to have been a part of this. As a fellow mental health professional, I related strongly to what he must have gone through with trying to be both a healer and a soldier. Major Leso had been thrown right into the jaws of what had been for me mostly a theoretical, what-if type of debate.

He witnessed many harsh and inhumane interrogation tactics, such as sexual humiliation, stress positions, detainees being stripped naked, and the use of K-9 dogs to terrorize detainees. He had no command authority, meaning he felt as though he had no legal right to tell anyone what to do or not do. There were no guides or reference books he could refer to, nor old college professors he could consult. This young officer was dropped in this

horrible situation without the training, informational background, senior military rank, or experience that would be necessary to derail this broken downhill train. Nevertheless, he had
garnered the trust of the interrogators over time and was able to
make some changes. Though the changes sometimes came only
after a fight, he had convinced the intel unit that he should be
involved in the interrogation process as a consultant and was successful in cutting back on some of the abusive practices.

I spoke with John for a long time that first night, letting him
pour out a lot of frustrations and offering advice on how to cope
with the difficulty of being both a soldier and a doctor. I shared
with him my own concerns about how to balance those two roles,
and he was relieved to hear that a colonel with years of experience still struggled with that dilemma.

Major Leso told me he would remain in Cuba for two weeks,
completing the administrative processing prior to his departure
from JTF Guantanamo and his return to Walter Reed. That was
ideal, I thought, because this would give me about two weeks to
uncover what in the hell had happened on this island. As I would
often do with others around me, especially those in pain, I began
telling Major Leso old stories, filled with laughter and good fun.
His emotional pain paused for the time being as we got back in
the SUV and headed for the chow hall.

We had been driving for a few minutes when he looked over
to me and said, "Colonel . . ." and then paused, obviously wanting to tell me something important. I will never forget the hurt
in his eyes.

"Colonel, you need to be real careful down here, sir," he said
softly, but intently. "You can step in a minefield every hour of
the day at this place."

For a second I thought he was talking about actual mine-fields, warning me with another housekeeping detail about life in Cuba, but I quickly realized he wasn't talking about explosive ordnance.

"Thanks, John," I said. "I'll keep that in mind."

3

An Infidel in Guantanamo

January 2003

The first Saturday I was "on Island," as they say there, Major Leso took me to the intel headquarters building for a 9 a.m. meeting with the commanding general of JTF Guantanamo, Major General Geoffrey D. Miller. He was now the bigwig at Gitmo, the head honcho in charge of the military prison and anything else in Cuba that came with an American flag attached. It was clear who was in charge, there was never any debate about who had veto authority on General Miller's post. Unlike the previous two-star general, Miller was in charge of everything in a typical Army hierarchal style. Second in command was a one-star brigadier general who was the deputy commander at Gitmo. This mirrored both the typical Army hierarchal command in structure and process. In other words, when Miller spoke, we never, ever heard the one-star general disagree or second-guess him.

The room was packed with the key leaders of the command, and the psychologist—that would be me from now on—was required to sit right behind the general. Major Leso introduced me to General Miller while he and I stood up to talk.

"Welcome, Colonel," he said, with a nod toward me. "You'll have big shoes to fill as the new biscuit."

That caught me off guard and I'm sure everyone saw the puzzled look on my face. Outside of a cheerleader I once knew back in college, I had never been called "biscuit" before, let alone by a male, two-star general artillery officer. Major Leso saw the confusion on my face and leaned over toward me.

"I'll explain later, sir," he whispered. "Trust me, it's actually a good thing, Colonel."

The meeting lasted exactly one hour, and after years in the halls of Walter Reed, it was a pleasure to be among infantry and operational officers again. This appealed to the soldier side of me. General Miller was the kind of commander you wanted to be around—a soldier's soldier, all business and no bullshit. A minute with him was worth two hours with any PhD or MD. He was focused, and could provide more information with eye contact alone than any medical-officer general I had ever worked for in the past. But at the same time, he had a keen awareness of the value of what the psychologist brought to the fight. In a hospital, we were only called when a patient had committed suicide, a staff physician had a meltdown, or one of our patients was seen on post with no pants or talking to his shoe. Not so under General Miller. He knew that an Army psychologist could contribute much more than that. His meeting was organized, and I saw that everyone serving under him had already learned a key lesson: one better not stutter when questioned by General Miller. Fulfilling objectives within his timeline and bringing your "A game" to his meeting were the only things accepted by him. General Miller made it clear that he expected you to put your feet on the line but not to cross it. Spending all your time on interoffice politics, as was common in some Army medical centers, was not an option. I loved it.

Later on in the meeting it became clear that a special mission was about to occur in February 2003 and I was going to play a key role. Our guys in Afghanistan had captured three teenage terrorists and I was chosen to fly to Afghanistan with a special unit to secure them and return them to Gitmo. This mission was to jump off in less than a month. "Colonel James, you got flight lead on a plane for the juveniles," Miller told me. He made it clear that he did not want them in the general population, and that I needed to plan how to interrogate these "juvenile enemy combatants" (JECs) posthaste.

"Got it, sir," I replied, quickly and with conviction. "I'll have the plan by next Saturday."

"No, I need it by close of business on Monday."

"Roger, General," I said without hesitation. "I'm tracking on it, sir. Consider it done."

During the meeting, General Miller had discussed how I would be replacing Major Leso, and that it would be my job to teach the interrogators how to get intel without yelling, slapping, sleep deprivation, humiliation, or food deprivation. There was no comment or discussion during the meeting, of course, but as I sat there looking out at the other officers in the room, I knew I had been given a tall order and that not everyone was going to welcome my guidance. After all, the yelling, slapping, and other abuse that I was supposed to help them avoid was actually allowed by the Army Field Manual on intelligence collection. I knew some of the men and women in this room would at some point ask me, "Hey, the manual says it's okay, so why not?"

When the meeting was finished, Leso explained to me that

"biscuit" was an affectionate nickname taken from the initials for Behavioral Science and Consultation Team (BSCT). It was the special behavioral science unit formed when Major Leso was brought over by the previous general to work with the interrogators. Anytime someone needed me or Major Leso, they said, "Where's the biscuit?" I was the senior psychologist, so I was known as Biscuit 1.

"Okay, I get it," I told Leso. "I've been called worse."

Everything about General Miller screamed "action." You felt like you should always be on the move around him, doing something productive, getting things done, not standing around like a slack-ass. So with that in mind, I didn't waste any time getting to my main task at Gitmo—improving the way we interrogated prisoners. I had already had a long talk with General Miller and I knew that our views on this issue were not too far apart. We had a much better understanding than I would have had with the previous commander. Though General Miller looked at interrogations through the eyes of a soldier, relying largely on the Army Field Manual to determine what was and wasn't acceptable, I was able to explain to him how an Army psychologist sees it.

"Here's the problem with the field manual," I told him. "There's a difference between what's legal for a soldier to do under the field manual and what a doctor can do under his ethics code. Now, I'm a soldier, sir, and that guides everything I do here, but the ethics code for a psychologist says we can do no harm to a human being."

"So you can't do both," he said, tracking with me.

"I can't, but the thing is, there isn't really a reason to do it that way anyway," I explained. "What's in the field manual isn't necessarily the best way, and what I can bring to the table, sir, is my knowledge of psychology and how to best get people to talk. There are better ways, more effective ways, to get this intel."

The conversation went on for some time, but luckily for me I wasn't starting with a superior officer who thought the only way to get intelligence was to beat it out of the prisoner. General Miller knew from the outset that we needed to reform the interrogation process and that was the main reason I was on his island. He was looking for me to get to it and make it happen.

Major Leso showed me around Gitmo over the next few days, starting with Camp Delta, the permanent 612-unit detention center that replaced the temporary facilities of Camp X-Ray, used when the detainees first started arriving in 2002. Leso explained to me how Camp Delta was broken down into four areas with different levels of security. Newly arriving detainees were first sent to Camp 3, the maximum-security camp, then to Camp 2 if they cooperated with the guards. After more cooperation they might be moved to Camp 1. Prisoners who were considered to be a minimum security risk and who cooperated with interrogators were moved to Camp 4.

Moving from one camp to another had its advantages, and Camp 4 was the choice accommodation, with showers and four communal living rooms for ten detainees each. In Camp 4, each detainee had a bed and a locker for personal items. It even had small common recreational areas for playing board games and team sports. The detainees at Camp 4 also shared communal meals, and wore white uniforms instead of the orange worn by other detainees.

The next two weeks went by fast. I became occupied with the plan for the JECs and Leso was already out-processing. During this time period, I met up with an old friend, Dr. Mike Gelles, who was in Gitmo for an official visit. Mike and I had been interns together many years ago at Bethesda Naval Hospital in Washington, D.C. He had long since left Navy active duty, but he had worked his way up to be chief psychologist for the Navy Criminal Investigative Service (NCIS) Behavioral Science Unit. Mike was not happy with the abuses at Gitmo and filed a formal complaint through Navy channels. It pissed off a ton of people. He and I agreed to work together to turn this ship around and teach interrogators how to interview with respect, decency, and humanity. I trusted Mike as a person and as a forensic psychologist. Likewise he trusted me, and so we charted a course for the future of the BSCT at Gitmo.

As I took on more of Major Leso's duties by the day, he began to detach himself from the Joint Task Force, which is the normal process for a departing soldier. Over the course of the next two weeks, he and I had many talks and I helped him work through and process the emotions, ethics, and morality of what he had been through. Through hard work, consultation, and the relationships he established, Major Leso was able to help right a sinking ship out in the middle of the Caribbean. I reminded him that it was through his efforts and determination to do the right thing that he was able to help craft a command policy to outlaw the harsh and abusive tactics. Rather than focusing on the net negative, I emphasized to Major Leso the importance of what he had done. He had convinced the chain of command that there was another way to get a prisoner to talk instead of employing harsh tactics. I felt it vital that he could hear this and grasp this emotionally. Otherwise, he would return to Walter Reed a broken man and a shell of a human being. Unknown to him at the time, he had paved the road for me, and the interrogators were ready for more guidance on how a psychologist could help them accomplish their mission and get detainees to talk without abuse.

He had a huge going-away party on a Friday night put on by the Intelligence Control Element staff, and I was pleased to see that he actually enjoyed himself. He was immensely relieved to be leaving Gitmo, and I was glad he could go back to the States and get himself back together. I drove him to the ferry Saturday morning, on his way to the airport. When we said our good-byes, he repeated his earlier warning to me.

"Sir, you gotta be careful down here," he said. "Don't step in anything."

I promised him I'd watch out. As I watched him leave, I was both heartened to see that his mood had improved somewhat and dismayed that such a short time at Gitmo could do that to a man. I wondered if he would ever bounce back to the bright-eyed officer I knew at Walter Reed. John did not know it at that time, nor did I, but in the coming years many horrible things would be written about him without any data to back up the charges. I would not see Major Leso nor have any contact with him again for four months. For his own well-being he just needed to fade away, but his time in Cuba would continue haunting him.

"Larry, you got flight lead. You're the tip of the bayonet for the juveniles." Those words from Major General Miller rang in my head over and over. "Flight lead" meant that I was responsible for putting together a team to handle the three juvenile enemy combatants who would arrive in February 2003 at Guantanamo Bay, and the building of a specially designed facility for them to live in.

How am I supposed to work with teenagers in this place?

There was not a computer lit search I could do, nor were there any other PhD colleagues I could consult with on how to manage teenage terrorists. There was no one in the country with any experience on this.

You're it. You gotta figure out something.

I didn't have the time it would take to develop the usual PhD planning committee. There was no time. The plane was leaving for Afghanistan in a matter of three weeks and the general demanded a plan by yesterday.

Don't panic, Larry. You spent a few years growing up in a New Orleans housing project where you became good friends with some hardcore teenage sociopaths. Surely that's got to be some help here.

Plus, I decided to draw upon my experience working with male juvenile patients I had encountered earlier in my career. Some of these boys were genuine in their desire to hurt others—they liked it and felt no remorse. From these experiences I would build the components of the rehabilitative plan. I realized early in my thinking that I would need a child psychologist to provide the needed psychotherapy, and a pediatrician to serve as the medical director.

With every passing day I ramped up my involvement in planning for the arrival of the three juveniles. My recommendation was to house these teenagers separately from the adult prison population. Major General Miller agreed. Next, I coordinated with a reservist who in civilian life was the warden of an Indiana state prison. Command Sergeant Johnson was the senior-ranking enlisted adviser for the military police brigade in Gitmo. He brought with him nearly thirty years of experience in the prison field. His task was the physical reconstruction and rehabilitation of a house separate and away from the main prison facility, much like a halfway house, and I was charged with building a team for the academic, medical, psychological, and intelligence collection efforts for the juveniles. My guidance to everyone was that we could never house these teenagers in the general adult prison population—not for a minute and no matter how inconvenient it was to keep them separate. We busied ourselves with the plan to retrofit an already existing house that was isolated from the rest of the camp. We named it Camp Iguana, after the two- to three-foot-long lizards that are as common in Gitmo as squirrels are back home, to differentiate it from the rest of the prison known as Camp Delta.

We needed to devise a plan for the correctional custody, medical care, and psychological treatment of these young people, and we had to determine just how one can safely and morally interrogate teenage terrorists. And they were indeed terrorists, according to the intel we had on them. Their age didn't make them any less so. Fortunately, there was a Navy child psychologist assigned to the hospital, Dr. Tim Dugan, who was an old friend of mine. I valued his judgment and trusted him, so he would be ideal for this task. Tim's skills would be especially useful because our intel indicated that two of the three boys had been brutally raped, were clinically depressed, and suffered from severe post-traumatic stress disorder (PTSD). These prisoners were in bad shape.

Soon I boarded a small military C-12 prop plane out of GTMO and headed to a classified military location on the East Coast of the United States. The next morning we loaded up a huge C-17 with a medical team, military police, and a team of Air Force Special Forces shooters. These guys were a special reserve unit with two purposes in life: 1. Kill anyone who messes with our plane, and 2. Kill anyone who messes with the runway while the plane is on it. Those guys were focused.

The Army MPs were on board for the custody and control of the prisoners. They had more damn guns and weapons than any SWAT team I had ever seen in any city in America. We took off and were in the air for twenty hours, which required us to refuel in midair two or three times. In the darkness, an Air Force KC-135 refueling tanker showed up out of the clouds for the rendezvous with our C-17. From the cockpit I watched the steady hands of the pilots and crew connect these two huge aircraft and complete this dangerous task. We landed at Bagram Air Base in Afghanistan and remained on the runway for a short while, with the Special Forces shooters on high alert, watching for any sign of trouble. Then the back ramp in the tail of the plane was lowered and a truck approached with prisoners, both adults and the teens I was there for. We separated the teenagers out from the other prisoners. I immediately felt sympathy for the young prisoners, though I knew they were far from innocent. They looked not only terrified but also disheveled and lost. The adult detainees looked and smelled repulsive. They smelled like shit or a foul stench of body odor—it was hard to tell the difference. Their hair was uncut, raggedy and long, with long, unkempt beards. The tailgate was closed and we headed back to Cuba.

Twenty or so hours later we landed and I had the teenagers separated according to plan, away from the general adult population. They were in fact never seen by any of the adult prisoners. The command gave me two male interpreters who were fluent in the specific language spoken in the villages where these three boys were raised. The two interpreters had master's degrees in education, were soft-spoken, and had in fact been teachers in Afghanistan for many years prior to emigrating to the United States. Their age was also an important factor. Both were in their fifties, which would engender some respect. They were kind, well educated, and dedicated to helping these three fragile boys. They were exceptional as surrogate fathers, teachers, and protectors.

Back in Cuba, after we had fully processed the incoming prisoners, I was able to get a really good look at the teenagers. I couldn't help but ask myself how these pitiful-looking boys could be a threat to any U.S. soldier. Did they just wake up one day and say, "I want to be a terrorist" or "I want to kill soldiers"? I couldn't connect the dots in my head, so I started to simply ask each of them the questions "how?" and "why?"

The answers that came back through the interpreters were shocking. In the United States we do not use what are known as conscripts. In today's military, you have to volunteer to fight. And even in the past in our country, we drafted people legally and usually not at gunpoint, at least in modern times. But in Afghanistan, young boys are literally dragged from their homes by the local tribal gang lord in a conscription of sorts. Parents watch helplessly in horror, knowing that to intervene would only end in death for the parent, child, or perhaps both. The young teenage boy would usually be brutally raped on the first night of captivity and afterwards made to perform female domestic chores like cooking, washing dishes, and performing sex favors for the gang lord or visiting male guests. It would not be unusual for a thirteen-year-old boy in Afghanistan, after he was forcibly taken at gunpoint, to wear girls' clothes and live in a sex harem.

Bizarre, I thought. *I thought these guys were all supposed to be religious fanatics. How do they do that to young boys?*

All three boys were fragile psychologically, and my job was to ensure that they were never harmed in any way whatsoever. Also, it was a requirement by Major General Miller that in order for any interrogations to be conducted, I had to be present the entire time. We found out that the youngest of the three, who was approximately twelve years of age, had been kidnapped by his province's Taliban gang lord and forced into sex slavery. He was required to wear Afghani girls' clothes, to walk and talk like a girl, and to do domestic chores such as cooking and washing dishes as well as bathing male guests and performing sexual duties as required. The next oldest was approximately fourteen and also had been kidnapped by another Taliban gang lord at gunpoint, literally dragged from his home while his parents watched helplessly, and forced to be the houseboy at the home of the gang lord. On the first night of his captivity, he was held down by three members of this Taliban gang and brutally raped all night. He and the youngest boy would have nightmares and other symptoms associated with post-traumatic stress disorder. The homosexual rape seemed incongruous with what I knew of strict Islamic culture, but sadly, our intelligence from Afghanistan indicated that the boys' experience was not that unusual. It was hard for my mind to process how terrible it must have been. The third teenage terrorist was physically healthy and unharmed sexually, but he was academically the most illiterate of the group.

I asked Hassan, one of the older Afghani translators, to explain more about the prevalence of homosexual rape in the Afghani culture.

"It just doesn't jibe with what I thought about Muslim culture," I said. "When does it stop? Can the boys ever stop being sex slaves?"

"Sir, the custom is that once the boy grows a beard he is no longer seen as attractive to his captors," Hassan told me.

I was being introduced to a new type of enemy we were encountering in this new war, the global war on terrorism. In Afghanistan at least 10 to 20 percent of the soldiers were teenagers. The boys were either forced into the service of a gang lord or were indoctrinated at a younger age at a mosque by radical fundamentalist religious training. Perhaps in a manner similar to the brainwashing of the Ku Klux Klan in our country, radical religious teachers taught these young boys that anyone who was not Muslim was an infidel, and that it was his duty to kill all infidels. Just like the indoctrination of the KKK at the height of its membership in the United States, or the Nazi Party in Germany, the youth members were taught to hate with such ferocity and certainty that it became second nature. For the KKK, all nonwhites and non-Christians were the enemy, and in the group's interpretation, the ethnic, racial, and religious cleansing was justified by scripture. Similarly, the Muslim fundamentalists believed that all nonbelievers had to be put to death.

What developed was a rigid, almost delusional mind-set, so that by the time the boy became a young adult all who believed differently were evil. To complicate the scenario, the rest of the Afghani culture could be cold and brutal. Killing, torture, rape, the opium drug trade, bombmaking, and weapons trafficking were normal for many teenage boys in Afghanistan. After their initial experience with the gangs, these young boys often graduated into trafficking weapons and on to actual war fighting.

One of the boys talked about being raped and seemed to have reframed his experience. He believed that his rape was a "rite of passage" and really had nothing to do with him. The older men had a physical need and he was there to meet that need, he explained. It was no more than that, not sexual, and most certainly not homosexual. The men who raped him were not gay, he said, and they had not committed a homosexual act on him. When the interpreters related the boy's way of looking at his rape, I couldn't really understand.

"Hassan, how can he think that? I mean, he's not homosexual because he was raped by other men, but how can he defend them and say they didn't commit a homosexual act?"

I could tell that Hassan was struggling to explain a part of his culture that was very difficult for outsiders to understand. Without trying to defend the boys' attackers, he patiently explained to me that Afghanis and Americans look at the situation from very different perspectives. In a fundamentalist Muslim culture, homosexuality is strictly forbidden and can result in death, he said, but sex with another man or boy was not seen as homosexual if it was done simply to satisfy a physical need and there was no female around to use instead. In the mountains of Afghanistan, particularly with the tribal gangs that often lived in remote locations and were on the run, looking for women or keeping a woman around camp was not practical. The boys served that role instead.

"But if a man has the opportunity to be with a woman and chooses to be with a boy or a man, that is different," Hassan explained. "That is not the same thing."

I was reminded of a similar philosophy that can be found in prisons worldwide. Sex with a same-sex cellmate doesn't necessarily make you gay, many prisoners will tell you; it's just the only option. It was a lesson in how one's cultural perspective can shift how different people view the same set of facts. But at the same time, my Afghani friend acknowledged that the boys were also just denying some of the terror they had experienced. Hassan explained to me that in their country, good fortune was rare, and putting firm boundaries or compartmentalizing their bad emotional experiences was a requirement to survive. "Colonel, there are no Oprah talk shows in my country. In the U.S. you got a talk show for everything, and if an American can't see it on TV you even have people calling in to strangers on radio shows talking about their personal problems. That's not how it is in my country," he said. "First, you don't talk about your problems with strangers in public, and second, why talk about it or think about it at all? It will not make your problems go away. Sir, this is why it seems like these kids have just put this away in the back of their minds."

Once we learned a little about their pasts, we decided that it was important to get the juveniles healthy before we did anything else. Gathering any intelligence from them would have to wait. Like many children from rural Afghanistan, these three boys could not recall the last time or if ever they had been seen by a doctor. So we had our pediatrician conduct thorough physical examinations and follow them for their medical care.

After getting their health on track, we then had to focus on interrogating them. I realized that talking to these kids was going to be different from the way we talked to most prisoners. How can you interrogate teenagers who can't read and write and who have little exposure to anyone or anything outside their immediate family and village? Most Americans have never even talked to a person who cannot even spell "cat" or add one plus one, but none of the boys could read or write, not even in a rudimentary way.

None of the three had ever ridden an escalator, an elevator, or a plane, and they had never even heard the phrase "video game." They were the most fragile—psychologically, medically, and academically—children I had ever met. Whatever problems they had when they were picked up in Afghanistan, language and cultural barriers exacerbated the problems. Most schizophrenic teenagers in the United States were in better shape.

The biggest problem I had was selecting interrogators who would not be abusive, raise their voice, or use any fear tactics with these boys whatsoever. More so than with other prisoners, we had to approach the interrogation of these boys gently. They were young, scared, and very traumatized, so any harsh tactics would have exactly the opposite of the desired effect, making the boys shut down even more and tell us nothing. I soon realized that these boys exemplified why the methods I wanted to employ at Gitmo were necessary, a case study in how a softer approach will yield more results than brutality. Major General Miller had handed me exactly the type of prisoners I needed to test my philosophy on interrogation.

Fortunately there was an FBI agent on the island who had some limited experience with teenage gangs in Texas, and his experience and style served the process well. We also had a civilian contract interrogator who had many years working with adolescents and teenage boys. The Army did not have enough military interrogators so it hired contractors to do this job, most of whom were retired military or had had many years of military experience as interrogators. The two interrogators bonded with the juveniles like they were their younger brothers.

Though we were dedicated to a gentle approach with these juveniles, there was no mistaking our intentions. We needed these boys to talk to us, and we established a program that would help us get to know them and encourage them to trust us. The boys worked with the Muslim chaplain from 8 a.m. to 9 a.m., were seen by the interrogators from 9 a.m. to 11 a.m., and then they would break for lunch and rest. The rest of the afternoon was reserved for academics, recreation, group prayer, visits as needed with the pediatrician, and instruction on the Koran. Though I hoped they could provide intel that would be useful, I still cringed at using the word "interrogation" with these three boys. The word typically denotes terror, torture, or abuse. After some thought, I instructed everyone at Camp Iguana to use the word "interview" instead—to change both the attitude of those doing the interrogation and the perception of the boys.

My days were intense, trying to make sure the boys were not abused or unnecessarily stressed while also facilitating their interrogation. Each morning I went to physical training, showered, ate breakfast, and spent 9 a.m. to 11 a.m. at Camp Iguana with the teenage terrorists. Afternoons from approximately 1 p.m. to 3 p.m. would be reserved for meetings and consultations with military police, interrogators, and other staff members. It was a daily struggle to keep the staff who had contact with these teenagers mindful and hypervigilant. One of my greatest fears was that, in my effort to help these juveniles heal from their traumatic experiences and to trust us, I would inadvertently encourage the staff to relax too much around them and let their guard down. I worried that I might sound like I was trying to talk out of both sides of my mouth, but I frequently reminded the staff that these juveniles were not sweet kids. All three had been captured while fighting in a combatant role against U.S. forces in Afghanistan. It was easy, because of their youth, disheveled appearance, illiteracy, and poor health, to see them as innocent little boys. This was not the case. On occasion, I had to remind staff that a thirteen-year-old right index finger could pull the trigger on an AK-47 or fire a rocket-propelled grenade as easily as a thirty-year-old finger. It was a constant struggle to find the right psychological balance between seeing them as either terrorists who happened to be fourteen or harmless boys caught up in the tragedy of their third world nation's plight.

The juvenile prisoners consumed much of my time and energy, but they were not my only tasks. While working with them, I was still expected to oversee the rest of the interrogation process at Gitmo and to fix what had gone so wrong in the past. It was clear to me that if I was going to stumble across the abuses and torture Major Leso talked about, I wouldn't find it during the daytime when supervisors were around. I needed to walk the grounds and see what went on at the interrogation booths in the late night. One day I decided to pay an unannounced visit that night to observe interrogations.

However, before leaving work to rest prior to my midnight return, I began to see what Major Leso was concerned about. I went into an office to talk with an interrogator by the name of Luther. Luther was a good old boy from Georgia, a retired warrant-officer interrogator who stood about five feet five inches tall and was built like a fire hydrant. He had trouble in his eyes, anger that he directed at anyone in his path. He was pissed about something, but I didn't know him well enough to broach the subject. I had a brief conversation with Luther as we went over some of his notes from his previous interrogations. As I turned and left his office, I noticed a pair of women's pink panties and a pink nightgown hanging on the back of his office door. Thinking I might do better than to simply ask what the lingerie was for, I made a point to find the schedule for interrogations instead. I wanted to observe Luther's next interrogation, and as luck would have it, he was scheduled for that night. Interrogations were regularly conducted at night as a way to screw with the prisoner's head, to keep him off balance when he was tired.

That night at about 1 a.m. I was making my rounds in the building that housed most of the interrogation booths. The interrogation buildings were prefab trailers with several small rooms about ten feet by ten feet in size. Each had a table, usually three or four chairs, and a metal hook welded to the floor. The hook served as the anchor to fasten a detainee's leg irons during the interrogation.

As I walked toward the observation room with its one-way mirror that would allow me to peek into the interrogation booths, I heard lots of yelling, screaming, and furniture being thrown around. I saw Luther and three MPs wrestling with a detainee on the floor. It was an awful sight. I wanted to run back to my room and wash my eyes with bleach. The detainee was naked except for the pink panties I had seen hanging on the door earlier. He also had lipstick and a wig on. The four men were holding the prisoner down and trying to outfit him with the matching pink nightgown, but he was fighting hard.

My first instinct was to rush in and start barking orders at the men, demanding they stop this ridiculous and abusive wrestling match. But I managed to quell that urge and wait. I opened my thermos, poured a cup of coffee, and watched the episode play out, hoping it would take a better turn and not wanting to interfere without good reason, even if this was a terrible scene. I waited several minutes, but with no good end in sight I had to act.

Someone is gonna get hurt, I thought. *I need to stop this right now.*

I knocked on the door and stepped in, trying hard to look like this crazy scene didn't bother me in the least.

"Hey Luther, you want some coffee?" I asked in a calm, low voice.

Luther, who looked like he'd been wrestling a pig and wasn't coming out ahead, got up off the floor and walked over to me. "I sure do, Colonel," he said, breathing hard. "I'll take you up on that, sir."

I asked the MPs to let the detainee up and put him in the chair for a break. Luther and I poured coffee from my thermos and went outside. We talked about catfishing and the criteria for determining when a hog is properly roasted. This segued into hunting and then why the 1911 .45 caliber pistol is a far better weapon than a 9mm pistol. I never once said anything about the lingerie or the interrogation. My purpose was to build a relationship with Luther rather than to attack him as being wrong or as a human being. What eventually came out was that he was frustrated because the detainee, two days ago, had spit in his face and screamed something lewd at him.

"'I'm gonna butt-fuck your wife' is how I think the interpreter said it, sir," Luther told me. I could tell he took it seriously, probably bundling up all his frustrations and anger about a dozen different things into that one obscene sentence from a prisoner.

He asked me if I would be willing to review the case tomorrow with him and I said yes. We had the detainee taken back to his cell for the night.

The next day, Luther and I met for about two hours. I had read all the background files on the detainee prior to our meeting, so I knew this prisoner was a hardcore terrorist and had been difficult during interrogations. But I asked Luther how the interrogation process had been going.

"Sir, the problem is that the fucker just won't talk to me," Luther said. Just answering my question brought back the frustration for him, and I could see that he was starting to get anxious and angry again. I responded as calmly as if we were just talking about how to get your dog to come when called.

"Hey, I have a couple of questions for you. What is this guy eating every day?"

"The bastard is getting MREs, Colonel," he said, referring to the Meals, Ready-to-Eat that soldiers eat in the field when hot meals aren't available. In some areas, the U.S. military also hands them out to locals in need of food. They're nutritious, but not exactly tasty. "He hasn't had a hot meal in a while because he keeps throwing piss and shit on the guards every time they try to serve him food on a tray."

"Okay," I replied, still avoiding any hint of criticism in my voice. "Are any of the guards pretty females?"

"No way," he said. "He hasn't seen a woman in at least a year. All the corpsmen and medics are fat ugly dudes."

"Well, Luther, here's what I recommend. Go to McDonald's and get a hot fish sandwich. Just one. Then stop off at the PX and get a *Sports Illustrated*, the swimsuit edition."

Luther looked at me like I was crazy. "Where you going with this one, Colonel?" he asked. "You don't want me to give that stuff to him, do you? 'Cause that just ain't right, sir . . ."

"Just stay with me, Luther," I replied. "Luther, I would like for you to go and see this detainee two or three times next week. But don't even bother trying to get anything out of him. Just put him in the booth, eat your sandwich with some pistachio nuts and some fresh hot tea. You know how they all crave tea. And read the *Sports Illustrated* swimsuit edition. Don't say a word to him, but repeat this each time you bring him in the booth. Don't yell at him or be rough in any way."

Luther was looking at me like I'd lost my mind. He didn't see where this was going. I told him to make sure he sat so that the detainee would be able to look over his shoulder and see the hot girls in the magazine, close enough that he could really smell the fish sandwich and the tea. Mind you, the prisoner wasn't being denied food or left hungry. The detainees were fed quite well at Gitmo and almost all of them put on "Gitmo pounds" during their stay. The meals were regular, filling, and culturally appropriate, but a fish sandwich from McDonald's would be a real treat, especially for this guy who was eating MREs at the moment because of his behavior.

"Well hell, I don't mind eating and looking at girls, sir, but that's not doing my job. I'm supposed to be getting intel from this guy. You telling me to just forget that?"

"Only for a while," I told him. "At the end of the week, bring an extra hot fish sandwich. Let's just see what happens."

Luther grinned just slightly and I could tell he was starting to understand the point I was making.

Two weeks went by and Luther reported back to me that that during the first week the detainee seemed as confused as Luther had been at first, then he started showing some interest in the

McDonald's fish sandwich. When Luther held the magazine so that the prisoner could get a glimpse of the scantily clad women, the prisoner perked up and strained to see.

After a week of those silent sessions, with no interaction at all, Luther brought in a second fish sandwich and offered it to the detainee in a casual way, not like a bribe but just as a non-chalant gesture from one person to another—"You want this? Here you go." He continued bringing sandwiches for the prisoner, and on one of those visits he also left the magazine on the table for him. On my instructions, Luther soon told the prisoner, in a very hushed, conspiratorial tone after checking to make sure no guards were watching, "Here, you take this magazine back to your cell. Just hide it in your pants. I understand you're a man like me, and you need this." The guards, of course, were in on the ruse and didn't "find" the hidden magazine.

The prisoner's attitude improved so much that he looked forward to his interrogation sessions and enjoyed seeing Luther walk into the room. Slowly over that second week, Luther started talking to him.

It wasn't long before the rapport between Luther and the detainee led to useful intel. There was no need for me to lecture and hammer home how this approach could work so much better than trying to wrestle a detainee into a pink nightgown; Luther saw the results for himself. Luther shared his experience with the other interrogators and soon most of the noncompliant detainees became cooperative. Incentive-, respect-based interrogations began to catch on. I saw Luther in the parking lot late one afternoon and he told me the new strategy was continuing to work.

"But Colonel, I still can't figure out why your recommendations worked so well with that son of a bitch," he said. "I mean, it sure as hell worked, but why would a mean bastard like that open up just because I gave him a sandwich?"

"Luther, my momma taught me that a good meal among enemies can cast good fortune," I told him. "Luther, remember all human beings have the capacity to appreciate and understand acts of decency and kindness, even that dude who says something nasty about your wife. 'Treat a man the way you want to be treated' is what Reverend Johnson would say."

"Sir, who in the hell is Reverend Johnson?"

"Luther, he was my Baptist minister many years ago," I said. "I learned a lot from him."

The technique I taught Luther was just one way we got prisoners to talk without anything remotely abusive. Much of the culture at Gitmo in 2002 and 2003, perhaps due to the anger over 9/11, involved projecting one's rage onto the detainees. My role was to teach rapport and relationship-building approaches between the detainee and the interrogators without the abuse. Simple things like kindness, sweets, pizza, cigarettes, movies, tea, and magazines went a long way in fostering these relationships. If a fish sandwich and a girlie magazine didn't work, then there were other plans we could implement. For instance, if the prisoner was an older male it would sometimes be effective to have a young, petite female interrogator work with him in a very calm and reassuring manner, rather than a more aggressive male interrogator.

I had a hundred scenarios we could try. No matter which strategy we employed, the goal was always the same: get the prisoner to say something in response. *Anything.* Once the prisoner said, "Okay," or "Thank you," or "Praise Allah," I knew we had him. From there it was only a matter of time before he told us something useful.

There would be many more challenges to come at Gitmo, and I had no idea at the time that how we handled those challenges would shape the future role for military psychologists in this global war on terrorism. For example, one afternoon I was having lunch in the chow hall and a female nurse who was a Navy lieutenant commander came to see me in a fit of anger. Her name was Lieutenant Commander Pearl Henderson from northern California. "Commander, I have been hearing about you and I've been looking forward to meeting you," I said with a smile. "Pour yourself a cup of coffee and let's see if we can work this thing out."

She began talking really fast and I regretted offering her coffee. This was an intense woman. I captured enough of what she was saying to understand that she was upset with how interrogators were coming over to the medical clinic and demanding unhindered access to detainees' medical records. This was a surprise to me, and a disturbing concept to a psychologist. I had to ask her to slow down and give me a better understanding of what was going on.

"I'm not tracking with you at all," I said. "They're doing what with the medical records?"

She explained to me that there was a federal regulation that made it perfectly legal for any interrogator, regardless of rank, educational background, or age, to have legal open access to any detainee's medical record. What I discovered was that on any given day, FBI, CIA, Army, Navy, and contract interrogators would go to the hospital and demand to see detainees' records immediately. If any of the doctors or nurses hesitated — and they naturally would as medical professionals — these interrogators, some of them only eighteen or twenty years old, would simply walk into the medical records room and help themselves. It was allowed by federal law but it ran counter to everything the doctors and nurses held sacred about the privacy of medical records.

I told the lieutenant commander that in spite of what the regulation or law said, from a practical standpoint this system just didn't seem to be working. Not only was I sympathetic to the staff's desire to protect those records, but I also could see that the animosity generated by interrogators snatching records from the clinic was counterproductive to our overall mission. So Lieutenant Commander Henderson and I devised a plan that would keep the interrogators from having any physical access to the records. We painted an invisible red line around the entire medical hospital by declaring that the hospital and all doctors and nurses were completely off-limits to anyone from the intel community. The biscuit staff were the only members of the Joint Intelligence Group or the entire intel community who would have any access or discuss any medical information with the doctors and nurses. Even though the interrogators were incredibly pissed at this, and though technically it circumvented federal law, the plan actually worked. It streamlined the process and stopped thirty or forty interrogators on any day of the week from storming over to the hospital and creating havoc.

Now, we thought this was a fine solution to a real problem. But then the media got hold of the story and, of course, they completely distorted what was happening. We later saw and heard reports in the news media about how biscuit was supposedly stealing medical information and using it to help interrogators craft interrogation plans. On June 10, 2004, the *Washington Post* reported that "Military interrogators at the U.S. detention facility at Guantanamo Bay, Cuba, have been given access to the medical records of individual prisoners, a breach of patient confidentiality that ethicists describe as a violation of international medical standards designed to protect captives from inhumane treatment."

The newspaper went on to say, "How military interrogators used the information is unknown. But a previously undisclosed Defense Department memo dated Oct. 9 cites Red Cross complaints that the medical files 'are being used by interrogators to gain information in developing an interrogation plan.'"

The October 9 memo, however, contained no information or proof to support these accusations. In fact, the intent of the biscuit was to be the keepers of the relevant medical information so that no detainee would ever be harmed. We had to have that information because if someone in our position did not know of a detainee's disease or medical condition, detainees could be harmed. So we, the biscuit, became the gatekeepers of this information in order to protect it. We used the information to make sure all prisoners received their medications and that detainees with major psychiatric illnesses, such as psychotic patients, were not interrogated at all. Most importantly, we used this information to eliminate the possibility that any ill or fragile detainee would be harmed as a result of some abusive interrogation technique. So what came out of the new arrangement was that any time interrogators needed to know if there were any medical complications, they would first come to us before starting their interrogations. But the International Committee of the Red Cross and the media reported the exact opposite—that we were hoarding the information for nefarious reasons and using it, in effect, to tell interrogators exactly where to poke the prisoner with a sharp stick.

The next month seemed to go by in a blur. I was starting to feel some satisfaction that we were making progress in turning this ship around, and especially when I stepped out into the dark Caribbean night air, the stillness and quiet could lull me into thinking that all was well. On one particular night, I learned this was just an illusion. I decided to make some rounds on one of the cellblocks. *It's always good to see what's going on at night,* I thought.

I entered the prison building and started looking around. Everything seemed relatively calm, nothing out of the ordinary. I figured I would look through the rest of the cellblock and then head back to my place for some sleep. But as I walked toward the cellblock the detainees started throwing feces, urine, and other bodily fluids all over the place. It was a full-scale, all-out riot. I had heard this was a pretty common occurrence, sometimes sparked by an action like one of the detainees being taken out of his cell for interrogation, but just as often by nothing at all. The cellblock would be quiet and suddenly erupt into chaos. On this night, I had no idea what started the riot, if anything, but I could see that the guards and other staff were trying to dodge urine, feces, and other bodily fluids thrown at the nineteen- to twenty-one-year-olds. I was amazed at the level of discipline shown by the guards. There was no yelling, no cursing, and none of the guards threw the cups filled with feces back at the detainees. They were better Americans than me, I thought as I watched. Night after night for twelve-hour shifts, the guards stood stead-fastly on duty to cope with the horror of these attacks. There was no way at nineteen I could have handled this, a foreign prisoner spitting in my face only to be followed by the same knucklehead hitting me in the back of the head with a cup of feces. On many nights I asked myself, where did we get these young Americans from? As I watched, a Styrofoam cup filled with feces and urine hit a young female sergeant directly in the face. She calmly turned and instructed the detainee to "knock it off."

I was tense and worried about what else might come flying through the air, maybe something that would do some real dam-age instead of just disgusting me. One of the guards ran to me and took me by the arm in a firm grip, yelling in my ear to be heard over the noise of the riot in the background.

"Don't worry, Colonel. We'll get these shitheads under con-trol. And Colonel, it will get a whole lot uglier before it gets better."

My escort rushed me to the exit and I burst outside, the door slamming behind me as the guards continued their efforts to quell the riot. Standing there alone in the Cuban breeze, cov-ered in Taliban feces and urine, I was utterly disgusted and couldn't decide if it was better to ride in my car to my hooch or walk. I decided walking was a better option to avoid getting this foul smell permanently imprinted into my car. As I walked, I had to acknowledge the absurdity of the situation I found myself in, and it was actually a relief to laugh at myself and give myself a few moments of respite from the deadly serious thoughts that occupied my mind the rest of the time at Gitmo. I kept coming back to the young men and women we had serving as the guards on the cellblocks. They were an amazing, untold story, steadfastly doing their duty without ever retaliating. By the time I reached my hooch, I had created a new term for the military—the TOW. The TOW acronym was not new to the Army, but it usually stood for "tank offensive weapon," a missile launched from a Humvee designed to kill Russian tanks. After that night, I always thought of TOW as the Turd Offensive Weapon. I learned from talking to the MPs afterward that the prisoners also had a variation we came to call the SOW—the Semen Offensive Weapon. No matter which primary ingredient was used, the methodology was the same: make the deposit in a cup, add some toilet paper for stability when throwing, douse liberally in urine, and hide the concoction in your cell for a while to let it ferment. Then wait for an opportune moment when the guard lets his attention wander and suddenly—wham!— fling the TOW or SOW by reaching through the "bean chute" used to pass in meals. One detainee explained to a guard that he omitted the toilet paper in his preparations because that promoted a better dispersal on impact. And he insisted that he had done "scientific studies" to confirm the benefits of his approach.

I went home and took the longest shower of my entire time in Cuba. As I stood there scrubbing and scrubbing, I realized that though I could laugh about the insanity of that moment, the riot reminded me that I still had plenty of work to do. The next day we had many long meetings to come up with safe ways of disrupting the detainees' tendency to throw TOWs at the guards. The first move was to take away all their cups and water bottles, followed soon by the erection of Plexiglas walls that would prevent them throwing anything into the middle of the cellblock. My experience that night also gave me a newfound respect for the guards who watched over the detainees and who were subjected to that kind of abuse day in and day out, yet still found the discipline to be professional and not respond the way most people would when someone throws shit at them.

I decided I needed to get back to walking the halls of the interrogation buildings on a regular basis. A few days went by and I showed up at about 2 a.m. to see what was going on in a particular building. Like on many of the nights before, I heard a noise, yells and screams, and decided to check it out.

As I watched through a one-way observation window, I saw a detainee being held straight up in a corner by two large, mean, badass-looking MPs, an interrogator, and an interpreter. The four of them yelled at the prisoner as loudly as they possibly could. The interrogator decided it was time for a break after the detainee spit in the left eye of the shortest MP. They put the prisoner down and started exiting. Once the interpreter, Hakim, came out of the room, I asked him how long had they been going at it and he told me it had been three hours.

"Three hours of that?" I asked.

"Yes sir," he said. "This one won't talk, so we're on him pretty hard, sir."

"Okay . . ." I said, trying not to signal any criticism. "Hakim, has the detainee been to the bathroom or had anything to eat or drink during this time?"

"No sir."

When the interrogator returned from wherever he'd gone for a break, I asked if it was okay if I came into the room and simply observed. I didn't really need his permission, but I wanted to let him retain his authority in the interrogation and not lose face in front of the other men. He replied that he wouldn't mind. We all went into the interrogation room and the prisoner immediately noticed that there was now a fifth person to scream at him and toss him around the room. Before the interrogation began again, I pulled the interrogator aside.

"How about if you get the detainee something to eat and drink? And maybe he could be allowed to go to the bathroom?" I said. "What do you think?"

The interrogator seemed a bit surprised by the suggestion but he didn't want to argue with a colonel, so he said yes. After about another half hour the detainee was allowed to go to the bathroom and get some water. When the MPs brought him back to the room, he looked directly at me and said something in broken English that sounded like a thank-you.

I asked the interpreter what he had said. "He said, 'Thank you,' sir," the interpreter confirmed.

The comment didn't impress me much, because I wasn't looking to coddle the prisoner. If anything the expression of gratitude just confirmed to me that a softer touch might get more intel out of this guy. But then I looked from the interpreter back to the detainee and found him staring at me intently, with a dark, piercing look that did not convey appreciation.

The prisoner continued looking into my eyes as he began to

speak to me in Arabic. When he paused, I kept my eyes on him and asked the interpreter what he had said.

"Sir, I don't know if you really want to know what he said to you," the interpreter said.

I turned to the interpreter and said, "Tell me exactly what he said, Hakim. Word for word."

"Sir, the detainee told you thank you for being kind to him but he said he was going to kill you as soon as he got out of here."

Hmmm . . . well, that's an interesting sentence.

"Ask the detainee why on earth would he want to kill me," I told the interpreter. "I've done nothing to harm him."

The detainee responded quickly and forcefully as soon as he heard the question in Arabic. "He says you're a Kaffir, sir."

"A Kaffir? What does that word mean?"

Before he could reply, the detainee screamed, "Infidel!" The prisoner was growing agitated, as if he had to get through to me why I had to die.

I was a bit confused about why the prisoner would react this way after thanking me for a small kindness, though I was not unfamiliar with the mindless, singular fanaticism that possessed this man and most of the other prisoners at Gitmo. The man was talking to us, and that was progress of a sort, so I continued the exchange.

"Why am I an infidel? Is it because I'm an American?"

The prisoner shouted and slobbered some more.

"No, you're an infidel because you're a nonbeliever," the interpreter said. "In order for me to get to heaven, I must kill you as soon as possible."

"Well, okay. Good to know," I said, getting up to leave.

I told the men to continue talking with him about whatever he was willing to talk about, which would probably be a lesson in why we're all infidel pigs who must die, and he's going to fuck your mother, and America is the Great Satan, blah, blah, blah. As long as he's talking, you might be able to steer him into giving up some intel, I reminded them.

This Taliban prisoner was more confusing than most I had seen in my career, but he was not that unusual among the detainees we were encountering in the global war on terrorism. They could be disarmingly gentle and appreciative seconds before pledging to kill you and your whole family. I wondered to myself if this detainee I had just seen was a sociopath, mentally ill, or delusional. Was he unique or just goddamned crazy? I was coming to understand that America was at war with an enemy like no other we have ever faced. Moreover, it became clear that with people like that dedicated to our destruction, even if we terminated the threat from Al Qaeda tomorrow, the larger war could go on for the next fifty years. This new enemy had as its goal the total destruction of all "nonbelievers." And if this would mean killing themselves in the process, that would be fine and be their pathway to heaven and a life of eternal bliss. That is a hell of an enemy to fight.

My work with the juvenile detainees continued, and over time the boys did start talking to us, providing some useful intelligence about their experience with the Taliban in Afghanistan. We were quite proud of the work we did with these three boys, who stayed with us in Cuba for about a year before returning home far better off academically, medically, and psychologically than when they were brought to Gitmo. When U.S. forces captured them in Afghanistan, those boys were flat-out dumber than a bag of rocks, in poor physical health, and one of the three had severe PTSD. The educational, medical, and psychological staff worked tirelessly each day to restore their humanity, mental health, and physical health. By the time they returned back to their home, they were all functioning at the sixth to eighth grade academic level. They were medically healthy and doing well psychologically.

This is how my country handles prisoners, I reminded myself. *It's not all about abuse. We can take juveniles like that and send them home better than we found them.*

My tour at Gitmo flew by as we continued making progress in righting the wrongs that had brought me there. The interrogators and MPs came around to the incentive- and respect-based approach, seeing for themselves that they could get better results than they had been getting with the methods that danced on that knife edge of what was acceptable and what was abusive. On May 5, 2003, I boarded a military chartered plane and headed home. Although ultimately I enjoyed my tour at Gitmo, confident that I had done good work and accomplished a great deal, I hoped that I would never see the island again. As I walked off the plane at Naval Air Station Jacksonville, Florida, I felt I had done something meaningful in the global war on terror.

It took us a while to get it right at Gitmo, but now that the war in Iraq will be ending soon, that should be it, I thought. *I'm glad we won't be sending any psychologists to POW or detention fa-cilities in Iraq. This global war on terror thing will end soon and my world will return to normal. I'll be seeing patients, teaching, conducting research, and lying in the comfort of my wife's arms each night.*

I had no idea what was coming.

4
Long Flight to Hell

April 2004

Almost a year had passed since I departed Gitmo in May 2003 and returned to Walter Reed. My wife and I were living at Fort Meade, Maryland, which is the lush military housing area for senior officers assigned to Walter Reed. Springtime at Fort Meade arrived on a Sunday in April 2004. The sun was bright and I could see early signs of spring in the budding trees and lawn emerging from the melting snow. The soft chill in the air coupled with the comforting heat from my brick fireplace somehow seemed to quiet my usually active house. I was determined to be a recluse on this day. My wife was away for a conference, and my chores were done by about 10 a.m. After a slow four-mile run at the track at Fort Meade, I found myself on the sofa drifting off to sleep while CNN faded away in the background. Oddly, my thoughts found passage again to Guantanamo Bay, Cuba. I sighed, tried to put these memories aside, and wondered if my duties would ever call me to such a place again. I thought not, as I sank into a two-hour sleep.

I awoke abruptly to a reporter's voice, seemingly loud even

Indianapolis-Marion County Public Library
www.imcpl.org
Phone:(317) 275-4450
Telephone Renewal:(317) 269-5222

Title: Fixing hell : an army p...
Due: 11/20/10
Item: 31978070911409

Title: A beautiful mind
Due: 11/02/10
Item: 31978075072256

Total items checked out: 2

though the TV's sound was but a whisper. The volume and urgency in his voice spiraled up, signaling more than just the routine report to fill time on CNN. I turned my head and saw the first images of a horrible place called Abu Ghraib. In my groggy state, I could only make out fuzzy images of prisoners and American soldiers. I arose, staggered to the TV, remote in hand, turning the volume to high, my attention focused—and watched. Even in my half-awake state, I almost felt I was there; I could see the sights and hear the sounds clearly at this diabolical place, even though it was on the other side of the world. At that precise moment, images of naked dog piles, an Iraqi prisoner standing with a hangman's noose around his neck, and K-9 dogs terrorizing detainees were forever etched in my memory and humanity.

I felt both sick and furious. As I lay back down on the sofa, I wondered how this could have happened after everything we did at Gitmo.

What dumbass psychologist at the prison let this happen? Didn't he read the standard operating procedures I wrote at Gitmo a year ago? I'm gonna track that bastard down and kick his ass!

I nearly yelled out loud as I was thinking what I would do to the lousy doctor who let this happen on his watch. Then I calmed myself.

This has to be a misunderstanding. No American soldiers would do these things. Tomorrow I'll call Colonel Banks and get to the bottom of this debacle. There's got to be some kind of explanation.

The exhaustion and fatigue that was a constant state of being from working at Walter Reed Army Medical Center engulfed me again. It occurred to me that maybe, just maybe, these TV images were a part of a dream fog that is common in early hypnogogic states while awakening.

What the hell . . . Maybe I'm just dreaming.

I put the CNN report out of my mind and fell back into a deep sleep.

When I woke up again, CNN was still on and they were still talking about Abu Ghraib. It wasn't a dream. On Monday morning, at 7:30 a.m., I called Colonel Morgan Banks at his office at Fort Bragg, North Carolina, Special Operations Command. Morgan was the command psychologist with whom I had worked to get Major Leso some better training for the tasks he faced in Gitmo. Morgan was intimately familiar with the work we had done in Gitmo and the steps we put in place to prevent further abuses. He was a good friend and the nation's most respected psychologist at the Special Operations Command, but as soon as he picked up the phone, I barked at him.

"Morgan, what in the heck is going on at Abu Ghraib, and who's the dumb son-of-a-bitch psychologist we have out there?"

Morgan replied in his crisp military style. "That's the problem, Larry. We don't have a biscuit psychologist at that place. You and I know what the standard should be, but until now, the leadership wouldn't listen to me."

I was dumbfounded. All the possible explanations I had running through my mind hinged on why the psychologist at Abu Ghraib had dropped the ball. But there was no biscuit psychologist? It took me a minute to even process that.

"Larry, look, I can't talk now," Colonel Banks continued. "I'm on the run and lots of shit is happening, but I do need to talk to you. I'll be coming to town real soon, and I'll call you when I get to D.C."

There was a pause on the line. Then Colonel Banks added,

"Larry, some shit is about to hit the fan over this thing. I'll be in town for some Senate committee hearing."

I felt bad for my friend having to deal with this growing mess, but a big part of me was just happy that it wasn't me. Over the next month, my time at Walter Reed accelerated like gas on a barn fire. I had recently learned that I was being reassigned to Tripler Army Medical Center in Hawaii—a respite from the East Coast, I naively thought. I had been at Walter Reed for five years, and knowing that I'd be heading to Hawaii was not only welcome news for me, but for my lovely wife, Janet. I had been the chief of Walter Reed's Psychology Department for five years. I was burned out and needed the tranquillity of Hawaii. The simplest matters of one's day were difficult stuff at Walter Reed, and I was psychologically spent. I felt I had done my share of hard work in recent years and was looking forward to some time on the beach with my wife.

As my wife and I headed toward our departure date in the beginning of May, the headlines were dominated by more pictures and reports of abuses at Abu Ghraib. As it became a commonplace story on the news each night, I worked to distance myself from the tragedy.

Don't get yourself wrapped up in this, Larry, I told myself. *This is somebody else's task. Let them deal with it.*

I foolishly thought that somehow, this would work itself out without me. I could escape to the paradise of Hawaii—my tropical psychological home. I had survived Walter Reed and a tour at Gitmo. My duty was done, and my wife and I were ready to move on.

On Thursday, May 6, 2004, we had only four days before I

left for my new Hawaiian post. That day, the phone rang at my office in Walter Reed. It was Colonel Banks. We engaged in the type of conversation that senior military officers reserve for discussing sensitive information on an unsecured phone line. These conversations were similar to a chat with Sergeant Joe Friday of the old *Dragnet* TV series—just the facts, ma'am, just the facts.

"Larry, are you gonna be in town this weekend? Man, I *really* need to talk to you."

My thoughts were elsewhere as I glanced at pictures of Bellows Air Force Station beach in Hawaii, my granddaughter who lives in Hawaii, and the ocean. I was going to be there so very soon. For a second, I almost forgot I was on a serious phone call. I snapped back into it, "Morgan, you can just call me on my cell anytime."

"No, man," he stressed, "I need to talk to you in person. I'll call you at home this weekend."

Clearly, the unsecured phone line he was on would not allow him to detail the seriousness of the issues. But I could tell from the tone of his voice that he had a real mess on his hands and needed some help.

On Saturday, May 8, I attended to the details of moving 22,000 pounds of furniture (why the hell did we need so much furniture? I wondered to myself), two cars, and all of our worldly possessions 10,000 miles from D.C. to Hawaii. On Sunday, my wife and I decided to take the train to Union Station in Washington, D.C., one last time before we flew to Hawaii. Even though I longed to experience the peacefulness of Hawaii again, I had already started to miss the unique aspects of the District. While downtown, we walked to the Smithsonian Museum of Natural History, one of our favorite sites in D.C. On this gorgeous blue-sky day, my wife and I wanted to just stroll along the Mall, visit the souvenir booths, and experience the life of this great city before leaving. We were eager to go back to Hawaii, but we would miss this home too.

Unknown to me at the time, Colonel Banks was already in town for the Department of Defense inspector general committee meeting on Abu Ghraib that he had mentioned on the phone. Later this would become known as the Taguba report, after Major General Taguba, the officer in charge of the team that went in to evaluate Abu Ghraib. At exactly 1 p.m. that Sunday afternoon—just as I was heading up the stairs to the museum—my cell phone rang. It was Banks.

"Larry, where are you?" he said urgently. "General Miller wants you in Abu Ghraib. He needs your help to fix the mess. Larry, I need to talk with you ASAP."

My heart sank. Instantly I began to see clear images of Gitmo all over again. "Morgan, can't we just talk now on the phone?" I asked.

"Larry, this is a conversation we need to have in person. Where are you right now?"

I answered as much for my wife's sake as for mine. "I'm with my wife, and we're at the Smithsonian, the Museum of Natural History." I was hoping he would tell me to just enjoy the afternoon with my wife and he'd get back to me later.

"No shit, Larry," Morgan shot back. "Are you kidding me? I'm on the second floor with my wife. I'll meet you outside of the museum's main entrance in fifteen minutes."

Only in D.C., I thought, shaking my head at the coincidence. At 1:30 p.m. on the steps of the Smithsonian, I spotted the colonel. Even when he was in civilian clothes, a blind man could see that

Morgan Banks was a Green Beret and a soldier to the core. From the moment he shook your hand you knew the situation and the plan; he always reminded me of Lee Marvin in *The Dirty Dozen*. Without wasting any time, Colonel Banks laid out the horror of Abu Ghraib, the details that an unsecured phone line would not allow to be shared.

"Larry, it's a fuckin' shit mess at this place. We learned at Gitmo that we needed to have a psychologist in place the next time around. Well, man, they fucked this up good."

He paused, then continued. "Larry, you need to read the General Taguba inspector general report ASAP. There is a declassified version you can download off of CNN. Here's the problem in a nutshell: they have had poor leadership, poor facilities, and piss-poor supervision."

I couldn't get the classified version because 99.99 percent of all computers in military hospitals have unsecured computers and unsecured phone lines. Banks explained that I was a "by name" request from Major General Miller, my old boss in Gitmo, to deploy to Abu Ghraib to put procedures in place to fix these problems. Major General Miller had once said that I was the best operational psychologist in the Army and that he trusted me. This wasn't a matter of me simply being named a good candidate; Major General Miller had specifically said I was the one person who could and should go fix this fuckup in Abu Ghraib. Twenty or thirty years earlier in my career, I would have relished being singled out for such an honor, but now I could only focus on the practical side of what it meant for me and my wife.

"Will you take the assignment, Larry?" Colonel Banks asked me. "You need to be there soon."

"Of course, yes," I said.

But I still was not getting the picture. My innocent thought was: *I'll fly to Hawaii, and I'll have three to six months to buy a home, get my wife settled, relax, and then go to Abu Ghraib.*

Colonel Banks thanked me, we shook hands, and he asked me to give him a call when I arrived in Hawaii.

As soon as the official business with Colonel Banks was complete, I joined back up with my wife, and we visited the Smithsonian Asian Art and African American museums, just like any other couple enjoying a Sunday afternoon jaunt in downtown D.C. Military husbands and wives have a way of compartmentalizing worry, fear, and the normal emotions that paralyze most couples, so we spoke little about my conversation with Colonel Banks and what it would mean for us.

The next morning, Janet and I boarded a United Airlines plane out of Reagan National Airport to Honolulu and headed west for what we thought would be a needed break. We arrived in Honolulu late that Monday night and were greeted by our son and granddaughter and a close family friend at the airport. How I had longed over these long five years at Walter Reed to be with my son and my granddaughter again! My three-year-old granddaughter held a striking resemblance to my son. Her intense brown eyes, engaging laugh, affection for all living things around her, and energy would capture the hearts of many. We went to Anna Miller's All Night Restaurant and had breakfast. My granddaughter sat on my lap the entire time and must have said my name fifty times. My son, as usual, lamented the many problems with his antique cars, spoke excitedly of his new job, and told us of the splendor of now being a college graduate. I couldn't have been happier.

I reported for duty bright and early the next morning, May 11, at 7:30 a.m. I had no downtime to get my bearings, but that was okay. At least I was in Hawaii again. On the way to my office I met my secretary, whom I knew from my earlier work at the hospital, in the hallway. I expected to exchange some pleasantries. But instead she looked at me strangely.

"Colonel James, we're surprised to see you," she said. Her voice was tinged with an unusual seriousness, as if she were worried. "You're not supposed to be here . . ."

"Ms. Judy, what on earth are you talking about?" I asked.

The look on her face was growing more and more serious. "Colonel, you have orders on your desk that say you should have been at a place in Iraq called Abu-something by *yesterday*. We thought you must be there already."

The blood drained from my head. *Awww shit* . . . I stumbled into the office of the chief psychologist, the officer I came to Hawaii to replace, and demanded an explanation. "What in the heck is going on?"

Meeting my forceful language with his own, he replied, "Larry, you need to call Colonel Banks ASAP. All hell has broken loose up on the Hill with this Abu Ghraib thing and Congress wants it fixed *now*!!"

Dazed by the sudden acceleration, I could only think over and over how I had naively counted on three to six months before I headed down range to Iraq. I found a phone, called Colonel Banks, and informed him that I felt a tad misled.

"Morgan," I said, trying hard to keep my voice light, "you have a new definition of the word 'soon.' You just talked with me yesterday about this." He briefed me on the urgency, how the pressure on President Bush and Defense Secretary Rumsfeld was mounting and the Army needed to send me there to put a plan in place posthaste. The colonel reminded me that, regardless of what either the president or Rumsfeld wanted, it was the right moral thing to put procedures in place quickly so that the abuses would never occur again. I couldn't argue with that.

I made some phone calls to get more details. In between each call, I dialed my wife, but hung up before the call went through. This talk with my soul mate of thirty years needed to be in person. I realized that the loneliness of being away from her had already begun to haunt me deep in my soul.

My wife was a seasoned veteran of the madness of military life and I knew she would roll with this latest punch just as she had done many times in years past. But we both would later learn that this deployment would try and test both of our souls in ways we had never experienced before. As I walked into our hotel room, even before I spoke, she knew something was amiss. She saw an intense seriousness, perhaps the death stare all soldiers have in their eyes when they know their pending duties may be their last journey in life. She already knew I was going to this faraway, wretched place, but like me, she hadn't realized it would come this soon. She also knew this deployment was different and the perils were greater. Unlike any previous field assignment, I was heading right into a hot combat zone where American servicemen and -women were dying every day. Though we never spoke of this possibility, she knew that she might never see me again.

Yet, after I told her the news of the imminent deployment, she came through as strongly as I expected. It was like watching her change the tire on that little car again. She looked at me with determined eyes.

"Not a problem," she said. "I'll stay in the hotel for a few

months until we close on a house. But Larry, there's more we
need to talk about. Mary was notified this morning that her Hawaii Army Reserve unit is deploying in June. That's less than one
month away."

Mary was my son's ex, the mother of our gorgeous three-year-
old granddaughter. She was a personnel clerk in her reserve unit
and her deployment meant that our granddaughter would be
staying with us until Mary returned. Now that I was going to be
away, that meant that my wife would be living in a hotel with
our granddaughter. All of our furniture and the two cars were on
a slow boat across the Pacific, and her entire social network was
on the East Coast. Janet had so much on her shoulders, and yet
she managed to stand tall.

Later that day, when I returned to my office, I received an e-mail
from Dr. Philip Zimbardo saying he wanted to meet with me
when he came to Honolulu to lecture at the University of Hawaii. Zimbardo was considered perhaps the most famous psychologist alive, best known for his studies on how good people
turn evil—most notably demonstrated through his controversial
Stanford Prison Experiment of 1971. In this study, discussed in
psychology classes throughout the world, he divided young men
into prisoners and prison guards to demonstrate the powerful
situational forces on individual behavior. Zimbardo found that
even good people, when put into positions of authority under
certain circumstances, can become abusive and lose all restraint.
I had already been thinking that Zimbardo's experiment, and
what he learned from it, would prove useful in helping me fix
what was wrong at Abu Ghraib. So his call, and his upcoming

trip, turned out to be serendipitous. I needed to craft a plan in a hurry to stop the craziness as soon as my Black Hawk helicopter touched down at the Abu Ghraib compound. There was little time for literature searches and committees with my academic colleagues; both activities would occupy my time and would be futile efforts. I knew that Phil had lots of real-life information to share from his prison study. Hell, even he had gotten caught up in the madness of his experiment gone wrong, so he could speak from experience, not just as an observer. I needed to pick Zimbardo's brain about what went wrong with his prison project, and how he would do the study differently to prevent abuses. Perhaps, I thought, this might help us down the road in Iraq at Abu Ghraib.

Zimbardo came to town that very week. We met and discussed what went wrong in his study. From what I already knew of Abu Ghraib, the situation there seemed to have a lot in common with Zimbardo's experiment. In both cases, what started as a legitimate, necessary endeavor—supposedly with controls in place to protect the participants—went very, very wrong. Zimbardo had to terminate the experiment when the college boys assigned to act as prison guards became abusive—and when he realized that in his role as the prison "superintendent" he was condoning it. Something similar was happening in Abu Ghraib, I suspected, and I needed Zimbardo to guide me in the right direction.

I met up with Zimbardo for breakfast early one morning at a sidewalk café right in the heart of downtown Waikiki, Honolulu. Phil and I ate pastries and drank strong Italian coffee while we discussed what he had heard about Abu Ghraib and the unclassified intel I knew about the situation.

The timing could not be more perfect, I kept thinking.

Zimbardo, a tall, dark-haired, handsome man, had a gift for telling long stories filled with moral dilemmas and a concern for social justice, the same as myself. He had traveled the world many times over and had volumes of knowledge in his head about what had gone wrong at many prisons around the world. I was but a rookie compared to his skills. I wasn't interested in the gory stories and the big picture of torture. Rather, I was curious about the early signs of abuse and how it would lead to outright torture. After some friendly chat to catch up with each other, I got right to it.

"Phil, tell me about your study at Stanford, your prison project. How did things get so fucked up so quickly?" I asked. I was searching for whatever I could to help me in my mission at Abu Ghraib.

In his Stanford Prison Experiment in 1971, the goal was to assess the effects of prison life on normal young men. As described on Zimbardo's Web site and in his book *The Lucifer Effect*, Zimbardo and his team wanted to test the hypothesis that guards and prisoners tended to come to their roles with certain inherent traits that would promote poor prison conditions—in particular, the idea that people with sadistic tendencies gravitated toward jobs as prison guards. Zimbardo recruited students through a newspaper ad and paid them $15 a day ($75 in 2007 dollars).

All of the subjects selected for the study were normal in every way; they all came from good families, were well-educated and financially secure, and had no history of alcohol or drug abuse or psychological problems—this was key to what Zimbardo wanted to test. Anyone who had a history of psychological or drug problems was carefully screened out. Zimbardo emphasized to me that the selection of participants was very important.

"We wanted to make sure that no one could throw out the study by saying one bad thing about how we designed it because students in the sample had preexisting psychological problems," he explained as we ordered more coffee. "So we excluded anyone in our study who had any hint of mental illness. Out of seventy-five applicants, we selected twenty-four."

The "prison" was in the basement of the Stanford Psychology Department in Palo Alto, California. Zimbardo explained that he had flipped a coin to randomly assign one group of young men to be prisoners and the other group to be prison guards.

With wooden batons, khaki uniforms, and mirrored sunglasses, the guards looked the part. While the guards could return home during off hours, many would later volunteer for added duty without additional pay. The prisoners wore muslin smocks with no underwear and rubber thong sandals, both chosen to be intentionally uncomfortable. Zimbardo explained that the uncomfortable clothing had a subtle but important effect, forcing the men to adopt "unfamiliar body postures" that helped to disorient and agitate them. They were referred to by assigned numbers instead of by name. These numbers were sewn on to their uniforms, and the prisoners were required to wear tight-fitting nylon pantyhose caps to the simulate shaven heads often found in prisons. A small chain around their ankles served as a symbolic reminder of their status.

Zimbardo briefed the guards before the experiment began and gave them only very simple instructions: no physical violence was permitted against prisoners. Other than that, it was up to them how to run the prison. Zimbardo also told the guards this:

"You can create in the prisoners feelings of boredom, a sense of fear to some degree, you can create a notion of arbitrariness that their life is totally controlled by us, by the system, you, me, and they'll have no privacy . . . . We're going to take away their individuality in various ways. In general what all this leads to is a sense of powerlessness. That is, in this situation we'll have all the power and they'll have none."

In *The Lucifer Effect*, Zimbardo explains how the "prisoners" were told to wait at home until the experiment began. Suddenly the Palo Alto Police Department, which was cooperating with Zimbardo at this point, showed up and "arrested" them. They were "charged" with armed robbery and after a full booking procedure by the police, including fingerprinting, having their mug shots taken, and listening to information regarding their Miranda rights, they were delivered to Zimbardo's prison, where a strip-search and delousing awaited them.

The behavior of both the guards and prisoners was shocking. Zimbardo found that even though this was only a study simulating prison life, the guards inflicted extreme abuse upon the student prisoners—and the prisoners took it. The guards forced sleep deprivation, food deprivation, and simulated homosexual acts on the prisoners. They raged against the inmates, humiliated them any way they could, and used isolation cells.

It was clear that the student guards sought to break the prisoners' wills and leave them with a sense of psychological hopelessness, as is common in real prisons. Zimbardo learned that even though none of the students had ever worked as prison guards before, within thirty-six hours of the study beginning, these "perfectly normal college boys," as he frequently referred to them, began to demonstrate typical abusive behaviors documented in many prisons around the world. And as is seen in real prisons, the high level of stress progressively led the prisoners from rebellion to inhibition. Within days, many of them were completely submissive and showed severe emotional disturbances.

Prisoner counts became hour-long ordeals in which guards tormented the prisoners with forced exercise. The prison became filthy, with guards often denying bathroom rights to the prisoners. Prisoners sometimes had to clean toilets with bare hands, and guards would remove mattresses from cellblocks as a form of punishment or harassment. Some guards also inflicted forced nudity and sexual humiliation on their charges, *The Lucifer Effect* recounts. A rumor of a planned escape attempt on the fourth day prompted Zimbardo and the guards to try moving the prisoners to a more secure facility—the real Palo Alto police station jail. When the police department refused, Zimbardo could not understand why his law enforcement "colleagues" would not help him with the escape problem. Still deeply absorbed in his role as "superintendent" of the prison, Zimbardo reacted with anger and disgust at the lack of professional cooperation between his prison and the police jail.

As the experiment proceeded, several guards became progressively sadistic. But interestingly, the prisoners had taken to their prescribed roles just as seriously. During the experiment some prisoners were offered "parole"—release from the prison—on the condition that they forfeit all of their experiment participation pay. But when Superintendent Zimbardo denied their parole applications, none of the prisoner participants quit the experiment. Theoretically, any prisoner could have said "To hell with this!" and walked out of the experiment at any time, Zimbardo told me. But he admitted that, as the experiment actually played out, walking away was not a simple proposition—not in a physical sense and certainly not in terms of the psychological effect on the prisoners.

Zimbardo explained that he thought the subjects continued participating because they had internalized the prisoner identity. Amazingly, this fake prison scenario had very quickly created a prisoner mentality for them. They considered themselves prisoners, and prisoners stay in prison. So they did not leave even though they could have.

But the prisoners were not entirely compliant. In *The Lucifer Effect*, Zimbardo describes how one prisoner, Number 416, went on a hunger strike in an attempt to force his release—again, trying to force the release of his prisoner persona, since in theory the experiment participant could have quit at any time. The guards responded by forcing the man to stay in a small closet and hold the meal he refused to eat. After three hours, the guards left the man's fate up to the other prisoners. If they would give up blankets, the man would be let out of the closet. If not, Number 416 would stay in solitary confinement overnight. The other prisoners ostracized Number 416 and all but one kept their blankets.

With the abuse continuing to spiral out of control, Christina Maslach, one of Zimbardo's graduate students, was allowed into the prison for the first time to interview the participants. She was appalled by what she found and strongly advised Zimbardo that the experiment had crossed a line. She told him that what he was doing was harmful to the students, possibly unethical, and must be ended immediately. Finally able to pull himself out of the scenario and see it with more objective eyes, Zimbardo agreed that his graduate student was correct. After only six days instead of the planned fourteen, the Stanford Prison Experiment was shut down. In the years since, it has been cited as a classic demonstration of the impressionability and obedience of people when provided with a legitimizing ideology and social and institutional support, plus the power of authority. Hundreds of papers have been published dissecting the Stanford Prison Experiment.

One of the key revelations from the experiment was that the situation caused the participants' behavior, rather than anything inherent in their individual personalities. The "guards" weren't sadistic bastards who seized on the opportunity to abuse others, and the "prisoners" weren't submissive weaklings predisposed to accept their abuse. In both groups, they were normal young men turned into those personas by the situation.

I asked Zimbardo questions about the oversight and the basic level of controls, and the checks and balances for the study. The first major failing was that Zimbardo assigned himself the role as the prison superintendent. This meant that he was supposed to be the overall director of the study and at the same time serve as the head of the simulated prison—supervising the role-playing while also role-playing himself. He admitted that this was a problem. As the director of the study and head researcher he was supposed to be sort of a third party, a detached, objective observer. He admitted that by being a participant he became blinded and missed some of the problems that occurred early on. Another problem was that there was no medical monitor with expertise in the effects of sleep deprivation and food deprivation upon the prisoners. That made me think that having physicians assigned to work for me at Abu Ghraib would help ensure safety at all times. We would need medical experts to monitor the welfare of the detainees who were being interrogated.

Zimbardo went on to talk about the vagueness of the instructions that he gave to the guards, and it was clear that this became a major problem within a matter of days.

"When I told them not to physically harm the prisoners, I thought I was setting some limits. It turned out that my instructions should have been much more explicit," he said.

I remarked on how, no matter how much I study the Stanford experience and similar experiments on human behavior, it's hard to accept how normal people, good people, can be driven to inhumane treatment of one another under certain conditions. Zimbardo told me the idea chills him also, and he probably knows the truth of that more than any other professional in this field.

"About a third of the guards exhibited genuine sadistic tendencies. And most of the guards were disappointed when the experiment concluded early," he said. "Hard to imagine, isn't it? And it's not just the participants either. Out of more than fifty outside persons who saw the prison, who actually saw what was going on inside and how things had gotten out of control, Maslach was the only one who questioned the morality of the whole thing."

Zimbardo emphasized to me that the rules and policies for what should and should not happen must be made clear, and that there has to be firm and constant oversight from the leadership at all prisons. Moreover, he went on to explain that the living conditions, the overall environment, could have been important in steering guards toward abuse.

"You have to look at how these people are living. When you live in a hellhole, your mind is going to go in that direction too," he said. "Perhaps the generals and colonels and senior leaders may have never told anyone to torture a prisoner, but if this Abu Ghraib is as horrible an environment as I've heard, the living conditions and the tacit approval of higher-ups may have combined to set the conditions for what occurred there."

We marveled at how the human mind could jump the rails so quickly and with such intensity. After a while we moved on to talking about the Confederate prison in Andersonville, Georgia, during the Civil War, a sort of precursor to Abu Ghraib in which Americans held other Americans in the worst conditions. As noted in *Battle Cry of Freedom* by James M. McPherson, Andersonville was the most notorious of all Civil War prisons, hastily constructed in early 1864 in southwest Georgia to corral the growing number of Union soldiers taken prisoner. Built to accommodate up to 10,000 captured soldiers, it was soon jammed with over 32,000. The open-air stockade with twenty-foot-high log walls was a horrible place. A stagnant stream named Sweet Water Branch ran through the camp and prisoners were forced to use it as a sewer as well as for drinking and bathing.

Prisoners were forbidden to construct shelters, and most had to survive while fully exposed to the elements. Prisoners starved on a diet of rancid grain and mealy beans or peas. Sickness often was a certain road to death, as there was no medical care, McPherson explains. During the summer, more than a hundred prisoners died every day, while others were killed by marauders among their own ranks. More than 30 percent of the 45,000 who entered Andersonville never came out alive. The Union had similar prison camps, including one in Elmira, New York, where the death rate approached Andersonville's, despite the North being much better equipped to cope with captured soldiers.

After the war, the North accused the Confederacy of deliberately abusing Union prisoners at Andersonville, and the prison's commander, Captain Henry Wirz, was hanged in November 1865. His crime was cited as "impairing the health and destroying the lives of prisoners."

Abu Ghraib was not unique, Zimbardo and I agreed. We knew we could take lessons from the past and apply them to this current problem. We agreed that underlying the overall problem was a leadership failure. By not putting procedures in place to prevent these abuses, they were inevitable once Abu Ghraib received the very first prisoner. Not only had this occurred at Abu Ghraib and Andersonville, but it had also happened in many other prisons around the world when the proper procedures were not put into place. In Brazil, for instance, the military dictatorship in the 1960s and 1970s used its prisons to torture those who spoke out against the government. We began to reflect back on my work at Guantanamo Bay in 2003. My staff and I wrote standard operating procedures (SOPs) and briefed many leaders on how to do this right. Defense Secretary Donald Rumsfeld visited Cuba during my time there, as did other senior leaders. The system had the knowledge of how to do it right, how to manage prisoners without resorting to the abuses we saw at Gitmo.

We already fixed this, I kept thinking. *Why the hell is it happening all over again?*

The more we talked it over, the more Zimbardo and I arrived at the same conclusion. Clearly, the leaders at the highest levels never thought that we would be in Iraq for more than three to six months so there was no need to prepare and establish a proper prison system. All my guidance was there in black and white, ready to be implemented, but the head honchos must have figured we were just going to be in and out of Iraq in a flash, so why bother?

We finished our breakfast and I finished my notes. Zimbardo gave me a big hug and I told him that I'd keep in touch with him as best I could while I was at Abu Ghraib. We tentatively set plans to meet again at the upcoming American Psychological Association convention that was to be held in August 2004, in Honolulu. I told him if I was able to attend the conference, I would like to sit down with him again and compare notes about my experience.

My talk with Zimbardo reaffirmed that no amount of professional discourse with another psychologist can make some things clear. You may understand it in some intellectual sense as a medical professional, but you still have to deal with it as a human being. As I headed back to my car I couldn't help but ask myself, *How could any American soldier do that? How could the environment be so bad that it would lead any red-blooded American soldier to do the things that I saw in those horrible pictures of naked dog piles and prisoners being tortured at Abu Ghraib?*

I knew that I could not answer these questions yet, that I would have to wait until I arrived at Abu Ghraib. The trip would be long and exhausting, taking eight days in all. First I would fly from Honolulu to San Francisco, then to Fort Bragg, North Carolina, for some additional briefing, then on to Germany, Kuwait City, and finally to Abu Ghraib.

I went back to our temporary hotel room at Fort Shafter, Hawaii, picked up my wife, and headed for the beach at Bellows Air Force Station—a gorgeous area that is accessible only to military personnel and their guests. Janet and I had spent many days there, alone and with our son and granddaughter. It was a place that always brought me immense peace and satisfaction. But on this day, as I lay on that sandy beach, staring up at that beautiful blue Hawaiian sky, I couldn't stop asking myself the same thing, over and over. *How could any American soldier torture another living human being?*

I did my best to focus on enjoying the time with my family, but I was busy preparing for my trip to Abu Ghraib. Within days of my seeing Zimbardo, a package arrived in the mail. He had had his staff mail me a copy of a DVD entitled *Quiet Rage*, the definitive video account of the Stanford Prison Experiment, with extensive footage taken during the experiment and commentary from Zimbardo and others. I was glad to have it in hand because, like most psychologists, I had read about the experiment in graduate school but had never seen the video.

Within a week, I was wheels up and en route to Iraq. All told, it would take about twenty-seven hours in the air for me to arrive at Camp Victory, Iraq, the headquarters of the U.S. forces. I flew to Fort Bragg and then to Kuwait—on commercial flights, thank God. Military flights lacked the comforts of even the most budget-conscious commercial airlines. Soldiers flying with heavy loads and all sorts of gear made them even less comfortable. Plus, even when I flew in civilian clothes on military flights, the young soldiers still knew that I was an officer. That usually wasn't a problem, but for this flight I needed anonymity and solitude to have a well-crafted plan in place by the time my wheels touched down.

Once my United Airlines plane was en route to the West Coast, I popped in Zimbardo's *Quiet Rage* DVD in my laptop and watched it several times on the five-hour flight from Honolulu to San Francisco. When I got off the plane in San Francisco I had a good three-hour layover, so I headed for the USO lounge because I knew that I would find comfort and friendship being around other soldiers and sailors. There was only one empty seat available in the lounge, so I put my gear down and sat in the soft brown leather chair. I was expecting to just drift away for a nap. But after a few minutes, I overheard a soldier talking with his wife on a cell phone. I glanced over in his direction and saw a big beefy soldier hunched over, elbows on his knees, phone pressed to his ear. This tall, bald-headed kid, who must have been 230 pounds of muscle mass, was crying like a baby. Overhearing bits and pieces of the conversation, I ascertained that he was struggling with the death of his father. When he got off the phone, I gave him a moment to regain his composure, and then I walked over to him. I reached out and put my hand on his shoulder as I spoke.

"Son, I'm so sorry for your loss," I said. "Thank you for serving your country at this very difficult time in your life."

He thanked me for the concern but tried to brush it off, probably feeling uncomfortable showing such emotion in a roomful of soldiers and sailors. I introduced myself and he told me his name was Danny. We chatted and I learned that this sergeant had come home from Abu Ghraib to bury his father, who had suddenly died of a heart attack in the middle of the night, and now he was headed back to the combat zone. He and I got up and walked over to the counter, poured ourselves large cups of some awful coffee, and talked some more.

"Danny, what was your favorite memory of your dad?" I asked.

"Sir, that's an easy one. My best memories of my dad were fishing or when he taught me how to throw a football for the first time." He smiled and the tears disappeared. He began telling me about the peacefulness of fishing and that he had actually gone fishing while in Iraq.

Eventually, Sergeant Danny asked me, "Colonel, where ya heading down range?"

"Well son, I'm going to Abu Ghraib and see if I can help fix that shit mess out there."

His face brightened. "Hell, Colonel, we can use all the help we can get, sir. The higher-ups at that place . . . Heck, I never see 'em. I don't even know if we have any colonels at Abu Ghraib."

I was shocked at the coincidence. Out of all the soldiers I might have talked to, I happened on one heading back to Abu Ghraib. Then Sergeant Danny started telling me about how rough the area was, how he had lost some of his buddies because they got hit by mortars, roadside IEDs, or were shot by snipers.

"Sir, when you get there, make sure you stay in one of those prison cells rather than a tent or a trailer," he said.

"Why the hell would I want to stay in a prison cell instead of a tent or trailer, Danny?" I asked. "Even a shitty trailer's got to be better than a prison cell."

"Hell no, Colonel," Sergeant Danny said. "Those prison cells have a cement roof and the mortars and rockets hit the roof and bounce off. Now sir, you'll have one hell of a headache from the blast impact but you won't get your head blown off. Sir, if you stay in a trailer and that son of a bitch gets hit by a mortar, your ass is dead. A mortar will peel back a trailer like a tuna can."

"Message received," I said. "Stay out of the damn trailers."

Sergeant Danny appeared to be in better spirits after our two-hour conversation. We shook hands and he headed for his plane that would take him to the military air terminal at the Baltimore-Washington International Airport, then to Baghdad via Kuwait. Not long after, I was on my commercial flight to the same place.

While in the air, I watched the fifty-minute *Quiet Rage* DVD about twenty times. In Zimbardo's video, he provides a synopsis of his famous Stanford Prison Experiment. I marveled anew at how these bright, well-educated students transformed so drastically that the experiment ceased to be a simulation and instead assumed real dimensions. The video showed the guards subjecting the prisoners to countless forms of abuse, including sleep deprivation, humiliation, and solitary confinement. They sadistically paraded the prisoners around with bags on their heads, some of the guards even seeming to enjoy performing for the camera. The images were eerily similar to the snapshots taken at Abu Ghraib, the deplorable pictures of Iraqi prisoners being humiliated and abused while U.S. soldiers smiled and smirked for the camera.

I asked a flight attendant for a napkin and found a pen. "How did Zimbardo fuck it up?" I wrote in big black letters. This was my basic question, the starting point. *Answer this riddle and you can fix the mess in Iraq*, I thought to myself. I knew Zimbardo's experiment held the keys. I felt that if I could list the primary things that went wrong in his famous study, that would guide me in correcting the abuses occurring in Iraq.

Drawing on what I had seen in the video and my conversation with Zimbardo, I worked at answering that question, which would in turn help me outline a plan to fix the problems at Abu Ghraib. Scrawled on that napkin, I identified four major errors that led to the harm Zimbardo unleashed in his study:

1. **There was no detached observer.** Zimbardo himself was the principal investigator and simultaneously played the superintendent role. He got caught up in the madness.

As a result there was an inherent conflict of interest. I had to avoid the same mistake. If I was to be successful, my role at Abu Ghraib had to be clear at all times. I had to stay out of the interrogator role and be the detached, objective consultant and observer. If I were to get court-martialed for doing something stupid while at Abu Ghraib, it would be because I had assumed the role of an interrogator and lost my objectivity, as Zimbardo had done in his role as superintendent. I must be conscious of remaining firmly in the role of consultant.

2. **In the Zimbardo study, he did not clearly define what behaviors were prohibited and what behaviors were allowed.** Thus, the "guards" in his study made it up as they went along. The only rule that was firmly stated was that you couldn't harm the prisoners. But harm was never clearly defined. I would need to review processes at Abu Ghraib, and if rules were not crystal clear, I'd need to set forth new, detailed guidelines.

3. **There was no medical monitor to assess the psychological consequences of the sleep and food deprivation that occurred in the prison study.** I would find out what monitoring was occurring in the Iraq prison on my arrival. I suspected not much.

4. **Zimbardo's study lacked tiers of supervision.** The guards were the final law. It seemed as though they supervised themselves because Zimbardo—the "observer"—was also role-playing as the superintendent. This told me that superiors needed to be present at Abu Ghraib, and their roles needed to be clearly delineated.

Keeping these four lessons in mind, I devised five major goals and a plan for turning this misguided train around at Abu Ghraib:

Goal #1. Do no harm. This is the first rule every doctor learns. I wanted to leave Iraq knowing that no prisoners were physically or psychologically hurt while I was there, and that the structures I put in place would ensure that none would be hurt after I left. I also felt that it was my duty to improve the physical and psychological safety of the Army prison guards and interrogators. It was clear that the guards who observed the torture but did not participate in it were themselves tortured psychologically and harmed by what they had witnessed. They would need mental health care.

Goal #2: Nobody dies or gets injured on my watch. Keep everything safe at all times and put procedures in place to prevent torture.

Goal #3: Nobody goes to jail on my watch. Be certain that everything remains legal at all times. Stay within the Geneva Conventions and the Uniform Code of Military Justice.

Goal #4: Be ethical. As a psychologist, never do anything that violates the ethical code of the American Psychological Association.

Goal #5: Improve the effectiveness of the operation by teaching these young men and women how to interview—rather than interrogate and torture—prisoners.

For the first ten hours of the long flight, I focused on these goals, watching the video again and again to look for clues about how to achieve them. After I had firmly established the goals in my mind, I began to ask myself, *How are you going to accomplish these goals?* I then turned my efforts to crafting my eleven-step action plan. My napkin was getting filled up:

1. **Have one boss and only one boss for myself: the commanding general.** I needed to be a separate observer/consultant and not have to report to the commander at Abu Ghraib nor to the intel unit commander. Why was this so important? If I reported to the intel unit commander, I knew that I would lack effectiveness. Reporting to one or two other officers prior to discussing anything with the general would significantly dilute my concerns. Instead, I needed to be a special staff officer who was part of the general's staff, and who reported only to him. I would request that Major General Miller have me report to him and only him.

2. **Be an active, positive influential force at all times.** I learned from my tour at Gitmo that I needed to be visible, involved, active, solution-focused, and not blame any of the young soldiers for the previous failures. Bad leadership was to blame, first and foremost, not the poor efforts of the young Americans that I had the privilege of serving with.

3. **Actively engage leadership in the work.** My briefings on Abu Ghraib suggested that one problem that led to abuses was that junior enlisted men and women operated under the cloak of darkness, without supervision by senior officers or senior noncommissioned officers. I resolved, as the new leader, to become actively involved in all aspects of the mission.

4. **Provide 100 percent supervision at all times to the soldiers overseeing the prisoner interviews.** I would advise the intel leadership that if a psychologist was not present, we could not do interrogations—plain and simple. By having a psychologist present, the prisoner would be provided a level of protection. In the beginning it might be hard to accommodate this step due to massive understaffing of psychologists, but I intended for it, in time, to become standard practice.

5. **Add cameras in all interview booths** so that all interviews could be monitored simultaneously from one office.

6. **Add multiple layers of supervision.** Have a supervisor observing at all times either from behind a one-way observation mirror or on a video monitor.

7. **Institute a medical monitoring process to identify abuses.** If all detainees were given a brief physical prior to being interviewed, and then another one directly afterwards, it would be easy to identify if any overt physical abuse had occurred during the interview.

8. Perhaps most important of all the steps: **Bring on board a military lawyer with expertise in the Geneva Conventions.** Interrogations and plans must be reviewed to determine if the procedures and techniques were harmful, illegal, or violated the Geneva Conventions in any way.

9. **Institute specific training for all interrogators.** Similar to what I had found at Gitmo, my briefings indicated that most of the interrogators in Abu Ghraib were nineteen to twenty-five years old and had attended a three-month training school. The skill levels varied greatly,

and as a result I would want to start holding training
seminars to improve interviewing techniques.

10. **Put clear policies on acceptable and unacceptable
behaviors into place in writing.** What constituted
"abuse" needed to be defined precisely—and not tolerated.

11. **Add roaming military police patrols.** These MPs would
make rounds at the intel facility for the entire time interrogations were being conducted.

My two days at Fort Bragg with Colonel Banks seemed to fly by.
I read all the necessary classified reports, reviewed the classified
and unclassified versions of the Taguba inspector general report
and had several long conversations with Colonel Banks, who was
disgusted with what we were seeing from our soldiers in Abu
Ghraib but, like the rest of us, was not yet sure how to explain it.
He did tell me that, from what he saw, one thing was clear: there
was no effective leadership at the prison. He was sending me to
determine the details of what had gone wrong and how to fix it,
but he was already sure that the photos of abuse were evidence
that no one had the reins in Abu Ghraib, that no one was exert-
ing any control.

"Larry, remember, people will do what their leaders allow
them to do," he said.

I thought about that comment quite a bit as I continued my
journey. I boarded a plane from the Raleigh-Durham, North
Carolina, International Airport that took me all the way to Germany. There I transferred planes and boarded a chartered DC-10
with four hundred other soldiers headed for Iraq via Kuwait City.

As we flew, there was nothing but silence in the cabin. It seemed odd that we were flying into the heart of a dangerous combat zone, where death could await some of us, and most of these twenty-year-old boys and girls slept while listening to their iPods.

We arrived to a pitch-black abyss in Kuwait City at the Air Force Military Air Terminal. It was Zero Dark Thirty—impossible to know the day and time. I glanced at my young comrades and realized that even this darkness was strange to most of them. Most Americans have never experienced the level of darkness found in these countries.

We exited from the plane and a tall Army first sergeant yelled, "Fall in!" All four hundred sleep-deprived soldiers fashioned themselves into a crisp military formation. We remained in formation for about forty-five minutes until the semi truck with our bags arrived. Arranging ourselves in a long line, we passed the duffel bags down the line, stacking them side by side. Despite the orderliness of the process, it was indeed a shit mess. Finding my five Army green duffel bags among the identical five Army green duffel bags all four hundred soldiers brought took three hours. Finally, bags safely in my possession, I headed to the nearby huge tin warehouse that housed about one thousand Army green cots. I threw myself onto a cot, desperate for sleep.

It was hot as hell, despite being 3 a.m. As I dozed off to sleep, I didn't feel right. It was hard to determine if it was the 130-degree heat or if I was getting sick. Finally, I sank into unconsciousness. The next day, I didn't feel any better, and for the following forty-eight hours I did nothing but eat and sleep—and neither very efficiently. I was losing my voice but I couldn't tell if I actually had a fever because it was 125 degrees outside and rising, and everything felt overheated. I had a hard time figuring out if I was sick or just plain miserable from the heat like everyone around me.

From Kuwait I boarded an Air Force C-130 cargo plane into Baghdad. As I boarded the plane I noticed there were three female MPs loading their gear onto it. The tallest of them could only have been five feet. The senior sergeant of the three picked up a .50 caliber machine gun—that's a big, badass weapon—and slung it over her right shoulder while she carried an M16 and a can of ammo in her left hand. The other two female MPs had a double-barreled shotgun, an M16, and a 9mm pistol on each hip. The crew chief asked me, "Colonel, where would you like to sit?"

"Son, I want to sit right between those three rough-and-tough gals over there."

"Sir . . . but you can sit up in the comfortable seat, up by the pilots," he said helpfully.

"Partner, if this bird goes down and we get in a gunfight, the pilots won't be able to save my old ass like those three girls right there," I told him. "I want to sit right between those female MPs, and I'll sit real close to the one with the .50 cal machine gun."

I nestled in nice and cozy with the heavily armed soldiers and waited out the long ride into Baghdad. A few miles out from Baghdad, at 10,000 feet, the crew chief stood up and yelled, "Don your helmets and vest!" We did, and within minutes I felt the plane pick up speed. I knew what that meant: this big bird was doing a combat approach.

Here we go. This is gonna be some wild shit here, I thought.

A combat approach is used when landing at an airport in a combat zone, and it is truly something to experience at least once in your life. Instead of a gentle, slow descent to the runway that would make your big fat plane an easy target for anyone on the ground, the pilot brings it in fast and furious, juking and jiving up and down, left and right. In an instant, this mammoth aircraft picked up speed and banked sharply at a 45-degree angle in a downward motion to my right, like we had suddenly gone over that first big hill on a roller coaster. It was wicked! The huge lumbering plane was dancing like it had delusions of being a nimble fighter jet. The sailor across from me barfed on the floor of the plane and then started shouting prayers loudly with puke all over his chin. The twenty-eight-year-old pilot leveled the aircraft for what seemed to be three seconds. Then the plane suddenly angled straight down and it seemed as though we were plunging nose first to the ground. Then we leveled out at the very last second and came to a *sudden* stop. I never knew a C-130 could land so fast and come to a complete halt in so little time. When the plane finally stopped moving, it felt like my nuts were in my throat.

"Welcome to Iraq," somebody on the plane mumbled amid the groans as we all tried to get our shit together again. I was finally here and now it was time for me to get to work. The hell of Abu Ghraib still awaited me, but now it was just around the corner.

5

House of Strange Fathers

June 2004

When I arrived in Baghdad, I was greeted by General Miller's staff and the Abu Ghraib intel center's acting commander. We loaded into an armored Humvee and drove to the tent reserved for high-level military personnel for the night. It was just another tent with cots on the floor, not a big step up from the tin shed with cots in Kuwait, but with one big difference. With the outside temperature still around 100 degrees, this VIP tent was a frigid 49 degrees. I slept in my clothes because it was so damn cold.

The following morning, I met with General Miller, my former commander at Gitmo, to get my marching orders. Just the sight of him reassured me that we had a good soldier in charge here. If the late great Marine Corps general Chesty Puller had ever had a twin brother, it would have been General Geoffrey D. Miller. I welcomed the opportunity to work for him again. You never left General Miller's office unclear about your purpose in life or what your exact mission was to be. He was about five feet five inches tall with a notable underbite. He would have been a better choice as an actor for the colonel than even John Wayne in the 1960s film about Vietnam, *The Green Berets*. Despite his small size, General Miller could organize soldiers with passion and a clear sense of purpose. We respected him and wanted to work for him. He measured every word with an uncanny efficiency. This gift, coupled with his telling movements and expression, provided the observer with volumes of information.

Inside the general's office at Task Force 134 headquarters, Miller immediately focused on the mission—he was not one for much small talk. He launched into business, with his customary drawl.

"Larry, we could sure use your help," he said, growling out the last word so it sounded more like *hep*. "The JIDC [Joint Intelligence and Debriefing Center] doesn't have a lot of good leaders like you. I want you to teach them how to do this the right way, teach 'em how to get prisoners to talk without all the harsh stuff. You know how to do it. You will report to me and only me."

With his instructions on the table, he looked me in the eye. "Now, what are your questions?"

I had none. It was exactly clear what he wanted me to do: save this rapidly sinking ship.

At 2 p.m. the following day, General Miller, the acting director, and the five-man security team for the general and me boarded a Black Hawk helicopter. Because of the dangers in Iraq, all generals traveled with a well-armed security force. Twenty minutes later, we landed at Abu Ghraib. I tried to brace myself for whatever I would find here, knowing it wouldn't be good.

As I stepped off the helicopter, I recalled Truman Capote's description of the small, remote Kansas town in his book *In Cold Blood*. Americans didn't "happen across" Abu Ghraib. Before the news of the abuses, most Americans had never even heard of this place, and the few who had rarely gave it a passing thought. This was a place you forgot as soon as possible.

Abu Ghraib was a wasteland, nothing but sand and rocks and run-down buildings, with garbage and raw sewage everywhere you looked. This was a terrible place to be, for anyone.

As I stood there surveying the scene, it struck me that I didn't even know what this place was named for. Was it named after somebody or did the name mean something? I asked Sam, an Arabic interpreter from the intel center, and found that the meaning of Abu Ghraib held a very ominous and dark metaphorical message, even prior to the beginning of the global war on terrorism. The actions of U.S. soldiers here were not the first abuses to be attached to this name.

The word *Abu* refers to "father" in Arabic, and *Ghraib* has been interpreted to mean "strange." Loosely translated, Abu Ghraib was interpreted by the locals to mean "the house of strange fathers." It was built by the British in the 1950s and '60s. Since its beginnings, it took on three or four ominous and sinister purposes in the Saddam Hussein regime. Initially, it was an insane asylum much like those found around the world before 1956. Before then, psychiatrists lacked the ability to control schizophrenics with medication, leading to many of the horrible scenes we think of from the worst mental hospitals of that time. Then Thorazine, a very effective antipsychotic medication, hit the market in the United States. It became the most effective clinical tool of its time in managing hallucinations, paranoia, and other symptoms of schizophrenia. But not in Iraq. Even in the modern era, psychiatrically ill patients were sentenced to Abu Ghraib without these modern advances, locked away, and the keys discarded. These patients were strapped to beds and beaten or tortured into submission by Iraqi guards.

Later, Abu Ghraib functioned as the torture chamber for those who either disagreed with Saddam Hussein or created a quiet discontent with his wishes. Iraqi citizens were hanged, mauled by animals, tortured, and brutalized in ways most Americans could never fathom. Some of the very worst of Saddam Hussein's atrocities occurred right here, in these wretched buildings at Abu Ghraib.

Third, Abu Ghraib served as the center of the Hussein-era maximum-security prison system. Even a country abused by a bloodthirsty dictator has its share of hardcore criminals, and this is where Iraq sent them. Abu Ghraib housed the worst of the worst criminals — rogue degenerates, murderers, rapists, and sociopaths.

Fourth, the Abu Ghraib prison was to sequester away husbands and fathers who resisted turning their wives or daughters over to Saddam or his two favorite sons to satisfy the Husseins' perverted sexual desires. If either Saddam or his sons sought the company of a man's wife and the husband did not consent, the husband was arrested by a member of Saddam's thug guard and brought to Abu Ghraib for convincing sessions. The husband or father would be beaten and tortured beyond recognition until he would consent to having his wife raped by either Saddam Hussein or one of his sons. Thousands of women were hidden away in sex harems across Iraq.

My God, this truly is hell on earth. The things that must have happened here, even before we showed up . . .

Sam waited for me to absorb all he had told me, finally adding his own commentary. "Abu Ghraib is indeed a house of strange fathers, a place of many strange fathers. It has had many ghosts," he said quietly. "The U.S. should not have come to Abu Ghraib."

I couldn't disagree with Sam, based on what I had just heard. I knew already that the Iraqi government told us not go to Abu Ghraib, that it was not the right place for any kind of U.S. operation, but I didn't really understand that warning until I was there at this "house of strange fathers." I came to think this phrase was a powerful metaphor for not only the prison of Abu Ghraib but also the half-assed, poorly planned postwar occupation. There really wasn't much of a plan. I remembered how, as the whole world watched, President Bush stood on that aircraft carrier and declared that the war was over. To us on the battlefield it seemed as though the administration believed that, like in the first Gulf War, the Iraqis would lay down their weapons and go home. But out on the front lines, it was clear there was no well-thought-out plan for what to do with the 20,000 prisoners we soon accumulated.

That's how we ended up in Abu Ghraib and why I was standing there wondering if I could fix the mess we'd made. Our leaders had expected the occupation of Iraq to be a very, very short-term venture and the prison at Abu Ghraib was already there, so why not use it? We soon found the answer to that question. As many soldiers would say, right from the beginning, the U.S. occupation of Abu Ghraib was a "Charlie Foxtrot," which could be loosely translated to mean a real shit mess. The big picture was that it was a failed postwar strategic plan. At the same time America watched our "strange fathers" lead us into a war that we now know had little to do with a real threat at that time.

Strained logic forced us to swallow the idea that Saddam actually had something to do with 9/11.

All of this was running through my mind as I was finally surveying the scene at Abu Ghraib. As the interpreter said "house of strange fathers" to me for the third or fourth time, I began to think that not only was this place a house of strange fathers but also that it took a bunch of strange fathers to actually believe this ragtag Iraqi army was any real threat to America's national security. I was not an infantry officer, but even I could see that the best Iraqi infantry unit would get their ass kicked in a fight with any Boy Scout troop in North Carolina.

As we walked from one side of the compound to the other I was increasingly lightheaded and nauseated. With an apology, I asked the general to excuse me because I didn't feel well. I found my way to my room, an actual old prison cell with bars, about thirty square feet in size. I remembered Sergeant Danny's warning to me to stay in an old prison cell, not one of the tents, so I at least understood why I had been put in such a shithole. In Abu Ghraib, apparently, this was high living. I collapsed onto the Army cot and passed out. Only later would I learn I was suffering from what was called the "Iraqi crud," which was soldiers' slang for the worst flu of your life. I awoke at 11 p.m., feeling no better than when I had gone to sleep. I resolved to see the physicians in the morning and get treated if need be. In the meantime, I had a job to do.

As I walked to the intel center, I was intensely curious to see what was really going on in this place, and more than a bit apprehensive. Walking past the sleeping soldier who was supposed to be guarding the entrance to the building, I entered and proceeded down the long hall. I moved toward the angry screams, cussing, and yelling that were coming from one of the interrogation booths. Peeking inside the door, I saw the twenty-two-year-old female interrogator being bested by a forty-year-old terrorist prisoner. The American soldier had tears in her eyes as the prisoner yelled with ferocity in Arabic and the interpreter translated.

Finally, having absorbed enough, I marched next door — about fifty steps away — into the headquarters building. The ratty cement building that held high-level intelligence papers and computers was unlocked. Inside, I found a twenty-five-year-old supervisor fast asleep with his feet up, a *Playboy* magazine clutched tightly to his chest. As I stood over him, I noticed he wore dark aviator sunglasses, despite it being 1:30 in the morning, and despite his being asleep. They reminded me of the sunglasses worn by the "guards" in the Stanford Prison Experiment. I tapped on his right shoulder to get his attention.

"Hey man, one of your soldiers needs some help in the booth," I said calmly. He woke and looked startled, as if thinking, *Where'd this guy come from?* He snapped to attention.

"She's getting her ass kicked and abused by this prisoner," I continued. "It might be a good idea if we call it a night and talk about this in the morning."

"I got it, sir," he said with a southern accent. "We'll shut it down for the night!"

As I walked away he called after me. "Colonel, who are you, sir?"

I turned. "Son, I'm Colonel James."

"Well sir . . . But sir, may I ask why you're here, sir? We ain't never had no colonel here this time of the night, sir."

"Yes, I can see that," I responded, with a bit of a grimace. "Well, I'm here to keep us safe and help make us all better."

Then I turned and went to disturb the nap of the sleeping MP guard at the front door.

Like the supervisor I had just roused, the MP was stunned to see a full colonel at 1:30 a.m. at the intel center. She would later learn to expect my presence at all hours of the day and night. On my order, the MP called for assistance and escorted the unruly prisoner to his cell.

As I was leaving the intel center, alone in Abu Ghraib's darkness, I could hear the young female interrogator crying outside the building. Ending the interrogation session had not ended her pain. The sobs I heard inside had progressed to painful heaves, with her gasps for air echoing in the quietness of the night. As I approached her, she made little effort to hide her distress, confiding in me right away.

"Colonel, I'm so afraid . . . and I'm no good at this." She got the words out between loud cries and gasps.

I shot her a big grin. "Well, you want to talk about being scared?" I replied. "Soldier, I thought I was gonna shit my pants on that helicopter this morning. But let's not talk about me. I need to tell you it took a lot of restraint not to smack that guy in the booth a few minutes ago."

"What do you mean, sir?" Her curiosity was distracting her, helping her calm down.

"Heck, I was impressed with the way you kept your resolve and didn't resort to yelling, screaming, and cussing. That took a lot of discipline," I explained, positively reinforcing her smart actions. She stopped crying and started pulling herself together.

"Thank you, sir . . . I guess that's something."

Within a few minutes, we were laughing and telling stories about the Midwest and how bad the food was at Abu Ghraib. I told her that we would need each other's help to get through this, and that I would get with her in the morning to review what went wrong and what went well with the interview. By the time I said good night, I felt like we'd made some progress with helping her cope.

As I walked away she said, "Colonel, you're the first full bird I ever saw come out here after dark."

That didn't surprise me, but it was disturbing nonetheless. In about forty-five minutes in my first visit to the intel center, I had already stumbled across a major factor in how the abuses and torture had occurred at Abu Ghraib. It was plain as day: these were young, unguided soldiers. How could anyone expect them to stay tough and controlled under these conditions and pressures without any supervisor to help them? I tried to take comfort in knowing that I was here to try and help guide us all back to some sense of decency.

Now, wide awake, I wanted to see the rest of the forward operating base (FOB). Knowing that prison escapes were common at Abu Ghraib, I chambered a round in my 9mm pistol before I walked around, in case I was attacked in the darkness. Buildings were far apart at the compound. Between each building there was only darkness—that deep darkness we don't usually see back home—sand, and the possibility of a desperate prisoner escapee stumbling upon me alone. The foul smell of Abu Ghraib coupled with the endless expanse of hot, dry sand created a frequent urge to gag. The place smelled worse than any U.S. dump or Iowa pig farm I had ever been on. I was amazed at how big the compound was. I must have walked around for an hour before I saw a single other guard or MP. This, I thought, might be just one of many reasons why there were frequent escapes. Once a prisoner made it outside the building he was in, there was little to stop him.

As I explored in the darkness, the constant state of readiness, watching for a crazed prisoner to jump out at me, kept my mind from noticing how long I was out looking around, and the hours flew by. Then I noticed that the chow hall was being opened, so I knew it must be about 6 a.m., even though the sun had not risen. As I walked toward the lights of the chow hall in the distance, there was nothing but silence in the hot air, a profound silence that seemed to be the right accompaniment to the utter darkness. Suddenly, the whole compound shook. *Shit! Incoming mortars . . .*

An all-out attack on the prison had started. At the gates, a massive car bomb exploded, shaking the entire compound, and as I'd learn later, killing a marine. The force of the car bomb was so powerful, even more than a hundred yards away, that I stumbled, lost my balance, and fell to the ground. I hadn't even been at the FOB for twenty-four hours and I had already learned that life could end in an instant at this hellhole. I stayed low as I scrambled toward the lights in the distance, hoping to find some place safer than out in the middle of the compound, waiting for a mortar to land right on my head. I was trying to move forward and watch for some indication of where the mortars were landing when, suddenly, the attack stopped.

With the last explosion, the quiet of the morning returned as if nothing had ever happened. The only sound was that of some personnel far in the distance responding to the car bomb. I resumed my walk to the chow hall, and when I got to the building, I found that the attack hadn't warranted much notice from the old hands at Abu Ghraib. Apparently, a few mortars and a car bomb were no reason to miss breakfast. I joined the line, but I was unimpressed with the food: scrambled eggs that didn't look like scrambled eggs and cream of wheat that didn't look like cream of wheat. I knew that all of the cooks and servers were foreign nationals, so I had to wonder if they even knew what they were making for these Americans.

Is there poison in the food? I wondered for a moment.

But I was too hungry to ponder that thought for long. Not hungry enough to eat those eggs, however. I got some fruit.

I took my tray and sat down at a table with some soldiers who had all been at Abu Ghraib for four to six months. The soldiers had experienced the fog of war and were not anxious as I sat with them. I tried to joke about being caught outside when the mortars came in, but my experience didn't seem to impress these soldiers, who probably had been through much worse before I arrived. While we ate and complained about the food, I introduced myself and told them why I had been sent to Abu Ghraib. Sensing that they didn't have any reluctance about talking to a colonel over breakfast, I asked them what they thought had caused the problems here.

The first answer came from a twenty-two-year-old male sergeant from Kansas with a face full of freckles from his time in the sun. He looked at me as if the answer were obvious, like I was really behind the curve for even asking.

"Those fuckers left us here, sir," he answered, as simply as that, and went back to eating.

"Who are 'those fuckers,' soldier?" I asked.

He put his fork down on the table and directed his full attention to answering my question. "Sir, there are about thirty generals at Camp Victory living in luxury. They are either too gutless or have no interest in coming to this place. Sir, this is a dangerous place and you can get your ass fucking killed out here."

Having already experienced the first morning's attack, I knew just how true the statement was.

I asked them about the different types of prisoners by ethnicity, wondering how many of the prisoners were Sunnis or Shiites. To my surprise, the soldiers informed me that there were more divisions than just ethnic ones, telling me that we had really made the war effort worse by arresting women and children. I turned to the sergeant, surprised by what I'd just heard.

"You mean we have women and kids locked up here?" I asked.

"Yes sir, we do," he said.

I was incredulous but kept cool, wanting to dig deeper. "Okay, but I'm not tracking with you. How does this make the war effort worse?"

The sergeant explained. "Sir, I can't get my arms around us locking up a bunch of grandmas. How in the heck is a seventy-five-year-old lady a threat to U.S. security?"

"Sergeant, you also said we have kids locked up here. Is this correct?"

"Yes sir, we have about ten to fifteen teenagers who are 'terrorists.'" The sergeant made quote signs in the air when he said this.

I was stunned and pushed aside my food tray, my appetite not as strong as it had been earlier. "Sergeant, can you take me to see the old women and these kids?"

"Yes sir, I'll take you to the camp right now."

We got up from the table immediately and put our trays away. As we left the chow hall, the sun was coming up and we could hear the Muslim prayers being played on the mosque loudspeakers across the street from the FOB. The sergeant picked up speed and motioned for me to keep up.

"Sir, we need to walk real fast," he explained. "When those fuckers stop praying, they get all fired up and start shooting at us."

We entered a dark, smelly building that served as a central lockup and screening facility. He opened the prison door. Inside, three elderly women were being held until they could be "processed." I asked the crusty and angry warrant officer in charge why these women were being held. It was clear that my presence there was a bother to the warrant officer. I later learned that he was angry because his retirement papers were rescinded by the intel superiors because they needed him to stick around. Back in the States, he had a new job and home lined up, and it all had to be placed on hold due to this deployment.

The warrant officer responded to my question matter-of-factly. "Colonel, when the infantry guys storm a building or house, they scarf up everybody in the house—Mom, Dad, little Junior, Grandpa, and the bad guy they're specifically targeting. They don't have time to sort it out, so we have to do it."

I was guided to another part of the FOB, a dog-pen-like place that held the teenage boys. In the 130-degree heat, without any air-conditioning, my country had around fifteen boys locked up in a tent much like wild animals. There was an overwhelming stench of feces. The conditions were so horrifying, so inhumane, that I struggled not to vomit in the presence of these soldiers. Each of the boys had a unique stare. Some simply stood in a catatonic state, others yelled obscenities, and some reached with their hands as to grab me as I walked by, desperate for me to listen to their story. It was clear from their decent weight that they were being well fed, but it was equally clear from the scarcity of personnel and foul surroundings that they lacked the medical attention of a pediatrician, psychologists, Arabic-speaking schoolteachers, Muslim chaplains, physical education activities, or any special needs consistent with what any U.S. juvenile correctional facility provided. Most animals in our country are afforded better. I was disgusted.

I later learned that at least half of these boys had been raped in captivity by other prisoners, or as a rite of passage in their hometowns, something I could still find hard to comprehend. Despite having heard of such rapes, and Hassan's patient explanation at Gitmo, it still was hard to reconcile the sad situation in my mind. Then, after that experience, we put those teenage boys in this shithole. Why? And why had we not provided them with the services of a child psychologist? The warrant officer and the sergeant had no answers.

As I left the area, I could not get past the criminal way we were treating these children. Even if they were involved in fighting U.S. troops, and that was not a certainty, they were still young people who deserved a minimum of dignity and care. I knew that even the hardest of convicted juvenile murderers in our country would be treated far better, far more humanely. I could not get their faces out of my mind—the haunting images, the young boys looking at me, reaching out to me, pleading with their eyes, hoping I would finally be the one to help them instead of walking away. I had to walk away that night, but it nearly killed me.

I found my way back to my room, dropped to my knees at my bedside, prayed, then cried my eyes out. *My God, how could a nation as mine, with so much good in it, with such a commit-*

ment to decency and the good of the individual, treat human be-ings this way? In my psyche, deep in my soul, I felt as though tonight I had seen the bowels of hell.

I couldn't sleep. The pain in my soul would not allow it. I went for a walk, hoping to find another soldier who could tell me if there was a commercial phone anywhere on the base. I needed to talk to my momma. My mother was an eighty-one-year-old, proper Southern Baptist Creole woman from New Orleans and I desperately needed to hear her voice in this hellish place. Her faith, her calm voice, and her warmth had quieted my anxiety during Hurricane Betsy in 1965, and in the years since, her steady, soothing voice had calmed my troubled soul on many occasions. I had never needed her more than I did that night in Abu Ghraib.

I found a soldier who directed me to the phone center, where I sat down and called my momma in New Orleans. As soon as she answered, she could hear the fear and loss of hope in my voice. Her voice instantly offered solace, but my voice still trembled as I told her this place was awful and that I was considering asking to be relieved, to be sent anywhere else but Abu Ghraib. My mother had never given me bad advice, and I needed to ask her if it was okay for me to give up, to admit that this was too much for me. My mother had a sixth-grade education and she basically taught herself to read and write by reading her Bible, got a GED, and went on to nursing school later on in her life. Whenever I was troubled, troubled in a way that it shook my soul, I would always call my momma.

Without any introduction, from her biblical library in her head, she began to tell me about Paul's journey to Macedonia and the trials and tribulations he found along the way.

"Son, Paul didn't know if he could do it either," she said in the most reassuring voice. "He wanted to quit, too. He didn't know what lay ahead of him or why God wanted him there."

I said yes, I remembered.

"Son, God has chosen you for this journey," she said. "Son, do not quit. Ask God to show you the way and he will."

6

Choosing a Path

June–July 2004

I went back to my room, exhausted. I had cried my soul out, and hadn't slept for well over twenty-four hours. But I still found myself restless, the wheels in my head moving too fast to sleep, so I left my room and started to walk around the FOB again. I ended up on the other side of the post. It was a godawful place. It looked like a prison camp in a third world country. I could not escape the odor of feces, dead animals, mixed with a novel, revolting scent my person had not previously experienced.

As I patrolled, I couldn't help but notice a big horse of a man walking toward me. It was Major Tom Smithon, the brigade surgeon. Major Smithon, an Army Reserve cardiologist from Mississippi, had a haggard, unhappy look chiseled into his face. Although I knew that he was a brilliant and dedicated physician, it was immediately clear that he was one who had experienced many of life's disappointments. I would come to learn that he was treated by his fellow officers like the chubby boy who was either selected last or never chosen at all for the schoolyard team. His wishes, ideas, or requests for improving Abu Ghraib in any way were always acknowledged by his superiors or fellow colleagues, but ultimately denied.

When Smithon saw me, he obviously realized who I must be. He grabbed me firmly and said, "Sir, I'm so goddamned glad to see you. I've been pinch-hitting as the post shrink since I got here. I have no idea what I'm doing. I medicate most of the psychotic patients and suicidal patients so they're not a danger to themselves or us."

"Is the post psychiatrist or psychologist not very helpful to you?" I asked.

He replied, "Shit, sir, there ain't none here."

For the umpteenth time that day/night, I was flabbergasted. "What is the population on this post, Major?" I asked.

"Well sir, we have about six to eight thousand prisoners, sometimes it's hard to tell because the numbers change every day, plus we have about two thousand soldiers and marines here as well, sir."

"Are you telling me, Major, that we have ten thousand people on this post and mental health services are not available?" My voice was rising despite my attempt to remain calm.

"Yes sir, that's exactly what I'm telling you," he replied. "The 322nd Medical Brigade sends a psychologist and a chaplain here once in a while, but that's only to see U.S. soldiers and marines."

"Well, why don't the psychologist and chaplain treat the prisoners while they're here?"

"Sir, they tell me that they were ordered by the commanding general of the 322nd Medical Brigade to not provide any services to prisoners. Their general thinks it ain't his mission to provide mental health care to prisoners."

I stood speechless. I struggled for words that appropriately described my emotions and none came. This wasn't even a conflict between my roles as doctor and soldier. Certainly in my position as a psychologist this offended me, but it outraged me just as much in my role as an Army officer. Deliberately withholding mental health care from prisoners—when they clearly needed it and the help was available—was inexcusable. I was filled with a rage and a deep sense of shame for my country that I had never before felt. At that moment, it occurred to me, I had just walked into a new mission.

On top of guiding the intel center out of the abyss of shame, I would need to build a mental health system for the prisoners as well as the soldiers. This would be a daunting task: nowhere in the entire country of Iraq could you find extra psychiatrists, psychologists, or social workers simply standing around with nothing to do. I was on my own in these early days, with no biscuit staff to share the workload.

But I did have support. From the first meeting I had with General Miller after arriving, he emphasized that he was behind me. This took care of Step 1 of my plan right away—have the commanding general be my only boss. He also stressed that he expected me to come up with the solutions that would set Abu Ghraib right. He made it clear to the leadership on post that I had open access to anything I needed to accomplish the mission. I was tasked with putting together for him a plan for what we needed to do in order to improve morale, interrogations, the work done by the MPs, facilities, health care for the detainees and the staff, post security, and how I would manage the overarching psychological despair at Abu Ghraib.

The second day I was in Abu Ghraib, I introduced myself to

the commanding officer of the Combat Support Hospital. Their mission was providing medical services for the roughly eight thousand prisoners and the approximately two thousand soldiers and marines at Abu Ghraib. The commanding officer of the Combat Support Hospital was a disheveled-looking, elderly colonel who was the senior physician of the medical team at Abu Ghraib. Colonel Barksdale was a well-respected physician back home in Fresno, California, but in this combat zone his soft-spoken style, depressed personality, and schizoid tendencies served neither the mission nor his team of doctors, nurses, and medics very well. Some would refer to him as a "quiet and distant leader."

That was a nice way of saying that the man's brain and heart were fried. The instant I looked into his eyes and shook his hand, I saw that empty combat stare—a stare that allowed me to see his pain, almost like a reflective mirror into his soul. I could see the deep, vast emptiness in his emotional reserve tank. I knew that Colonel Barksdale had become engulfed in the "fog of war." It's called a fog because it is like trying to navigate in a thick fog; a lack of clear vision and poor judgment were common and poor decisions would be made. Colonel Barksdale had become an ineffective combat leader and I needed to do whatever I could to help him. His eyes had that "deer in the headlights" stare, which was not a good look for the person in charge of the post hospital. He had a scruffy look about him with his hair uncombed and his uniform a mess. His words rolled off his lips from the side of his mouth in a mumble most of the time. He was angry and I would come to learn why. He felt abandoned by the commanding general of the 322nd Medical Brigade, who was living in luxury back in Baghdad's Green Zone. Like for Major Smithon, Colonel Barksdale's requests for additional staff, basic medical supplies, and support were denied or caught up in motionless bureaucratic red tape. It was as though the Abu Ghraib medical staff were either an inconvenience or an embarrassment for the medical leadership in the lavish Green Zone.

Colonel Barksdale's appearance and attitude were troubling, but I was gratified to see that he was not giving up on his mission. Even though the colonel and his medical staff were mentally fried, they continued to drive on and do the best they could with few resources from senior medical leaders. They regularly saw the horrors of war but their needs were constantly shunned by the medical leadership in Iraq. In spite of this, they still managed to save many lives and care for many prisoners and soldiers. As I saw them struggle on despite the circumstances, I felt privileged to know them.

Colonel Barksdale and his people were kept busy because, as I was constantly reminded, Abu Ghraib was a dangerous place. He told me about how one night before my arrival, Iraqi insurgents started aimlessly firing mortars into the Abu Ghraib compound. Rather than killing American soldiers, these mortars landed inside the prison camp that housed many Iraqi prisoners. On that night, twenty-nine Iraqi prisoners were blown up by their own people in that senseless attack. Colonel Barksdale and his medical team worked all night in the emergency room and surgery units of the Combat Support Hospital, saving many lives. Guts, brains, eyes, limbs, and raw human flesh peppered the prison camp ground. The Joint Intelligence and Debriefing Center, which bordered the prison camp, was almost overrun by prisoners running through barbed-wire fencing fleeing the mortar carnage. That seemed to be the turning point psychologically for both the medical staff and many at the intel center, the point at which their minds started sliding downhill fast. By the time I arrived, it seemed as though they were still performing their medical duties, but they had the facial expressions of firemen whose buddies had died when a burning roof collapsed from above as they all watched. Like these firemen, often their only choice was to stand and watch others die.

My days were packed with meetings, walking around the Abu Ghraib post, consulting with the military police, interrogators, and medical staff. In addition, I had to find two other psychologists in the United States and some enlisted psych techs to build a biscuit team. My goal was to fix hell—this place called Abu Ghraib—and it would require intense effort to not only build a team for the biscuit but to get the mental health resources that were needed for the detainees and the soldiers on the post. Frequent power outages, mortar attacks, broken computers, and crappy phone connections slowed the progress.

I spent several hours a day building relationships with suspicious interrogators as well as the military police leaders. They all wondered, "What is a psychologist doing here and how can he help me?" To this end, I had many cups of coffee with the more experienced officers on the post as well as the young men and women stuck in this place—the eighteen- to twenty-year-old privates. Soon we were able to start forging a policy and doctrine on how to manage detainees in a safe and humane way, and how to do interrogations without any abuse.

My mission frequently required me to convoy from Abu Ghraib to Baghdad, which could be an all-day affair. Traveling in Iraq was always risky business. Once you left the relative safety of the Abu Ghraib prison or any other American base, anything could happen. Even the folks back home had heard plenty about IEDs—improvised explosive devices—and knew that a great proportion of the American deaths in Iraq were caused by these bombs. The devices were usually hidden along the road and an Iraqi was hiding somewhere nearby, ready to set them off remotely when a military convoy passed by. Often improvised from standard bombs, mortars, and other ordnance, the bombs could produce a huge blast that would tear through even an armored Humvee. In addition, you were always at risk of being ambushed, particularly when the convoy had to slow or stop for any reason. Those dangers meant that traveling from Abu Ghraib to Baghdad, or anywhere else, was never as simple as hopping in a truck and driving off. It always required a convoy of Humvees in which every passenger was armed and ready to fight. When there was trouble, Army policy was to just keep going and drive through the kill zone as long as your vehicle was still operational. The Marines, on the other hand, would stop their convoy and go after the fucker who tried to kill them, even if it meant they might lose someone in the process.

Even though it should have been a thirty-minute drive to Baghdad, it often turned into an all-day event. You could get stuck out on the highway after an ambush or a bomb had been discovered. In these situations, the roads would be shut down and the bomb disposal units would take all day to find and dispose of the bomb.

While on a convoy I had plenty of time to sit in the Humvee, my weapon at the ready, and just think. I used this time to gather myself, my thoughts, my bearings. I began to realize the scope of my mission in Abu Ghraib. It was much bigger than just the interrogation cell. This undertaking would test every fiber of my moral compass. Each day, to remain sane, ethical, and moral, the challenges of Abu Ghraib would come to force a true north compass check. My beacon out of this darkness would be the question I asked myself over and over again: *Which road would a decent human being take?*

That question ran through my mind every time I talked with soldiers at Abu Ghraib who had been through so much already but seemed so unlike those we had seen abusing detainees in the pictures on CNN. One of those soldiers who had been through hell before my arrival was a seasoned Army warrant officer named Betty Patterson, whom I met on my tenth day in Abu Ghraib. This was no innocent young recruit or a soft desk jockey who'd never seen a moment of stress in the field. Warrant Officer Patterson was experienced and tough even before she arrived in Abu Ghraib, but she told me about how this place had nearly broken her. On Christmas Day 2003, she told me, thirty-three mortars landed inside the Abu Ghraib compound.

"Colonel, I sat in my room all day and night on Christmas Day with my helmet and body armor on. I just sat on my bed and rocked back and forth all day and night. It was fucking terror in my head I ain't never seen before."

What a way to spend Christmas, sitting on your bed wondering if the next mortar would kill you. She told me about another mortar barrage she had endured.

"Two Army interrogators who were friends of mine were killed standing right outside the interrogation booths," she said, her eyes getting that distant look as she relived the moment in her mind. "Sir, I heard the howling, screeching sound of an incoming mortar. The ground shook. I fell to the ground and heard my buddies screaming. The next thing, we were kneeling down and saying a prayer. They were gone. They were two very fine Americans. I still see their faces at night sometimes."

Betty spoke vividly of how she came to feel that she had no control over her fate, what social scientists have described as "learned helplessness." Learned helplessness is what happens to a person's mind when no matter what you do, or which way you turn, you get shocked or hurt emotionally or physically. I learned about this condition in graduate school through an experiment that involves placing a lab rat on an electrical hotplate that has a maze on top of it, then letting the rat try to find the route that does not yield an electrical shock. If the rat gets shocked no matter which way it goes in the maze, it will soon just stop and roll over and stop trying to determine its fate — the situation has convinced the rat that it is helpless, that there is no use trying. Learned helplessness is what Warrant Officer Patterson as well as many others I knew from Abu Ghraib described to me. No matter which way they turned in the Abu Ghraib maze, they were shocked with horror, death, poor leadership, inadequate facilities, and foul living conditions unfit for humans.

What can I do to fix this? I asked myself. "We need a hospital with not only a large staff, but well-resourced, fresh staff and with the necessary mental health services," I wrote down on the back of a *Stars & Stripes* newspaper. (I needed to learn to carry a notepad with me. My great thoughts were accumulating on airplane napkins and old newspapers.) So far it had been a battle to convince the medical leadership in Baghdad that the mission at Abu Ghraib warranted a large field hospital. It would have been easier talking to a camel out in the barren desert.

One of the roadblocks was Colonel Kerry Matson, the senior mental health officer in Iraq. Colonel Matson, an old friend of mine, was assigned as the coordinator for all mental health services and staffing in Iraq. She had been a mental health officer for nearly twenty-five years, yet I could not get her to see the need to have a permanent mental health team assigned to Abu Ghraib and the other prison way south, Camp Bucca. Colonel Matson just didn't want to hear it. She believed that it was a waste to send a full complement of mental health services to Abu Ghraib. I trusted Matson and saw this officer as a confidante and friend, but I disagreed with Kerry on the battle plan for mental health services at Abu Ghraib. We often had lunch together when I convoyed to Camp Victory in Baghdad, where Matson was stationed in relative comfort and with nearly everything the Army could offer at her disposal. Colonel Matson argued that if a soldier at Abu Ghraib needed services, we could just load him up in a Humvee and drive him twenty-seven miles to Baghdad to see a psychiatrist. After all, driving twenty-seven miles to see a psychiatrist wouldn't be considered unreasonable back home in the States, right? I couldn't help but think that Colonel Matson was seeing this issue purely as a health care professional, rather than through the eyes of a soldier. Colonel Matson didn't have a problem with loading one soldier up in a Humvee and sending him back to Camp Victory for a brief appointment with a psychiatrist. It was a dumbass idea and outright dangerous.

Colonel Matson had lost sight of the fact that we had many soldiers at Abu Ghraib who needed mental health services. The killings, the carnage, sexual assaults, depression, and fear were abundant at Abu Ghraib and the officer responsible for coordinating services at the compound failed to see the need for these services to be offered there. I had to try to appeal to the soldier in my friend.

"Kerry, you're forgetting one thing. Back home, that soldier can hop in a car by himself or with a buddy and go to the doctor. In Abu Ghraib, getting that one soldier to Baghdad requires a convoy of three armored Humvees. That's a total of nine soldiers to deliver one patient to the Army hospital in Camp Victory. You really think that's a good way to get mental health services to these folks?"

It took a bit more back-and-forth, with some arguing about how many soldiers really would need to take that dangerous convoy, but I won the debate, for the moment at least, when Colonel Matson gave in. This was only one small victory; there was plenty more to be done, and over the next few weeks my friend drove me up the wall by saying no to every request, every suggestion for improving mental health care.

Colonel Matson wasn't just trying to be obstinate when my efforts were resisted. She was in turn being pressured by the senior physician in Baghdad, the commanding general of the 322nd Medical Brigade, Brigadier General Thomas Huck. Huck believed that it was not his mission to provide mental health care to detainees. One reason Matson was being pushed around was that, although a brilliant mental health officer, she lacked the squared-away appearance required of all good military officers — a perfect uniform and an attitude to match. Matson's uniform was never quite right, just like her posture and the way she carried herself. It was all close enough to be technically compliant, but the West Point graduates in Baghdad instantly spotted any shortcomings. Without a real military bearing in her appearance and attitude, Colonel Matson might be considered a good mental health officer but would never be seen as "one of the boys" in a combat zone. But I also knew that her appearance wasn't the only explanation for why she was seen as an outsider. Her boss, the commanding general, wasn't respected much either, and that undercut her authority with the troops. Her boss *was* a squared-away type, but the troops questioned him for entirely different reasons related to his job performance.

After a while, it became apparent that I wasn't going to make much progress with Colonel Matson, nor the leadership at the 322nd Medical Brigade. I decided to work around these folks and go right to General Miller on this one. General Miller had little respect for the commanding general of the 322nd Medical Brigade, so he was receptive to my ideas. My staff and I wrote up a detailed report on the mental health needs at Abu Ghraib.

During one of our regular meetings a few days later, I went over my argument for why we needed a large complement of mental health staff, ready to make the case with some passion if necessary. But General Miller just listened to my explanation and said, "Tell me what we need, Larry, and I'll get it." The timing was perfect because there was a debate back in Washington, D.C., at the Office of the Surgeon General, that centered on medical resources at Abu Ghraib. Many felt that the prison was going to close any day now, so why put resources into it? But as long as the issue was being debated, General Miller said, there was an opening to make our case for better medical services. My belief was that we had soldiers on the ground and it was the largest prison population in Iraq. These were the imperatives one needed to justify the resources, I thought. I explained to General

Miller that the limited medical and mental health resources at Abu Ghraib were completely inadequate for this population. I told him we needed a team of psychologists, psychiatrists, and psych nurses to meet the need there. General Miller called the Army surgeon general that night and told him we needed more medical and mental health resources. The next day, Miller reported to me that by the end of July staff from the new 115th Field Hospital would start rolling into Abu Ghraib. And with it would be a complement of about thirty psychologists, psychiatrists, psych nurses, and psych techs.

Most of my medical colleagues in the region hated me for this. It would mean that some of them would have to leave the comfort and safety of their offices in the Green Zone in Baghdad by the U.S. embassy. Perhaps, just maybe, one or two of them would have to perform their medical duties in Abu Ghraib and risk getting shot at, or worse, not be able to watch TV. Let's just say I didn't shed a tear over their plight.

June was flying by quickly as I assembled a biscuit team of two psychologists in addition to myself and two enlisted psych techs. This was not easy. At this point there was neither a training course for a psychologist to acquire expertise in this area nor much that one could read. So Colonel Banks and I identified two solid reserve clinical psychologists who were willing to put their lives on the line and come to this hellhole. One of the officers was a senior ranking psychologist within the Federal Bureau of Prisons. The other was well trained as a psychologist. I told Colonel Banks, "Just send me two good officers and I'll do the rest." He did exactly that. The enlisted techs who were selected had both worked for me previously; one at Walter Reed and the other at Gitmo. I trusted them to serve as my eyes and ears with the enlisted soldiers. Now that we were fully staffed we were able to be present at the intel center twenty-four hours a day and seven days a week. The orders from the general, myself, and the intel center director were crystal clear: if the biscuit was not present, there were to be no interrogations. The additional benefit of having a full staff allowed me to spend a great deal of time walking the compound and grasping just what in the hell had led to the abuses at Abu Ghraib and the looming level of despair that was ever-present.

One of the first things I noticed was that these soldiers, who probably arrived in excellent physical condition, were starting to look like couch potatoes. I learned a long, long time ago as a psychologist that one of the worst things for a patient who is depressed is to be inactive and lie on the sofa most of the day, just hiding away from the world. We had a lot of that going on at Abu Ghraib, or at least the combat-zone equivalent of lying on the sofa. Most of the soldiers at Abu Ghraib gained ten, fifteen, or twenty pounds during their deployment. Many of them were attempting to hide and use food as their elixir. I knew that activity is one of the keys to getting a depressed patient turned around in the right direction. We got busy with putting together a physical fitness program, and I requested more equipment for the gym.

There were plenty of examples of how things had gotten so bad at Abu Ghraib. In addition to the lousy oversight by superior officers, the prison population posed challenges that would have been daunting even back in the States, with all the best resources available and without the fear of mortars coming at you. One day in early July, I was asked to see a teenage Iraqi soldier, a boy, who had been arrested for firing an RPG (rocket-propelled grenade) at some soldiers. This kid was apparently suicidal. I went to see him and once again my heart dropped at the sight of such a young boy in our custody. I knew, though, that being held by the U.S. Army was not this child's only problem.

His name was Abid, and though he was about fifteen years old, he could have passed for much older. He looked disheveled, smelled of feces, and wore tattered, torn clothes. He looked and smelled as bad as a sixty-year-old man living on the street in Washington, D.C. Through the aide of an Arabic interpreter, I learned that he had been kidnapped from his home by a local gang lord. Like most other teenage boys in his country, he was indoctrinated at a local mosque and believed that it was his duty to kill Americans and all other infidels. Also, he was angry because he felt that U.S. soldiers had wrongly captured his father and placed him in prison. The boy's father, a truck driver, had lost his business and their home because he was locked up for eight months. It was apparent to me that Abid was very ill and the translator explained to me that the boy complained of a stomachache as well as wanting to kill himself. I called the camp physician to examine him. While we were waiting I chatted casually with the prisoner, with the aid of the interpreter, Harim. Eventually I got him laughing about how ugly his first girl-friend was.

"Hey, if you're locked up here, at least you don't have to see her in your hometown, right?" I waited for the translator, and then I saw a small grin creep across Abid's face. He spoke softly to the translator, who then interpreted for me.

"He says he's hoping the girl's father will arrange for her to marry someone else while he is locked up," Harim said. I looked at Abid and we both laughed out loud.

Seeing Abid laugh was some solace. In a way, even after my

duty at Gitmo I was still sort of unprepared for this type of prisoner. Seeing a child in prison never seems right. But still, it's not
every day in the United States that you meet a teenager who was
arrested for trying to blow the head off a policeman.

The living conditions were inhumane at Abu Ghraib, and it
was particularly wrong for any youth to be housed in such filth.
I needed to develop a rehabilitative plan for these young boys
who were in our prison, to include their psychological, medical,
academic, religious, and athletic needs. Our military was equally
ill-prepared (medically, academically, in facilities/logistical planning, and in terms of mental health services) to manage the juvenile enemy combatant. No one was prepared for the large
number of teenage terrorists we would encounter in Afghanistan
and Iraq.

I worked closely with the camp physician and leadership to
form the nucleus for a rehab team. We put in an order to improve the facilities with air-conditioning, and we made plans for
adding recreational and educational activities. General Miller
brokered a deal with the Iraqi minister of education to provide
us with Iraqi tutors for the teenagers, and that helped us make
tremendous progress with their rehabilitation.

I thought a lot about Abid while I was in Iraq. He could appear
cheerful, kind, and engaging as long as you didn't talk about why
he wanted to kill Americans. That was when you realized you
didn't really want this kid hanging around your neighborhood.
Whenever anyone asked him about shooting at soldiers, building
weapons and IEDs, or bombmaking factories, he would sit up in
his chair and the pupils of his brown eyes would dilate. He went
from likable teenager to homicidal terrorist in an instant, like you
had flipped a switch. He would begin each sentence with "It says

in the Koran," but he could never tell the Arabic translator where in the Koran it said so. He couldn't read a lick! This was a common strategy of the Iraqi and Afghani leaders: deny people the ability to read. Illiteracy enslaved them in that they would have to rely on the Koran's interpretation from the gang lord or the tribal leaders. They couldn't read it for themselves and realize those people were feeding them a lot of bullshit to suit their own agenda. I learned that this was why so many schools in Afghanistan had minefields around them — to keep the children out of schools, to keep them dumb, to keep them useful.

The translator Harim would sometimes try to enlighten the young man about how he had been led astray by people who lied to him about the Koran. One afternoon he told Abid, "Islam is a peaceful religion. A good Muslim never hurts anybody with his hands or his mouth."

"Kill all nonbelievers!" Abid shouted in response, full of intense rage. It was almost like the mental rigidity of many delusional patients I had seen over the years. I couldn't help but ask myself on many occasions, *Is Abid crazy? Can this be more than just a wrongheaded dedication to his cause? Is he thinking this way because of a delusional disorder?*

These were questions our country was not prepared to answer, and even more so as they related to juvenile enemy combatants. The closest we had ever come to waging war against an enemy with a similar mind-set was when we fought the Japanese in World War II. The kamikaze suicide bombers would sign up for missions that required them to crash their planes into U.S. ships. We had never seen this prior to World War II — and the very idea of young people sacrificed by their leaders, and willing to be sacrificed, freaked us out at the time. The thought of such unstoppable fanaticism probably unnerved American service-men even more than the actual damage wrought by the suicide attacks. That was terrorism. This time around in the global war on terrorism, we were unnerved by the idea of these teenage terrorists coming at us in such large numbers. Like the Japanese suicide bombers, the JECs are rarely talked out of their mind-set of "kill all nonbelievers." In some regions, 10 to 20 percent of the Muslim fighters are teenagers. As the global war on terrorism spreads, we will have to dissect and analyze this issue. If we are to be effective in this war, we will have to ask, "Is this part of a mental delusion?"

The question has to be asked and the problem of teenage terrorists and their possible mental disorder has to be addressed. The first suicide bomber who walks into Madison Square Garden or Union Station may very well be a twelve- or thirteen-year-old with a backpack filled with C-4 explosives. I'm sure Abid would have been willing to do it.

Abid and the other JECs were constantly on my mind through June and July as I struggled to figure out how we should handle them, how I could care for their psychological needs as a doctor while fulfilling my duty to my country as a U.S. soldier. That was the type of question that often troubled me as I settled into operations in Abu Ghraib. I could never get away from the human suffering in this place. The screams and desperate faces of those young boys, and the smells of their filthy cages, came to me in my sleep, and they still do. And to this day, when I least expect it, I see the image of that young female interrogator being psychologi-cally tortured by the terrorist in the late night of my first twenty-four-hour period at Abu Ghraib. Sometimes I can clearly see her face and hear her gasping for air as though she were standing right next to me. If I could pick the one thing that was perhaps the most broken about Abu Ghraib, it would be those sailors, soldiers, and marines abandoned when night fell upon them. Rarely would there be any officers or senior enlisted soldiers providing oversight, supervision, or guidance to interrogators in the late-night hours. I knew that it would be an uphill battle to convince many of the supervising interrogators to come out of their cement buildings, stand over the shoulders of these young interrogators, and provide 100 percent supervision at all times.

I eventually asked myself why a supervisor would not want to come and work with their subordinates or provide the necessary oversight. There were really only two or three answers I could come up with. Perhaps fear, desperation, and hopelessness hung over the sand of Abu Ghraib like an early morning fog on a fall day. There was no respite from fear for the troops at this place. Most of us, when we experienced fear, could find a safe haven, a sanctuary—a psychological safe place. The fear doesn't just go on and on and on. Abu Ghraib lacked the usual things most American boys and girls grew to expect and experience in their lives back home—physical and emotional safety. I could see it in their eyes. As a child my mother's calm voice soothed me. "Son, it's gonna be okay. You'll feel better in the morning," she would say. No one here had their mothers to reassure them, but soldiers need the same thing from their commanders, the adult, military equivalent of hearing that someone is in control and watching over them and making sure everything will be fine. These soldiers lacked the comfort of their leaders telling them it would be okay.

Rather, the leaders would commonly express or show their sense of hopelessness and that things would get worse.

Toward the end of July it became clear to me that this was the answer. Many of the leaders at Abu Ghraib simply did not want to be there. They were angry and depressed, and not hiding it well. It was like a festering cancer. So my goal was to lead by example and sleep only perhaps three or four hours and spend the rest of my time at the intel center. I wanted those soldiers to see a colonel walking around all the time, to see me there at all times of the day and night, with a good word for them and a good attitude. This was the second of the eleven steps I had formulated for fixing this place—be an active, positive influence at all times.

I thought that leading by example would be what the doctor ordered. It worked. Over time it became the norm to see other officers and senior enlisted soldiers walking the halls, being there for the junior soldiers and even having a little fun. It made a difference for those soldiers.

7

I'm in a Zoo

Early August 2004

The 115th Field Hospital out of Fort Polk, Louisiana, was deployed to Abu Ghraib in mid to late July 2004. With it came surgeons, family practice specialists, a preventive medicine team, a full lab, and a sorely needed mental health team. I convinced the leadership that the mission required half of the mental health team to remain in Abu Ghraib and the other half to deploy south to the other prison, Camp Bucca, the newest detention center in southern Iraq. An inpatient psychiatric facility was built at Abu Ghraib for the detainees, coupled with outpatient services for the Army staff and prisoners.

We ended up with a psychiatrist, a psychologist, psych techs, and psych nurses to run the mental health services for the detainees as well as the soldiers. Likewise, we also got a psychiatrist, a social worker, psych nurses, and psych techs to staff a mental health clinic at Camp Bucca. We built a twelve- to sixteen-bed psych hospital at Abu Ghraib for the detainees and had more advanced mental health services for the Iraqis than anywhere else in the country. The standard procedure in Iraq—among the Iraqis themselves, not American soldiers—was to either beat a mentally ill patient, torture him, tie him up, or just drug the shit out of the guy so he couldn't cause any trouble. Finally, my staff and I had brought the mental health care standards of the American Correctional Health Services Association, the group that sets standards for health care in American prisons, to the prisoners at Abu Ghraib and Camp Bucca. Much of the good work in this area was done by a psychologist by the name of Captain Pat Bradleson, as well as the psychiatrist Major Martin Shorts.

Pat had trained under me at Walter Reed for a year. He stood about five foot seven and was a slender 160 pounds with dark hair. He wore gold wire-framed glasses that were as thick as a Coke bottle. Pat looked more like a nerdy store clerk than a rough-and-tough military officer. Perhaps this may be why some in the military shunned him—he just didn't look the part. His appearance, together with his slow-moving and deliberate style, would often get in his way at Walter Reed. But somehow he found his stride at Abu Ghraib and came out of his shell. A combat zone can make a soldier better or make him worse, and Pat grew as an officer, soldier, and man at Abu Ghraib. He developed the outpatient unit from the ground up for both the detainees and the military staff. Pat and I had many hilarious conversations and consultations about the camp's two most difficult patients. One was a psychotic, loudmouthed Moroccan Jew who had a penchant for telling the Arab prisoners what to do and how to do it, and on occasion he would remind them all that they were not God's chosen people. Needless to say, he got his ass kicked on a weekly basis. Undaunted, while in the midst of his schizophrenic stupor, he was determined to convert all of the Muslim fundamentalists and help them see the error of their ways. He was not successful. Pat and I would scratch our heads on many occasions, wondering how we could get this guy out of the camp alive and in one piece. He had lost his passport, had been divorced by his Moroccan wife, was flat-out crazy, and was Jewish in a place where that never helped ease your day.

Pat became a master at managing complicated patients like these with all of the cultural, medical, and State Department issues woven into it. He was able to help this patient who had neither a passport nor a birth certificate get home. His other cross to bear was a patient by the name of "Thumpy." Thumpy was a suicide bomber who changed his mind in midstream. We didn't know exactly how he abandoned the idea, but in the process he blew off several fingers, which somehow led to the nickname Thumpy. He was a walking personality disorder, just a chronic pain in the ass. He liked cutting on himself to ease his stress and, like the Moroccan Jewish guy, loved to confront the hardened killers in the detainee population. Well, like the Moroccan, he would also get his ass kicked on a regular basis. Pat was able to establish a rapport with this guy as well, which kept him stabilized and safe.

Major Shorts, the psychiatrist, was a former artillery officer prior to going to medical school. You could tell by his appearance and bearing that he was a no-bullshit military officer. This was what the mission needed, and Major Shorts excelled at developing the inpatient psych unit. From the moment I saw him in the hallway of our barracks building I knew he would organize the mental health team. We were now able to offer our soldiers at Abu Ghraib the same level of outpatient mental health services they would receive back home. At the same time, we brought on board enough well-trained mental health staff that our mental health department at Abu Ghraib could provide detainees with nearly all of the services delivered at any prison in the United States. Finally, soldiers and detainees were both covered.

But with more medical services came more newbies who assumed they knew how everything should be done. In August we saw more of those "terrorism experts" who had never actually looked in the eyes of a terrorist, but regardless of that minor detail, their PhDs or MDs made them the authorities on the subject. These experts tried to dismiss the idea that mental illness could help explain the terrorists' actions, arguing that there was in fact a low rate of mental illness in the terrorist population. Mind you, on a daily basis I would see "Abdul" or "Hassad" either talk to a turd in his cell or try to eat it. Then he would throw what was left of it in the face of the guard or make decorative pottery out of it—with a purpose, and with pride. We had built the inpatient psychiatric facility at Abu Ghraib over the objections of those experts who said there was little need for it, and then, in order to prove to the medical planners how sane they were, the schizophrenics at Abu Ghraib set the inpatient psych unit on fire in early August, the day after we opened it. The same experts who had tried to tell me that these detainees were perfectly sane now asked me why the psych patients had set the new unit on fire. I responded with just one line: *The voices told them to do it.*

By this time I was settled into the routine of Abu Ghraib and I felt like we had achieved a major goal by establishing the necessary mental health infrastructure. I had never stopped trying to understand how the abuse came to be, but in August I felt I had more time to focus on that question. I decided to start small and work my way up to the top as a process of trying to find what went wrong and how all of the many problems combined to create the debacle at Abu Ghraib. I was on the lookout for the many small indignities that can beat down any soldier in the field after a while, and they weren't hard to find. After chow one afternoon, I headed for the port-a-potty. I stopped short when I saw that it was literally overflowing with crap. Before I could open the door to the potty the smell just about knocked me over. I gagged, shut the door, and went to the next one. It was worse! There's nothing like the smell of an overflowing port-a-potty on a 130-degree day. I found the sergeant major in the headquarters building to report the problem to him.

Sergeant Major Clemens just looked up at me like it was the hundredth time he'd heard somebody say that. "Them boys ain't been comin' round that much," he said in his southern drawl.

"Sergeant Major, what in the heck are you talking about, man?"

Sergeant Major Clemens took a deep breath and explained. "Sir, a few months ago, those Eastern European guys who had the contract on the shitter trucks . . . Well sir, a couple of them were kidnapped and got their heads chopped off with a machete. Since then, if we can't provide them an armed escort they refuse to come on post with their big truck and clean out the shitters."

"Well, that's fine, but we still got to go to the bathroom," I replied.

"No problem, Colonel," he said with a grin. "I guess we'll just have to do it the old-fashioned way and dig holes out back, fill it with kerosene. Yup, doin' ya business and then setting it on fire. That's the old-fashioned way, Colonel."

I said, "Fine, whatever. Just fix it, Sergeant Major." A couple days went by and I began to see the Eastern Europeans show up and we didn't have to resort to digging holes and burning kerosene to go to the bathroom. But they still didn't come often enough, and the port-a-potties were so foul that you avoided going until you just couldn't stand it anymore.

Later, I was having coffee with a couple of infantry privates and we started grousing about the sad state of our toilets. One of them, Private Johnny Tolson from Arkansas, looked at me with a conspiratorial grin and leaned in a little closer. "Sir, you know, they got real shitters over by that got damn KBR building back there," he said.

I said, "Soldier, that can't be right. We don't have any real toilets here."

Private Tolson cracked a big smile and said, "Colonel, let me tell you a little secret. Once a month, we break in there just to sit on a real toilet. Sir, let's go on a mission tonight. We'll break into the KBR building and I'll show you the stuff those bastards got."

I declined, but at 3 a.m. Private Tolson and his buddies headed over to the KBR building for their "mission." When I saw him the next day, he asked me what the hell KBR stood for anyway, and I explained that KBR was a spin-off company of Halliburton. It was a huge company that benefited from the billions of dollars in federal contracts we outsourced to rich Republican politicians and friends of the current administration. I asked Tolson if they had accomplished their mission in the night. He said, "Sir, white porcelain never looked so inviting." Tolson and his buddies would break into the building for nature's respite once or twice a month. Small pleasures in hell, I thought.

There were other examples of downright mismanagement or just incompetence. One day in early August, the post commander started yelling again at the 4 p.m. briefing meeting. He had discovered that the KBR contractor had ordered a new $75,000 fire truck for Abu Ghraib—without any fire hoses. The commander couldn't believe the stupidity and the waste of taxpayer money. "What a dumbass . . ." he muttered, shaking his head. "Who in the fuck would order a damn fire truck without any shitting hoses?" he yelled at no one in particular. "I'm in a zoo."

My true enlightenment didn't come from those top-level briefings, however. The more time I spent with young soldiers and junior officers, the more the pieces of the puzzle began to fall into place. Not only were these soldiers and marines abandoned by their leadership, but they also were not allowed to defend themselves from the enemy, which is a basic human right that every American is afforded in the Constitution. Not long after that meeting with the irate post commander, I decided to go up in the main guard tower and visit with Corporal Kellar, one of the guards who had been there for a while. He was a pint-sized, freckle-faced marine—about five foot six and only 150 pounds—but he more than made up for his small size with a deep passion for serving his country. We talked about changes over the previous six months, since the abuses of Abu Ghraib first started getting attention back home, and he pointed out that there had been both good and bad changes.

"I can get to sleep a little easier at night, sir," he said. "I mean, at least I don't feel like I'm gonna be shot in the head while waiting for a phone call from Baghdad headquarters."

I wasn't tracking with him. "Corporal Kellar, what in the hell are you talking about?" I asked. "Son, I'm fairly new here, and I don't know how things were done six months ago."

"Heck, Colonel, now we can get in the fight," he explained. "A few months ago when I would see an Iraqi man put a mortar in the tube, getting ready to fire at us, we couldn't defend ourselves. I had to call the ops shop back in Baghdad and get permission to engage. The whole time I was on the phone I was staring at that dude and hoping he wouldn't fire before I got permission to engage him."

I just shook my head, amazed at the stupidity that led to such a restriction.

"Now sir, anytime I see one of those bastards pull up in a white pup truck and take out a weapon, I can defend myself. Dying for my country, sir, I don't mind that at all. Sir, it was just sitting on my ass and waiting to get permission, while I was gonna get blasted by a shithead, that's what took me for a loop, sir."

"I guess I can understand that, Corporal," I said. "Now, what do you mean by defending yourself? What do you do when you see some guy coming at you like that now?"

"I get to shoot one of those fuckers in the head," Corporal Kellar said with a grin.

Then, without any pause or change in facial expression, he went on to talk about his wife and three-month-old son back in Tennessee and how he would go fishing with his son as soon as he got back home. Defending his position didn't faze Corporal Kellar, and I saw a similar attitude with many other soldiers. These men and women were trained to fight the enemy, and one of the worst things you could do to them was to take them out of the fray, to make them stand idly by as threats loomed. A form of discipline at Abu Ghraib was to take a marine off guard tower duty if he was not properly performing his other duties. That punishment always produced quick results. All marines wanted to be in the fight.

As I climbed down from the tower, Corporal Kellar had a bright smile on his face. He yelled after me. "Hey, Colonel! Next time the shooting starts, come up here, sir, and you can see me shoot one of those fuckers in the head!"

A little disturbing, I thought, but if someone needs to be shot, I wanted men and women like Corporal Kellar up in that guard tower. I knew I could rest easy at night with Kellar up there, thinking about fishing with his son while he kept his eyes peeled for bad guys in pickups.

It was getting to be the end of the day and the sun was making a spectacular exit in the desert sky. I headed to the chow hall and sat down at a table with Major Quincy, the deputy director of the intel center, who seemed to be disliked by every person in the center. He lacked the social awareness to realize that everyone around him was either pissed at him or just saw him as "like a log in the middle of the road, in the way." That's how one of his subordinates had described him to me. Sitting down next to him, I instantly felt the same vibe that everyone had received from this guy. Major Quincy wore thick glasses, tried his best to speak as little as possible, and it seemed as though he shunned even the basic levels of human contact. I'm a friendly guy who could get just about anyone to talk to me if I tried, but this guy was sending off all kinds of signals that said "leave me the hell alone."

Like Colonel Barksdale and his medical staff, Major Quincy

was able to walk, talk, and put one foot in front of the other, but it was clear that he had emotionally disengaged from the staff and his mission at Abu Ghraib. It was a struggle for him to psychologically survive each day. I did my best to chat him up, and he begrudgingly responded to my efforts, probably only because I outranked him. After some pleasantries about the food and the heat and the usual bullshit, I moved into a more serious line of questioning.

"You've been here a good while, you must have seen how this place got the way it is."

Major Quincy paused and stopped eating. I could tell he was trying to decide whether to brush off my question or tell me what he really thought. He finally went for the second option.

"Sir, I doubt if you have enough time in the day for me to describe what's got me to where I am at in my head right now," he said. *Wow, he has some self-awareness about how messed up he is. That's good.*

"Major, I got nothing better to do," I said. "Take your time."

"Well, it's like this. I was brought here to do a job without the proper training, we were never staffed for the mission, the chain of command was never clear, the entire intel company had only one vehicle, and our equipment sucked."

He elaborated on some of those problems, venting about some issues that obviously had been gnawing at him a while. But it was when the subject of leadership arose that he really got pissed.

"Colonel, we have not had a commander or director for more than three months. How can you run any organization like that, sir?"

With the floodgates finally open, Major Quincy went on to describe a litany of serious problems he had witnessed in this hellhole. He began to describe the inappropriate sexual relations that were rampant at Abu Ghraib. He described a whorehouse that was run by some of the staff with the tacit consent of the leadership at that time.

"Heck, sir, one of the intel company commanders here got fired because he installed a wireless camera in the female soldiers' shower. And at night him and some of the enlisted soldiers would watch videos of their fellow female soldiers taking showers that very same morning. I doubt that he was ever court-martialed. The only thing ever happened to him that I recall was that he was simply reassigned."

Over the next few weeks, Major Quincy and I continued the conversation we started that first evening in the chow hall, often talking late into the night. We were talking one night and I felt like he had finally decided he could trust me, that he was letting his guard down more. I asked him to tell me what he thought was the psychological "marker" or line in the sand for him that he had crossed and that led to the debacle at Abu Ghraib. He talked about the military intelligence brigade commander, Colonel Paulsen, who also served as the post commander. The colonel had a meltdown after his driver got killed.

"Quincy, I wasn't here then," I said. "What on earth are you talking about?"

He described how the military intel commander's young driver was killed in a mortar attack right in front of the colonel's eyes. On that night, Colonel Paulsen, his driver, and some other young soldiers were in a tent. Paulsen was standing and talking to his driver when a huge mortar came in through the top of the tent and landed right behind his driver. The kid's body was sliced up like it was fed through a tree shredder. "Sir, that fella was probably dead before he hit the ground," Major Quincy said.

I could only shake my head at the thought.

"Colonel, sir . . . there's more," Quincy offered quietly.

"How could there be more to this awful story?"

"Sir, all the soldiers in that tent that night were either killed or torn apart with sharp metal fragments from the mortar, except Colonel Paulsen. He walked out of that tent without a scratch on him. You should have heard him describe how he just couldn't figure that out, how those young men were torn completely apart and he didn't even get a scratch. Colonel James, he was neither the same officer nor human being after that incident."

Other soldiers described Colonel Paulsen as depressed after that incident, but no one knew if he was ever seen by a psychologist. But soldier after soldier described how their leader, Colonel Paulsen, psychologically disappeared after that day. As a result, as night fell upon the post, this senior leader disappeared physically as well as psychologically, and unfortunately, his trauma-induced withdrawal gave permission for all his subordinate officers to follow suit. The vacancy at the top made it possible for the sociopaths to run unchecked and prey upon others.

During our long talks, Major Quincy shared many things that had happened with other officers and enlisted soldiers he had come to know. Through these many conversations I was able to conceptually weave a web and connect the dots in my head as to how the despair and hopelessness and defenselessness described by Major Quincy led to what the renowned psychologist Dr. Al Bandura has described as "moral disengagement." Simply stated, moral disengagement is what happens to human beings when they're stretched beyond their emotional and psychological capacity. Their bodies, psyches, minds, and souls disengage from events around them and they become detached, in an almost dissociative state. Unchecked, a person will "reconstrue," or use strained logic to justify their amoral behaviors. That's exactly what we had seen already from those involved in the abuse at Abu Ghraib. Some argued that "those prisoners had to be tortured so we could protect Americans." Moreover, moral disengagement produces a tendency to diffuse responsibility and blame the victim. Thus what we saw at Abu Ghraib was a process whereby the prisoners were blamed for the torture and the disengaged mind-set prospered. It was now clear to me, more than ever, that the biscuit staff and I needed to be present "twenty-four seven" if we were to identify and prevent atrocities from happening ever again.

One night in the first half of August, as I headed out back of my barracks building to the port-a-potty, in the dark night I could hear the sound of a woman crying. Specialist Molly Hansen, from upstate New York, was stooped over behind a Humvee with her head down in her hands. She looked as though she was about thirteen years old but I was to learn that she was actually a nineteen-year-old former cheerleader. Molly had joined the Army in order to acquire the funds to go to college, as her family didn't have the means. As I approached her and she caught sight of my rank, she stood to attention and tried to find her military bearing, issuing a feeble salute. Even in the dark Iraq night I could see the tears running down her face as she struggled to gather herself and find the military discipline she once knew, almost an eternity ago in boot camp. I placed my right arm around her shoulders and told her she could relax, that I just wanted to talk to her and see what was wrong.

She began to shake uncontrollably. I could feel that she was trying hard to contain an urge to break out in full-fledged hysterics.

"Colonel, please forgive me for crying like this, sir," she said in a trembling voice.

"Easy, soldier," I said. "Just catch your breath for a moment. Don't try to talk. Let's just walk so we can visit for a while."

As we walked, she regained her composure and was able to start talking to me more calmly. She explained that she had been pressured, although not physically held down and forced, into a sexual relationship with her sergeant in charge.

I asked if she wanted me to accompany her to the military police office right now or in the morning.

"Sir, it would be a waste of time because this stuff happens here over time and nobody will do a damn thing about it."

I wanted to tell her that I could make sure something happened, but I sensed that she didn't need another male superior coercing her into anything right now. So I told her it would be a good idea for her to go to the emergency room for treatment and documentation purposes, then she could decide later whether to go to the police. Molly felt that this wouldn't do any good either, because she was not held down and physically raped, so it would be seen as consensual.

After a good talk and walk, Molly was feeling better, and so I said good night to her after encouraging her to come to me if she needed help with this situation or just wanted to talk. I wasn't entirely satisfied with what I had accomplished, but at least I had reached out and let her know help was available.

The next morning, I made a point to see Molly in the chow hall during breakfast. She felt that she still didn't want to press charges. My heart ached to look at this young woman and know what kind of pain she was keeping locked inside. Molly was representative of the many soldiers abandoned at Abu Ghraib, their hopes and dreams darkened and dimmed by vacant leaders or preyed upon by others who masqueraded as soldiers.

Still not content to let Molly's situation go unresolved, I went to see the lawyer of the post without revealing her name. We discussed my concerns but the lawyer was not encouraging.

"Sir, unless the female soldier is willing to press charges, there's nothing I can do," he said. "We're in a combat zone and people get caught up in all kinds of strange relationships. Colonel James, I've been in country for almost a year now, and sir, sometimes when soldiers feel vulnerable, they seek comfort in a sexual way."

It sounded to me like he was either saying Molly had sought out the relationship or that her sergeant was justified in using her to satisfy his own needs. I took issue with this and bit his head off.

"Soldier, mothers and fathers from our country put faith and trust in us that we will protect their sons and daughters in harm's way. I will never accept your bullshit response!"

I walked to the office of the company commander, a young twenty-seven-year-old captain. We had a long talk about this situation and I convinced him that something had to change. After our talk it became our company's policy that all females would be escorted at night by a buddy system. We became hypervigilant and on the lookout for sexual assault, and I let it be known that this colonel would not tolerate some of the bullshit that had taken place in this camp before. The problem drastically decreased after the policy changes.

One of the enlisted soldiers who worked for me was a thirty-seven-year-old female from San Antonio, Texas, and she served an important role in our effort to protect the female soldiers. Staff Sergeant Kyra Denison, although not the most operationally minded soldier, became the matriarch to all the females in the intel unit. She provided counsel and compassion and served as a protective buffer to help thwart subtle sexual advances on the vulnerable young females at Abu Ghraib. She carved out new roles for the biscuit in addition to the work with the interrogators and MPs.

Another example of our multitalented resources was our other enlisted biscuit, Sergeant Jesus Realson. As a former tank driver, Realson brought valuable military skills many interrogators lacked. This guy knew the bread-and-butter skills of a soldier—how to kill and how to avoid being killed—better than most interrogators or Army specialists who hadn't practiced those skills since boot camp. Realson's tactical military skills proved extremely valuable in training our interrogators in defending the camp against the inevitable nighttime attacks. Sergeant Realson was gifted in his ability to teach anyone, even the most unlikely warrior, how to shoot. On one night when we were expecting a major assault on the camp, he actually taught a gay male interrogator, all of about 120 pounds, how to load and fire a .50 caliber machine gun—a big, badass weapon. I'll never forget the image of Sergeant Realson teaching the .50 cal to this soldier who was actually wearing makeup at the time. With helmet and Army gear on, this interrogator tested Sergeant Realson's patience as he became more preoccupied with his nails, makeup, and whether the helmet messed up his hairstyle than with how to target the enemy or how to load the machine gun.

Most Americans would find this odd—gay soldiers on the battlefield, and especially one so openly gay. The truth is that, just like in any city in America, about 5 to 10 percent of our soldiers were either gay or lesbian. While the military's "don't ask, don't tell" policy encouraged both the soldier and the military to just avoid making an issue of the individual's sexual orientation, sometimes in the field people let their guards down and their true selves came through. Then "don't ask, don't tell" became "pretend not to notice, just don't say anything." Once in a combat zone, the military usually focused more on how you performed your duties than anything else, so the same behavior that might have gotten you a reprimand or even a discharge at a base back home sometimes would result in officers looking the other way. And besides, at Abu Ghraib, the leaders usually weren't around anyway. That's how we ended up with a soldier in makeup manning a .50 cal. that night—quite effectively as it turned out. Most importantly, this young soldier was a good person, damn good at his job, and he was willing to give his life for our country. None of us cared at all about his sexual orientation.

I saw many other examples of how surprisingly diverse our troops are. A lesbian soldier once helped me unjam my M16 rifle while in a convoy. I didn't have to ask her if she was lesbian, but as a highly trained psychologist I spotted all the signals that made that a pretty safe conclusion. At the very least, this was one tough gal, no matter her sexual orientation. Her voice was deeper than mine, and if I had any tattoos I'm sure that I would have chosen more feminine ones than hers. Our convoy was stopped on the main road between Baghdad and Abu Ghraib and we thought we heard gunfire. As I tried to lock and load my M16, it jammed and I struggled to get it cleared. Sergeant Jackie saw the struggle on my face as I sat to her left side in the back of the Humvee. As she reached for my M16 with her left hand, I could see tattoos on the back of her left wrist and on her arms that might best be described as colorful and suggestive. She placed her own M16 between her legs and delicately balanced a Marlboro cigarette in the right corner of her mouth while firmly holding my M16 with her left hand. I said two things quietly to myself. *One, I'm glad she is on our side. And two, we have got to figure out a way to get gals like this up on the front lines.* Like the gay soldier manning the machine gun, Sergeant Jackie was impeccable at performing her duties and nobody really cared what she did after work.

Still, we had sexual issues on the post, and not everyone on the base was fine with what the civilian world calls "alternative lifestyles" and what military folk often call much worse. At the daily 4 p.m. briefing meeting one day, the post commander was enraged. He was briefed that there was a "friendly fellow" lurking around the marines' locker room in the morning. The guy was a civilian contract intel analyst from Oregon. This "friendly fellow" went on the other side of the post, into the Marine barracks locker room that morning, trying to be helpful with some buff young marines as they came out of the shower. The marines did not embrace him, to say the least. The post commander, a southern boy, had his hand on his pistol while I watched the veins in his neck expand and his face get redder by the second. He yelled out at us all.

"I can't have this on my post!" he screamed. "I ain't gonna have any monkeyshine like this shit here. I can't have some Peter Pan going into the Marine locker room offering to give a marine a massage as he comes out the shower. That fella's lucky he only got his ass kicked. I want that friendly fella off my post by sundown."

The friendly fella was packed up, loaded in a Humvee, and headed for a plane at the MAC terminal in Baghdad by 6 p.m. that same day. Unfortunately, most would remember this one incident and focus on it to cast aspersions on gay soldiers. We actually had more problems with heterosexual soldiers getting pregnant or sexually assaulted.

Indeed, the many unchecked bedfellows at Abu Ghraib contributed to the dark hopelessness there. My staff and I became the watchful eyes and ears of the commanding general. There were many challenges for us, from the abusive interrogators to the ones who lacked the social skills to interview a dead man in the ground. Teaching just basic interpersonal skills went a long way, as many of these young soldiers were right out of the Army's brief interrogator school, and high school right before that.

On top of this, the Army was running out of real, qualified MPs and began sending store clerks, artillerymen, truck drivers, and the like to a two- or three-week course, and then to Abu Ghraib where they would work as card-carrying MPs. Each found a steep learning curve where failure could mean getting shanked by a detainee.

Small things became big things in a combat zone, exacerbated by actionless leaders plagued by indecisiveness, moral corruption, a lack of expertise, or just good old-fashioned incompetence. Two to five detainees escaped every other week, and the strangeness of Abu Ghraib allowed the MP leaders to see this as normal. The last prison I worked at had one escape in ten years. The next day, the warden was canned.

The complicated conceptual, psychological, and emotional web that was woven at Abu Ghraib was like that of a venomous spider on the hunt. Most Americans' hearts sank, like mine, when they saw the dirty pictures of the naked detainees as Abu Ghraib. But there was no rational trigger for those abuses. The explanations usually put forth were that the actions were taken "to soften them up for interrogations," or "it was just rogue soldiers doing this stuff." I was learning that there was more—much more—to understanding how those despicable photos came to be. Desperation, hopelessness, poor leadership, depression, abandonment, rage, sexual exploitation, and a sense of defenselessness collectively yielded a climate of despair, which was exacerbated by the torrid, smothering heat, and unsanitary living conditions. Early on at Abu Ghraib, lack of e-mail, phone calls, and mail from home worsened the weaknesses in all of the soldiers—they were detached from their humanity. The Army and Air Force military stores refused to provide services in Abu Ghraib for fear of their employees getting killed. Only after they were given an ultimatum—"Come to Abu Ghraib or leave Iraq"—would they open a store there. Prior to this, female soldiers had no place to purchase feminine items and soldiers could not purchase condoms. Soldiers were reprimanded by their senior sergeants because of dirty uniforms, even though they lacked laundry facilities and a store on post to purchase basic uniform items. Over time, an Internet café with a phone center was built, along with a store, barber shop, movie room, and laundry. Yet regardless of the improvements in the facilities, emotional scars remained due to the tragic first year of our presence in Abu Ghraib.

Step 3 of my action plan—actively engage leadership in the work—was progressing well, in part because the commanding general was so supportive. By mid August, the new intel center director decided he liked what he was seeing from us and put a rule in place that the biscuit needed to be present at all times if interrogations were going on. Although I was glad to see him embrace Step 4—provide 100 percent supervision at all times to the soldiers overseeing the prisoner interviews—implementing it right away would be difficult. It was going to be physically almost impossible for us to observe all the interrogations because we had no way of monitoring all of them at the same time. So I convinced the leadership, with the support of the general, to go ahead with Steps 5 and 6 by installing video cameras in all of the interrogation booths and providing a video monitoring center much like we had in Cuba. This enabled multiple layers of supervision, with someone always observing the interrogation. Either myself or anyone from the biscuit staff could sit in one room and through the aid of video monitoring see what was going on in all interrogations at the same time. This became a critical safeguard.

Soon after the new cameras were installed, I was watching an interrogation that so far had been uneventful and frankly kind of boring. But we began to notice that the Arabic interpreter was starting to raise his voice in a manner inconsistent with the interrogator's voice. As things began to escalate, the twenty-year-old, 140-pound male interrogator had to break up a fight between the Arabic interpreter and the Iraqi prisoner. As we suspected from watching on video, the interrogator found out that the interpreter was interjecting his own comments as he interpreted. For example, the interrogator would ask, "How do you get along with your mother?" The interpreter would say, "How do you get along with that whore mother of yours, you fucking dog?" Not exactly the same thing. Or the interrogator would ask, "Are you married?" and the interpreter would say, "A homosexual pig like you must not be married, no?" When we realized what was going on, we sent in some help to keep things calm. It was only through the video monitoring by the biscuit staff that an all-out brawl was avoided. We explained quite firmly to the interpreter that his job was to just translate what we said, no more. There's a time to go for the throat when interrogating a prisoner, but the whole process of trying to ease our way in with the prisoner was being thwarted by an interpreter who thought he knew better.

It became critical for me to just walk about the compound at Abu Ghraib, at all hours of the day and night. I had learned that good leaders are "there" in the organization and have their hands on all aspects of the operation. When I was walking around the base at Abu Ghraib, ducking into buildings here and there just to see what was going on, I often thought of my time at Walter Reed Army Medical Center and the comment that probably sent the surgeon general of the Army to early retirement. During an interview, he said, "I don't do barracks inspection." He implied that it was beneath him and inconsequential to his duties. When I read that quote in the *Washington Post* I said to myself, "Why not?" If a leader wants to make a difference, he's got to go poking around in the basement and the closet. That's where I was finding the problems at Abu Ghraib.

Bad leaders never go to the basement, I thought. *Everything can look good from your desk, but that's not what's really going on.*

New gym equipment I had requested soon after my arrival finally arrived, and I made sure my biscuit staff and I led by example. We started working out at the gym every night until some staff were hit by mortar fragments. Then we moved the equipment and began working out in the hallway in our barracks building. Many of the soldiers at Abu Ghraib welcomed the chance to get back into an exercise routine, and I could tell that it was helping work off some of the anxiety and depression. But still, anger abounded among many of the senior enlisted supervisors and officers. They just didn't want to be there and as a result did everything within their power to not support the mission.

Much of my work was administrative and clinical in nature, but I was always looking for chances to make a difference with individuals, the guys and gals on the front line, because I knew how a bad attitude could fester if left unchecked. On one of my convoys to Baghdad in mid-August, I sat in the backseat of a Humvee with three other soldiers squeezed into this vehicle. In the vehicle with me was an officer by the name of Jim Carlson, a little guy who chain-smoked at every opportunity and was the stereotypical geek. Carlson was very angry and bitter about his deployment; resentment radiated from his presence. On this day we were stuck at Camp Victory for a good two to three hours waiting for a bomb to be cleared off the main road leading back to Abu Ghraib. The whole time, Carlson bitched, pissed, and moaned about how bad it was being in the Army, how bad the leadership was and how miserable his life was since he arrived at "this fucking shithole." I sat quietly, watching and observing the impact this angry officer had upon all the young soldiers in our vehicle. He had no idea how his bitterness, poor military bearing, depression, and rage negatively affected the young men and women around him. After I'd heard enough of his bellyaching, I pulled him aside.

"Jim, in any organization it is appropriate for you to complain up your chain of command, to your superiors, not down the chain of command," I told him. "Remember, this is a combat zone and for whatever reasons, we're here, good or bad. As a leader and a supervisor, you cannot give up hope and the mission. What I'm asking you to do is be a positive force with these young troops. They need this from you and they deserve it from you."

My talk snapped him out of his negative spiral for a moment and he was very apologetic. But still, he didn't think I understood how unhappy he was. "Sir, you're new here. You just have no idea how hopeless it can be at Abu Ghraib," he said.

"Jim, thanks for trusting me enough to let me know how you feel," I said. "But here's the deal: a few months from now, if you ever hear me pissing and moaning like you just did with your subordinates, tap me on my shoulder and remind me that a good leader needs to be a calm, levelheaded, positive voice at all times."

"Okay, sir," he said. "I got it and I'll hold you to it."

That appeared to be a turning point for us because after that interaction it seemed that people were a lot more cheerful. I did whatever I could do to help morale by being positive and improving living conditions for all the soldiers around me.

One day I walked into a meeting where a female soldier was very upset because she was told that she could not sleep with her husband, who was also stationed at Abu Ghraib. Sometimes in life, as you move about, you hear some shit that is so bizarre, so idiotic, it puts your thoughts on pause, and this was one of those moments. I couldn't help but start laughing and I went to the soldier's supervisor.

"Man, this is crazy," I told him. "Let me get this straight, Sergeant. You mean she can't sleep in the same room with her husband and she can't have sex with her husband, and they are assigned in the same unit, correct?"

"Sir, sex is off-limits and it simply violates one of the general's orders," he explained. "Sex is not authorized even between married couples who are in the same unit together."

I pulled the soldier aside and told her to let me work on it, that I would see what I could do. I was never able to arrange for these two married soldiers to work the same shift and live together, but we were able to arrange weekend passes to Baghdad for them.

Sex was a complicating factor in much of our work at Abu Ghraib. I came to know several single women at Abu Ghraib who got pregnant, received adverse legal action, and were sent home. Private Jeni Nelson was a short, fat, seriously ugly young lady. She looked as though she was crying all the time. Nevertheless, she got a boyfriend, got pregnant, and was promptly sent home by her company commander. Did she do it on purpose to get out of Abu Ghraib? Probably, and I'm sure she wasn't the first.

I couldn't help but have very bad memories of a conversation with a colonel at Gitmo back in 2003. I had walked into the little mini-mart during the lunch hour and Colonel Clements was bitching out the cashier for having condoms on the shelf. He was yelling, "Sex is not authorized in my camp!" and the cashier was stammering something about how he didn't decide what to put on the shelves. Later, outside in the parking lot, I stopped Colonel Clements and asked what the hell that was about.

"Colonel, why would we not want these boys and girls to practice safe sex?"

He was pissed at me! "Safe sex? *All* sex here is safe because there ain't supposed to be no fucking sex on this damn post!"

With a grin, I told him, "Colonel, if you put a boy monkey in a cage and the boy monkey in the cage is swinging on the vine with the girl monkey, sooner or later, you're gonna have little baby monkeys in the cage. It's only natural, Colonel. We would never try to outlaw sex on a college campus, now would we, Colonel?"

I could begin to see steam rise from his collar. He mumbled something, got in his car, and drove away. Colonel Clements didn't speak to me for a month after that, but I began to see condoms in the mini-mart again even though he had ordered the store clerk to remove all condoms from the shelf. We went through pretty much the same sort of debate at Abu Ghraib, and then in the middle of the summer the same change began to occur at the Abu Ghraib mini-mart. Condoms appeared, and before long we saw an overall improvement in the morale among the soldiers. I began to hear people laughing, telling stories, watching movies together, and simply having fun again.

Even though I was making slow progress in turning things around, I did not fathom that my biggest challenge still lay ahead of me. This one was an internal struggle, one that I would have to solve on my own. Now I was facing every day as a doctor in a combat zone, and I would soon have to determine, once and for all, whether I could be both a doctor and a military officer.

8

Is This the Day?

Late August 2004

*L*ord, *is this the day I will take the life of another human to save my own life or to protect the life of my soldiers? Is this the day I will die in combat?* After a couple months in Iraq I was asking myself these questions as I awakened each day. I was a combatant, not a healer, at Abu Ghraib. But still, I had taken an oath to "do no harm."

I asked myself these questions usually after having "the dream," as I came to call it. The demons would come for me nearly every time I went to sleep. No matter how well I felt as I lay down to sleep, I awoke with nightmares. Night after night, I woke up in a panic, startled and confused, my heart racing. I always calmed down quickly, but in the early days I rarely had a good idea what had frightened me so much. *What am I so upset about?* I would ask myself. *What is my struggle?*

I had asked these questions off and on since arriving in Iraq, but now they went round and round in my head each night, after I awakened soaking wet from sweat. I knew it had something to do with the psychological impasse of pain, a moral dilemma I could never seem to resolve in Iraq's dark abyss. Oddly, my nightmares were never about the sights and awful events, like seeing a soldier's guts blown out and lying on the ground, a charred body, or an Iraqi terrorist with his torso ripped open, blood pouring out. They were about me making the right decisions, finding a way to do the right thing in a wrong situation. My moral compass during the night seemed to be stuck in these nightmares, my mind stuttering like a VHS tape perpetually on pause at the critical juncture in a movie. As I considered the nightmares more, trying to piece together the bits I remembered as I lay in bed trying to catch my breath, their subject became clearer to me. They all tied in to the question that had been bothering me, in a much more conscious way, for some time now: how could I, as a doctor, a healer, knowingly kill another man? I was an Army officer in a combat zone. I might, at any moment, need to kill another human being. How could Dr. Larry James do that?

This quandary held me in a motionless pause each night, yet the nightmares spurred me to face this dilemma head-on in my waking hours, forcing me to cope with a predicament that I had always considered theoretical, something I could push to the back of my mind. I could not run from this question in Abu Ghraib, and unlike back home, sleep was not the customary respite period from such worries. Slumber catapulted me each night into a dialogue with my moral compass. In my head and in my heart, I was stuck on pause. I couldn't get past this.

For two months I had awoken each morning at about 5 or 5:30 a.m., showered, and then headed to the chow hall, for breakfast and to visit with soldiers. By the time I returned to my hooch at night at about 6 or 7 p.m., I would simply be flat-out exhausted. I showered again, cleaned my weapon, reloaded it, got on my knees and said my prayers. Within a minute I fell into a deep sleep. I slept deeply and soundly. But the nightmares still came, and after a few weeks in which I made a point of trying to remember them and analyze them, "the dream" became more consistent and clearer to me.

In this dream, it was as though I was up in the clouds on a beautiful sunny day—but I was hovering over Arlington National Cemetery in Washington, D.C., watching my own funeral. I could see soldiers from the Old Guard firmly raise the American flag from my coffin. Though it was gloriously sunny up in the sky where I was, my wife sat with the other mourners in the quietness of a dreary, cloudy, rainy day. Taps played and the bugler's sound echoed in the chill of the Arlington sky. I vividly saw the painful agony, the sadness in my wife's face, heard her cries and almost tasted the loneliness upon her lips. Surrounded by friends, family, and loved ones, she found difficulty in doing the simplest of things on this day. Then the color guard sergeant did an about-face, faced my wife, and slowly, in a deliberate manner, walked toward her with the American flag from my coffin. He extended his arms and, gently, with the flag in his hands, moved toward her with pensive steps. He stopped exactly one step in front of her, methodically and slowly leaned forward, and said, "Ma'am, from a grateful nation," as he extended his hands and presented her with the American flag from my coffin. He came to attention, saluted my wife, my flag, and returned to his post with the color guard.

The color guard sergeant, now back at his post, called everyone to attention. As the soldiers fired a volley from their rifles for the twenty-one-gun salute, my wife collapsed. That is the moment where, in a frenzied terror, I would awake gasping for air as though I were drowning. I sat up in my bed, drenched, soaking wet with sweat, heart racing, and tried to find my bearings in the darkness of my room. My watch would read 3 a.m. It would be a long time, almost three years after my return from Abu Ghraib, before I learned that my soul mate of thirty-one years also carried the burden of this same dream with her each night. Like me, my wife was never awakened with the image of her husband blown apart, nor visions of her double-amputee husband trying to walk again at Walter Reed. Rather, just as with my own nightmare, she would awaken at the moment the last volley was fired from the twenty-one-gun salute. As the sound from the rifle reverberated across the Arlington sky, she would awake in a night terror, gasping for air. I would learn that her panic was caused by a fear for my safety. My terror, on the other hand, was driven not by my potential death, but by my potentially doing the morally wrong deed as a doctor.

As time went on, I actually began to welcome the nightmares. They became my moral compass: as long as I had nightmares I knew that I was struggling with the wrongness of what I saw and the notion of how any psychologist could torture a human being. Better to struggle with doing the right thing than to blithely go about your business and not even wonder, never giving yourself a gut check about what you were doing.

But seeing the meaning behind my nightmares was for the daytime, in the light, when I could calmly assess them as I would for a patient. In the dark night, all alone, they were simply terrifying. When the demons came for me, I would reach for my weapon and check to ensure that it was loaded with the safety off. Then, after calming myself, I would drift back into the darkness of night, only to soon find myself haunted all over again by another nightmare. The second nightmare was usually different from the one about my funeral. It would involve an all-out attack on Abu Ghraib in which the perimeter walls had been breached by the enemy. Once again, in this dream I would find myself at the moral crossroads, standing with my M16 rifle with the safety off. As I leave the building to get in the fight, I see an enemy soldier stop, face me, and put his hand on the trigger of his AK-47, ready to blow my brains out. I position myself to kill the enemy and I squeeze the trigger. As the bullet leaves the gun's barrel, I awake again in a cold sweat.

After the second nightmare was over, I would climb out of my rack and get a drink of water, calm myself, and get down on my knees and pray the same prayer I prayed many nights. "Heavenly Father, thank you for not having me kill another human being today. Please wrap your gentle arms around me, keep me safe and calm at all times with a good heart, a steady hand, and a stable mind. Father, I would also ask that you not have me take the life of another human being tomorrow. In the event that you decide that on the battlefield I must take the life of another human being in the course of performing my duties, please forgive me."

In a way, this prayer would absorb my pain, soothe my disquiet for the moment, and calm the turmoil deep in my soul. I would get up to my knees, check my weapon, make sure the safety was off, get back in bed, and drift away into a deep, sound sleep all over again.

Early in my tour, I often wondered what it would feel like to get shot. What was it going to feel like if I got a leg blown off or had to spend the rest of my life with half of my skull blown apart? Would I find new strengths in order to function if I became blind from having my eyes blown out during an intense fire-fight? Would I recover? Would I be a better human being? Those thoughts had begun running through my head on the Air Force C-130 from Kuwait into Baghdad and in my early days at Abu Ghraib. But by late August I rarely thought about getting killed, shot, or blown up myself; I thought more about whether I would have to kill someone else. It was clear to me that I was no longer a doctor but rather a combatant with the sole purpose of helping the Army kill or capture the enemy. I knew that was appropriate in a combat zone, but it still troubled me as a doctor. *What's the difference now?* I would ask myself. *I've been a military officer for over twenty years. Why is it so difficult this time?*

In many ways the reason was simple. This was perhaps the first time in our nation's history where hundreds or thousands of doctors and nurses were put on the front lines in this manner. Doctors and nurses had been in combat before but most likely not in the same manner and with the large number of health care professionals we had far, far forward in the fight. In particular, for mental health professionals it was indeed a change. Simply be-cause of their proximity to the front lines and being smack dead in the middle of the fight, the options were clear and the choices few: kill or be killed. On a convoy, all soldiers were soldiers and the enemy bullets didn't care if I was a doctor or a Green Beret, nor could they discern the difference.

On one August convoy to Camp Victory for some meetings and other work, I saw a good example of how some medical pro-fessionals can take a while to realize what became clear to me in my first weeks at Abu Ghraib. After my work at Camp Victory, I was getting ready to join the convoy back to Abu Ghraib. We had about five new doctors and nurses who asked to ride with us back to Abu Ghraib. Staff Sergeant Jackson from Boone, North Carolina, was going from vehicle to vehicle prior to our departure to check the weapons of the medical personnel and field their questions. The Humvee in front of mine had a female nurse and a male physician in it. Neither had locked and loaded their weapons. The sergeant couldn't help but notice that the nurse didn't even have her 9mm pistol with her. It was at the bottom of her backpack.

"Where's y'all's weapons?" Sergeant Jackson asked.

The nurse replied in a condescending tone, "I try to never touch that thing. It's too heavy. We won't need it, anyway."

Without hesitation, this young soldier looked them both in the eyes and spoke plainly. "Ma'am, sir, with all due respect, you need to get the fuck out of my goddamn convoy because when the shooting starts, you shoot back or you're dead. Or even worse, people around you may get their goddamn heads blown off because of your moral dilemma. These hajis, frankly, don't give a shit if you're a doctor or nurse. All they know is they want to put a bullet right between your eyes. So you either lock and load your weapon or keep your butts out of my convoy."

They both got their pistols and loaded them.

We convoyed from Baghdad back to the compound at Abu Ghraib without a gunfight, but there was one incident that got my attention. A group of ten- to thirteen-year-old kids threw rocks and bottles at our vehicles as we drove by—not an unusual occurrence, but this time it triggered a question for me. As I watched one of the little bastards throw a rock, I asked myself, *Suppose that thirteen-year-old kid was throwing a hand grenade at your vehicle. Would you be able to shoot that child?* I decided that if it meant saving my life or the lives of my fellow soldiers, Colonel Larry C.

James could shoot the boy and would. But Dr. Larry C. James couldn't. If it actually ever happened, both the colonel and the doctor would be haunted by it for the rest of my life. I was terrified by that scenario and it occurred to me that I was never prepared psychologically, nor emotionally, to deal with this possibility, let alone cope with the reality of shooting a child. When the convoy arrived I went back to my hooch and dropped off my gear. It was now about 5 p.m., suppertime.

As I left my building and headed for the chow hall I bumped into one of the intelligence officers. This tall, lanky guy with dirty blond hair and wire-framed classes said, "Colonel! Welcome back. I'm glad I saw you because I need to talk with you."

We stepped to an area where we could talk with some privacy, and the intel officer passed on some interesting news.

"Sir, I was talking with some of the intel officers in our brigade back in Camp Victory and I have been briefed that you're on the most wanted list."

"Captain, what the hell are you talking about?" I asked, looking him right in the eyes.

"Well, you know Al Zarqawi, right?" he continued, referring to the most wanted man in Iraq at the moment, a high-level terrorist leader. I was quite familiar with him. "Well, he has a most wanted list and I was told that the four Army colonels at Abu Ghraib were named on this list. You're one of the four Army colonels here, so you're on the list."

I didn't know quite what to say. What does a person say in this situation? I just said something about how I appreciated the heads-up and left it at that. As I turned to walk away, the captain seemed to think that he hadn't really gotten his message across.

"Sir, you should be careful out here," he called after me. "There is also a $25,000 bounty on your head."

That got my attention again. "What in the hell does that mean?" I asked.

"Well, sir," he said, "if the perimeter wall on this post gets breached during an attack, the bad guys are gonna come looking for you with their machetes. Colonel, the first one to capture you and cut your head off with their machete will get $25,000 from Al Zarqawi."

Well shit . . . there's a thought that'll keep you up at night, I thought to myself. But after a moment, I considered that maybe, probably even, this young captain was embellishing the facts. Still not good news, but probably not as bad as the captain was saying. So I thanked him for his information and headed toward the chow hall.

Before I got halfway to the chow hall, I was soaking wet with sweat and it seemed to be unusually humid and hot that evening. I stopped for a moment, took my helmet off, and wiped the sweat out of my eyes. Before I put my helmet back on and buckled the chinstrap, I could see the intel center commander moving quickly toward me. He called out as soon as he was within earshot.

"Hey, Colonel James! Good to see you back. Larry, we need to talk about some pretty serious shit. The four colonels here, including you and me, have shown up on a pretty serious hit list."

Maybe it was my denial, but by this time I really wasn't in the mood for any more discussion about my name being on a hit list and getting my head chopped off, so I just told the commander I'd already heard and started to move on toward chow. The commander stopped me in my tracks, looked me in the eyes, and made sure he had my full attention.

"Colonel James, you're not tracking with me. So let me say this so you receive this message loud and clear. First, you need to know that you and I are high-value targets here and there's a goddamn bounty on our heads. You need to take your nameplate off of your front door, because trust me, the enemy already knows where you live, and if they come through the wall tonight, you better be ready because they're coming for you," he said, frustrated that I wasn't taking this seriously. "Larry, here's the deal: if you're captured, first those bastards are going beat you beyond recognition. Your wife will not recognize your face ever again. Then the fuckers are gonna butt-fuck you to the point where the docs will have to sew your asshole back together. Your asshole will be literally ripped apart. Man, after they're done with their group orgy with you, while you're still breathing, they'll get out the video camera and tape your execution. They will put you on your knees and cut your head off with their machetes and film every minute of it. After that, they're going to cut your nuts and your dick off with that very same machete and stick them in your mouth. Then they will take your head with your testicles and dick stuffed in your mouth and put it all in a paper sack and drop it off on the front steps of the Red Cross. This will be the special gift these bastards will give to your wife just in time for Christmas. Colonel James, from here on out you're ordered to always keep your weapon locked and loaded at all times. Are you tracking with me now?!"

I was. I got the picture clearly. This wasn't some bullshit threat that would never amount to anything. I really was on Zarqawi's hit list. (Our intelligence community would erase any lingering doubts in the coming weeks, confirming that Zarqawi had me in his sights.) I could be the next grisly video shown on

CNN and downloaded all over the world. If I still had any second thoughts about being a combatant, the intel center commander helped me get my head on right that night. After we finished our chat and I walked to the chow hall, I kept thinking about what the commander had described.

Is this the night that they will come for me? On this night will I have to kill another human being?

Clearly this was a new mind-set for me. This was a new way of thinking that I had never ever considered before. I wasn't worrying any more about whether I would have to kill or might be killed as a consequence of being here to do my job as a psychologist, sort of an unwanted side effect of just doing my job. No, this was now about me in a very personal way. I personally, Larry James, Biscuit 1, was now a specific high-value target for the enemy. It was freeing in a way, because the enemy had made it crystal clear that to them, I was a soldier, indisputably, no qualifications. My moral dilemma over being both a soldier and a doctor didn't mean shit to them. Part of me understood that already, but having your name on a terrorist hit list has a way of bringing the issue into great clarity.

My 9mm and M16 became permanent parts of my body and I could not follow the usual rule of always keeping my weapon on safe and not having a bullet locked and loaded until the shooting started. With what the commander described still ringing in my ears, I considered that for me, every single moment was now like being in a convoy. I had to be ready to fight at a moment's notice. My orders from the commander were clear: be locked and loaded at all times and don't keep your weapon on safe. But this created an additional layer of anxiety for the rest of my deployment that I had not anticipated. After a couple of days walking around with my gun always loaded I couldn't help thinking about a conversation I had with a former student of mine who used to be a Honolulu homicide police-man. John had retired after twenty-six years on the police force. I asked him once whether he had a pistol at home for personal protection, and he said, "Hell no, I couldn't wait to get rid of that damned gun. Dr. James, having a gun on your hip all the time is like having an extra-big dick. You always worry about whether it's hanging out. Is it showing or did you forget it some-where?" I understood now what he meant. Every soldier has to be mindful of his or her weapons, but carrying a locked and loaded weapon all the time creates a burden of vigilance that soon will wear you down.

The threat of having to kill someone, and being killed by Al Zarqawi's minions, became worse by the day. One evening in late August we all were put on alert and told that there was a high probability that there would be a major assault on the camp, and/or a prison break, that night. I asked a senior sergeant where the fighting position was for my staff and me and what our spe-cific duties were during an assault. He brought me over to a door inside my office that always remained locked. I had never asked any questions about this particular door, even though my own desk was right in front of it. We just assumed it led nowhere and we didn't need to use it.

"Your assignment is this door, sir," he told me.

I had no idea what he meant, so I asked him to explain. The young, redheaded sergeant told me about that door with a very flat, poker-faced expression.

"Sir, on the other side of that door are twenty-five hundred Iraqi prisoners."

"Son, that can't be right," I said in reply. "I think you got the layout of the camp sort of wrong."

"No sir," he said. This young sergeant went on to tell me that behind that door was the *other* prison at Abu Ghraib, the one that the Iraqi government was in charge of, not the Americans. I knew already that there were really two Abu Ghraib prisons, but I hadn't realized until this moment that this two-inch-thick door in front of my desk was the only thing separating me from the Iraqi one.

"Sir, the last time there was a real bear of a prison break, somehow those prisoners climbed up on the roof and were jumping down in the courtyard right outside your main door there. If they get out of that prison, sir, they'll be all over you in a heartbeat."

I told the sergeant I believed him now about my proximity to the other prison, but I still wasn't clear on my orders. What were my staff and I supposed to do?

"Sir, the first goddamn thing that comes through that door, or if you see something climb down from the roof, you shoot that motherfucker in the head."

All night we guarded that door and the roof. We stayed at our positions with our weapons pointed directly at the door, the roof, and the courtyard, locked and loaded all night.

Unknown to us at the time, we were exploring a new frontier for health care professionals in the global war on terrorism, particularly me. I had no idea that I would be thrust into the center of a national and international debate on the use and role of psychologists in a combatant situation. Sitting in Abu Ghraib, I had no idea that the debate over psychologists' involvement in interrogations was gathering a great deal of traction. Most Americans simply didn't understand our role and how simple yet critical it was to these young interrogators. We provided a great deal of guidance to the interrogators on how to interview someone without any yelling, abuse, or torture. These interrogators were young, inexperienced at life, and usually right out of their brief training school. We provided support and guidance on how to improve their interpersonal skills with the detainees and build a relationship.

We survived several attacks on the compound, but death was a constant visitor. Roy was twenty-five years old, married, and had a young baby at home. I would frequently see him in the chow hall and find time to visit with the marines who protected those of us inside the wall at Abu Ghraib. Through their patrols outside the post and vigil on the guard towers each night, I was able to sleep safely. One day in late August I had lunch with this young lieutenant and a couple of his men, and then he went out in his Humvee and got hit by a roadside bomb. The ground rumbled for a mile radius around the explosion. Even though he had on his body armor vest with the neck protector, a piece of metal from the bomb found its mark in the right side of his neck, in the small gap between the neck collar and the helmet, severing his spine at the base of his skull. He simply slumped over and died. When I learned of his death, I mourned his loss, but I reminded myself that this was part of the new battlefield mission for a doctor like myself.

Larry, that could have been you. The old Vietnam battlefield plan for health care professionals is gone. Now, in this new war, doctors will constantly walk the tightrope between being the soldier and the doctor. Kill or be killed, because it doesn't matter to the enemy if I am a doctor or a tank driver.

I began to see myself as wearing a white doctor's lab coat while at the same time I also wore a soldier's uniform. The change was that in previous wars usually the enlisted medics or corpsman would go forward with the field units. Never before in such great numbers had we seen psychologists and psychiatrists being so far forward in the battlefield. To psychologically survive, I could no longer try to keep them as separate but equal entities in my life, as most health care professionals in the military try to do, but rather I had to find a way to merge them into one. This new way of seeing the doctor on the battlefield would create many long nighttime debates for my doctor buddies and me. Even now, the answers and guidelines for doctors on the battlefield are evolving. Perhaps they always will.

9

This Is My Dog

September 2004

Some things were looking better as we headed into September, but we still needed more help with the medical aspect of our mission. We were getting our asses kicked on a weekly basis by the International Committee of the Red Cross. Most people hear "Red Cross" and think of the American organization that responds to disasters, but the ICRC, as it is called, is a very different group. The ICRC is a private humanitarian institution that monitors human rights abuses and compliance with the Geneva Conventions guidelines on how prisoners should be treated. The group is well-known throughout the world, having won three Nobel Peace Prizes in 1917, 1944, and 1963 for its humanitarian work.

The ICRC is based in Geneva, Switzerland, but we saw that, unlike the famously neutral Swiss, it is a long way from politically neutral. The group's mission statement says it is an "impartial, neutral, and independent organization," but the ICRC consistently takes a critical view of the United States. Like most other soldiers, I saw the ICRC representatives as a bunch of radical left do-gooders, mostly from Europe, who were as interested in giving America a black eye as they were in truly helping the innocent. Every ICRC rep I met had long, disheveled '60s and '70s hairstyles as well as Birkenstock sandals—the consummate hippie motif. They thought all of the detainees were completely innocent and only needed to be hugged more. I was seen as a devil by them, supposedly helping interrogators craft abusive interrogation practices. I hadn't been in Abu Ghraib for long before the ICRC accused me of torturing prisoners.

The ICRC claimed, very wrongly and without any evidence, that psychologists were stealing detainee medical information and helping interrogators craft torture. They made these claims in the media over and over without citing any evidence, and the misinformation took on a life of its own. Because of these false reports, many of my colleagues around the world believed that I stole medical information and used it to fashion torture plans. This was a lie, complete bullshit. Any medical information I ever had was used for safety and to protect the detainees. For example, if I knew that a detainee was psychotic, I would tell the interrogators to leave the guy alone. Or if a detainee had a serious medical condition, I would ensure that his medical needs were recognized and met by the doctors. Many of the detainees came to us right off the battlefield and had not ever seen a physician. So medically this could be a very ill enemy who needed medical and psychiatric care and constant surveillance. It was my job to make sure they were very well taken care of. This was Step 7 of my action plan—institute a medical monitoring process to identify abuses. If I became aware that a detainee had any untreated medical condition, I would speak directly with the doctors, and this worked very well. It was the ICRC who concocted the story of medical torture.

We instituted a new policy that required physicians and medics to conduct brief histories and physicals on all of the detainees before and after they were interrogated. The medical staff then would document on the appropriate forms any signs of physical abuse and report the abuse to the attorneys. This helped us tremendously and proved that no detainee was abused physically or psychologically while I was in charge of the biscuit at Abu Ghraib. At the same time, unlike in Cuba, I was able to get an attorney assigned to our staff who specialized in the Geneva Conventions and the rules of engagement as it relates to POWs and land warfare. With this young man, Captain Brown, we were fulfilling Step 8 of my action plan—bring on board a military lawyer with expertise in the Geneva Conventions. Captain Brown was simply brilliant. He had the right personality, and most importantly, he told great stories, was fun to be with, and was filled with humor. After consulting with the intel center director, we made it a requirement that all interrogation plans be reviewed by the attorney to make sure there was nothing in any interrogation plan that would be out of line with the Geneva Conventions or any of the existing laws or guidelines. Initially, the interrogators hated it because it was just one more extra step that they had to go through. But after a while everyone began to see that it was there for their own protection and to make sure that none of them could ever be accused, after the fact, of crafting a plan to abuse or torture someone. Captain Brown was able to help me put into place very, very clear policies and procedures on what were appropriate and inappropriate behaviors for all interrogators. It became clear that if there were any doubts in an interrogator's mind, he had to consult with the attorney.

By this point in September, I had been able to observe all of the interrogators and their skills. These skills ran the whole range from completely inadequate to very seasoned and competent. The intel center director was also aware of this range and wanted to capitalize upon having the biscuit present. He had us set up weekly training seminars on interviewing behaviors for the interrogators, fulfilling Step 9—institute specific training for all interrogators, and Step 10—put clear policies on acceptable and unacceptable behaviors into place in writing. It was mandatory for everyone assigned to the intel center. At first, it seemed to be overly burdensome for everyone, including myself and my staff. But after a while we just ended up having a whole lot of fun with it. We would frequently role-play scenarios with interrogators and teach them counter-resistance techniques and how to deal with these forms of resistance in legally and morally appropriate ways. Prior to our sessions, very few of these interrogators were taught how to build rapport and establish a relationship with a detainee. Private First Class Herb Coxan was so bad at just simply talking to people that he scared me. Coxan working as an interrogator highlighted the flaw in the screening and selection process for interrogators. Applicants were given a test to determine their skills, rough IQ, and aptitudes; it did not determine one's interpersonal abilities. If someone scored high enough on the test, he or she would be selected to be an interrogator. The nineteen-year-old was without the ability to appropriately establish rapport with another human being—in any situation. I didn't see how the man even ordered a hamburger at McDonald's without getting into a fistfight, much less extracting useful intel from a detainee. His first inclination was to always yell, accuse, and shame the detainee. He was about five foot eleven and was part Asian, with Coke-bottle-thick eyeglasses that magnified the crazed look in his eyes. One time I overheard him say, "That fucker ain't gonna get his medication unless he talks to me." My response was, "Son, if that guy doesn't get his medication, you won't have to worry about him not ever talking to you again."

"Well, why is that, sir?" he asked.

"Coxan, the detainee will die, and you'll spend many years in prison for detainee abuse. You can't withhold a prisoner's right to decent health care because he won't talk to you."

Coxan still didn't seem to get it. He worried me and we set up many training sessions for him. Eventually, we slowly assigned him more administrative duties. I told his supervisor that there is a reason why some physicians work with human beings who are alive and why some physicians are pathologists and only work with dead people.

Most of the interrogators were outright shocked and surprised when I would recommend going to the cafeteria and getting food, fruits and vegetables, desserts, and sodas and bringing them to the interrogation room. Most of them simply just wanted to go into an interrogation room and start yelling and screaming at the detainee. Eventually they would learn that building rapport was the way to go and that if you treated most detainees with decency and humanity, they would talk to you. Building rapport and establishing a relationship would soon take hold like it did in Cuba—it became the way to get detainees to talk and provide accurate and reliable information. It wasn't that we were giving them fruit and sodas to be nice to them; we were doing it because that is the way to get the information we wanted. Did they enjoy the treats we provided? Yes, but I didn't care as long as we were getting the intel. I'd rather be accused of coddling the detainees and getting useful intel than showing how badass and tough we were and not getting any information out of the prisoners.

We also instituted roaming MP patrols to fulfill Step 11, the last item on my action plan. The MP officers were a harder sell when it came to accepting my philosophy, but they really didn't have a choice in the matter because of my rank and my relationship with General Miller. One day I was walking through the camp and I could hear the guy who was second in command of the MP battalion, Major Townson. Townson was on a verbal and psychological rampage. He had two young MPs standing at his desk and he was yelling and screaming at them.

"You stupid fuckers! Both of you got shit for brains, I can't believe I have someone so goddamn fucking stupid working for me. I should just fire your asses right now."

I later caught up with one of these soldiers at the chow hall and she told me that Major Townson was a jerk and didn't know much about being an MP. This young, scared twenty-one-year-old redhead from Idaho said, "Sir, his only way to motivate you is to try to use shame and to ridicule us. I just want to cry every time I see him coming towards me." I was amazed at the insight this young reserve MP had about Major Townson and his leadership shortcomings. By age twenty-one, she had already figured out that a good leader praises in public and disciplines in private. She said, "Sir, I can't understand why Major Townson has to use the foul language all time and he can't talk to you unless he's yelling and screaming at you, calling you a stupid fucker. Colonel, I'm a Mormon and I'm not used to his type of hate." She went on to tell me that in her young Army career, Major Townson was the most "impaired" leader she had ever seen. Then she stunned me by saying, "Sir, my father is a retired Army sergeant major and it would hurt him deep down in his heart if he knew how his young daughter from Idaho was being treated on an almost daily basis by Major Townson."

My deputy chief of the biscuit happened to walk in the chow hall just as that young female soldier got her tray and left the chow hall. He sat down and said, "Sir, I've been meaning to talk with you about that guy Townson. He's an angry jerk and an awful leader. Colonel, I think he is harming and abusing many of the young MPs." I told my deputy chief that I would talk with the commanding general about this and see how he wanted it to be handled when I went back to Camp Victory on Saturday. That Saturday, I boarded a Black Hawk helicopter and flew into Camp Victory. I didn't know it, but the general had received many complaints about Major Townson. While at Camp Victory, I liked to visit the library, and so did the general. While I was hanging out at the post library Saturday evening, in walked Major General Miller.

"Larry, I'm glad I bumped into you 'cause I need to talk with you. When you get back over by the headquarters building stop by my office," he said. "I need to talk with you about an abusive officer over at Abu Ghraib."

Well, to my surprise and relief, General Miller wanted to talk with me about Major Townson. He wasted no time telling me he wanted to "fire his ass." Holding out one last hope for an improvement, he directed me to go and talk with this officer and see if I could "help turn him around," because otherwise he would fire him, put his ass on a plane, and send him home.

"Got it, sir," I replied. "I'll be back at Abu Ghraib on Tuesday afternoon and I'll stop in and have a chat with Major Townson."

That following Tuesday, I loaded up on a convoy and headed

back into Abu Ghraib. When I got back to my office I went to see Major Townson's boss, Lieutenant Colonel McNabb. Mc-Nabb, like Townson, was not the sharpest tool in the toolshed. He was a short, bald-headed reserve MP officer who told me that there was nothing wrong with Townson but that he was just an old rough-and-tough soldier.

"Well, McNabb, okay, thanks for sharing, but Major General Miller wants to fire his ass because he has received many complaints from the troops that Townson is an abusive jerk." McNabb didn't want to hear this and tried to interrupt me in midsentence.

"Stop!" I told him. "You need to hear me on this. There is no place in the Army anymore for this kind of bullshit. We're supposed to protect our soldiers, not tear them down. Destroying nineteen- to twenty-one-year-old kids was not part of the plan."

"Sir, I was not aware that General Miller received several abuse allegations and complaints about the guy."

"Well, McNabb, the boss gave me simple instructions. Meet with Townson on a daily basis if need be to help turn him around. Otherwise, if he gets another complaint, Townson will be out of here."

McNabb sighed. "I'm tracking with you, Colonel. I'll have Townson report to your office tomorrow morning."

Townson showed up at my office the next morning and he and I had a long talk. He was very apologetic, with tears in his eyes, and said that he was amazed that anyone would ever see him as abusive. He saw nothing wrong with yelling, "You stupid fucking idiot!" at the top of his voice. That's how he grew up as a soldier, he said.

"Townson, that was many, many years ago and these young

kids today are different from when you were an enlisted soldier twenty years ago," I told him.

Townson and I had many one-on-one conversations about leadership, supervision, mentoring junior soldiers, and life in general. He went on to finish his assignment at Abu Ghraib and was not fired by Major General Miller.

Out of this came many other opportunities to be actively involved in the development of other officers, helping to shape their style of leadership, molding their style of motivation without screaming, cussing, or belittling their subordinates. Not only had we been abusing detainees as America watched, but in the fray our senior officers and soldiers seemed to have turned on one another out of frustration, depression, hopelessness, anger, and rage. It was clear that the situation required me to be a level-headed leader. What was needed was for me to be a very calm, objective voice. As important, I needed to be there, to be an active, energetic leader who would be a positive force throughout every aspect of the operation—an officer people respected and also enjoyed being around.

In my fourth month at Abu Ghraib, I was beginning to think I could make a real difference. Having instituted some controls and stopped the downward spiral there, I had time to think more about what caused this mess. Who (or perhaps what) caused Abu Ghraib to occur? Was it an intentional, evil plan by the Bush administration? Was it just the natural evil in normal human beings coming out under stress? Was it an institutional problem or the actions of a few bad apples? Some argue it was the eight bad apples whom the Army court-martialed, while others would claim that the fault lay with poor leadership. Others, including social scientists (with Dr. Philip Zimbardo leading the charge), assert that it was the barrel itself (the military structure and the environment) that was bad and the not the apples (the individual soldiers).

"You're crazy. That's an illegal order and you can't make me do that shit. This is my dog and you ain't gonna tell me to make him hurt anybody." That was the quote Lieutenant Colonel Ray Frantz told me about. Ray and I were having one of our two-hour-long debates over the apple versus the barrel. Ray Frantz was a big strapping fellow from West Virginia and a proud redneck. He stood about six foot two and must've been on the heavy side of 230 pounds. I think we all felt safe around this big heap of a fellow. Ray had a way of getting things done in his country-boy, no-bullshit way of answering senior officers. It had a calming and refreshing sense of genuineness around it. This was rare for Abu Ghraib, where many of the officers either didn't know what they were doing, were burned out, or simply just didn't give a damn. Ray Frantz, on the other hand, got shit done. He would use his old storytelling, backslapping style of finding resources, turning strangers into friends, and rallying the troops around him.

"Apple versus the barrel?" Ray asked. "Sir, may I ask what in the shit are you talking about?"

"Well, Ray, America seems to be split as to what was the root cause of the problems here at Abu Ghraib," I explained. "Some folks say it was the apple, meaning the problems were caused by bad soldiers. Others claim that there are no bad apples but rather the barrel, meaning the environment, was so damn bad that it drove these decent and good young men and women to commit atrocities."

Frantz just about had a conniption fit. "Colonel, sir, keep in mind, sir, on this post we had twenty-two hundred soldiers and marines here. Sir, you need to know only eight of them did something stupid. *Eight of them*, sir. And they weren't even interrogators! They were just dipshit soldiers assigned to guard the prisoners. Colonel James, when I hear that stupid shit about the barrel and all that kinda shrink crap you guys talk, it makes my damn blood boil."

I could see clearly the rage was beginning to stew up. The veins of his neck were bulging and his face was turning beet red. I knew that part of his rage was coming from the righteous indignation of a soldier who is proud of the men and women he serves with, and the finer points of the apple vs. barrel argument weren't really sinking in with him. The barrel argument exonerates the soldiers, in a way, by saying that the bad actors were driven to what they did. But Frantz was hearing it as an accusation that any soldier would commit such acts when pushed. He vehemently disagreed. He leaned forward in his chair and looked me straight in the eyes. I could see the pupils in his green eyes dilate.

Frantz repeated, with real purpose this time, what the young, freckle-faced female MP had said. "Sir, she said, 'You're crazy. This is my dog, that's an illegal order and you can't make me do that shit. This is my dog and you ain't gonna tell me to make him hurt anybody.'" He said it again, just to make sure I understood, and then he began to explain all over again that this was a quote of a young twenty-year-old female MP whom America had never heard of. This young MP was a K-9 dog handler during the abuse period from August to October 2003. One night, she was called to the cellblock where all the abuses commonly occurred and was ordered to have her dog be used in the torture tactics. She refused, then calmly stated the explanation that Ray had committed to memory. Then she calmly told her dog, "Let's go," and walked off the cellblock, never looking back.

"How come nobody knows about this stuff?" I asked.

"Sir, it's because perhaps, you know, the good stuff never sells newspapers. Sir, the reality of it is most of the young soldiers here were trying to do the very best possible job that they could with little resources and crappy leadership. Heck, sir, eight of the 2,200 did a bunch of stupid shit. Now, Colonel, the way I figure, that means that 2,192 did the right stuff most of the time."

This was the common thought of most soldiers that I talked to over and over about Abu Ghraib: *Yes, we had crappy leadership and worked in a shithole, but I wouldn't have done what those eight knuckleheads did and neither would any of my buddies. There was something wrong with those eight people.* The average soldier walking down the street cannot imagine how any decent enlisted soldier or officer could ever torture another human being.

"Sir, not all soldiers at this place were immoral shitheads," Ray said. "*Eight.* Out of 2,200."

Many of my colleagues, such as Dr. Phil Zimbardo, disagreed and easily believed and asserted that it was the barrel that was bad and not the individual soldiers. I couldn't support that position. I would argue that in any prison in America you're going to find a small number of correctional officers who are impaired no matter how exceptional the prison facility and the leaders. The conditions at Abu Ghraib were the perfect storm whereby poor facilities, absent leaders, incompetence, depression, despair, fear, and hopelessness intersected and created a house of strange fathers. Whorehouses, alcoholism, sexual assault, and learned helplessness combined to fuel the moral demise at Abu Ghraib. I told Frantz that with my own eyes I could see that 99 percent of the soldiers were good, moral Americans who wanted to do the right thing but that all of their normal emotions were multiplied by fear and desperation, and left ungoverned by psychologically impaired leaders. The place became a cesspool in which people's most base impulses could be given free rein. And still, only eight gave in to their most craven desires.

Lieutenant Colonel Frantz agreed up to a point, but he still resisted the idea that the environment had much influence, if any. He was not convinced that the problem was anything other than some bad soldiers running amok, so I began to share with him commonalities from other prisons such as what occurred at Andersonville during the Civil War. Lieutenant Colonel Frantz pointed out that we could not find any evidence of the abuse and torture being condoned by the U.S. government, because at Abu Ghraib it was not prison-wide but rather was limited to one or two cellblocks.

I had to agree that this was totally different, for instance, from the pervasive torture mandated by the Brazilian military government from 1964 to the early 1980s, when an abusive military regime sanctioned the use of abuse in prisons to manage its political opponents and stifle free speech. What I could gather was that a small number of soldiers were allowed at Abu Ghraib unfettered opportunity to abuse and torture prisoners as a result of vacant and incompetent leadership. At Abu Ghraib, moral disengagement was at times like a plague and was too often coupled with sharp change in normal behavior. Soldiers were so traumatized that they would begin to depersonalize, dehumanize, and psychologically and emotionally detach from their surroundings and do things that under normal circumstances they never would. Were the eight soldiers personally responsible for what they did?

Yes, they were. Was there something wrong inside them, something immoral and pathological? Probably. But their demons might never have found their way to the surface if not for the terrible environment at Abu Ghraib, and they never would have had the opportunity to let those demons out if the leadership had been better.

I could see that Lieutenant Colonel Frantz was starting to see my point. He thought for a moment and then he tried to explain what it was like for the men and women at Abu Ghraib.

"Colonel, you have to remember, sir, we were getting the shit hammered out of us every damn day with mortars, rockets, and sniper fire. Sir, a big-ass mortar hit near and, man oh man, I was not myself for a while. It was like when Tom Hanks got blown off his feet in *Saving Private Ryan*. Colonel, remember at the end of the movie, the Germans were running over the town and Hanks got blasted by an incoming tank round? Sir, he was blown off his feet. Heck, even though he wasn't directly hit, his whole world was in slow motion and he was not right for the rest of the battle. Well sir, that's how it was for me. I had to deal with this place and at the same time I was in a mental daze all the time from the mortars."

He sat there quietly for a moment, reflecting in his own memories about how stressful that was for him and his soldiers. As I said good night to Lieutenant Colonel Frantz, I wondered how many other soldiers were just like him, outwardly strong and capable, but dealing with terrible memories and a type of fear that never really lets go once it gets hold of you. Our conversation also left me pondering where I stood on this apple vs. barrel question. After our talk I realized more clearly than before that the apple vs. barrel argument represented the two extremes, and I was settling into a more finessed point of view about what caused the tragedy at Abu Ghraib. I knew that the environment and the lack of leadership were driving forces, and Frantz even agreed with me that those were key to understanding why those eight soldiers did the wrong thing. But if we acknowledge the effect of the environment and the lack of leadership, aren't we buying into the barrel theory? Aren't we saying that it was the situation that was all wrong and allowed those eight people to give in to their most craven desires? But if only eight of them went awry, when so many more could have done exactly the same thing, doesn't that argue for the bad apple theory? I had to note the differences between this situation and the Stanford Prison Experiment, in which Dr. Zimbardo said the environment—the bad barrel—drove otherwise good kids to become abusive. In that situation, however, it was *all* the guards who went bad, not just some. At Abu Ghraib, it was eight out of thousands.

The more I thought about it, the more it seemed an Alice in Wonderland question that could be twisted in infinite ways. Could we really say that the environment was so terrible but that thousands of soldiers had the strength and moral fiber to resist it anyway, while eight did not? Or was it more reasonable to say that no matter how horrible the environment, it was not the primary cause, that most of the blame fell on the eight individuals who committed the crimes?

There was no doubt in my mind that the environment, the barrel, was terrible. But I was also certain that the individual soldiers had some predisposition to this immoral behavior. I was beginning to wonder if we had taken eight questionable apples and thrown them in a bad barrel. How would the results be any different than what we were seeing in Abu Ghraib?

10
Fighting the Terrorist Mind

October 2004

K affir! Kaffir!"

The detainee was shouting loudly and vigorously as Lieutenant Colonel Frantz and I walked by the razor fence line one afternoon.

"Did that bastard call me an infidel?" I asked Lieutenant Colonel Frantz, with mock indignation.

"That fucker sure did, sir," he replied. "Just breaks my heart to know those fuckers don't love us."

Lieutenant Colonel Frantz's dislike for the Iraqis was worn on his sleeve at all times. If you didn't notice it, he would be proud to explain it to you. The screamed insult prompted him to wax poetic about the Iraqis.

"Colonel, I just don't understand why we gotta be so nice to these bastards," he said. His face got really red as he kept talking. "Sir, I don't like their customs, and their language hurts my ears," he said, starting in on his list. "It's an ugly language. Man, it sounds like two guys are gagging when they talk."

It was clear that not only were the religion, language, food, battle tactics, and culture of these extremists different, but so was their thought process. *Is it a normal thought process?* I would ask myself over and over. And if the terrorists' mind-set is abnormal, what makes it abnormal? Is it a mental illness?

After making a detour to his office, Lieutenant Colonel Frantz and I headed to the chow hall for lunch. As we passed by the same part of the prison again, the same detainee saw us coming and yelled out "Kaaaaaaffirrrrrrr!!!!!" He was even louder this time and seemed to really be pissed. I stopped for a moment to hear what he said in broken English.

"I fuck you ass, I fuck you ass, you donkey, dog, dog, fuck you ass," he screamed, while he grabbed between his legs and shook his crotch at me. Then, as he pointed directly at me, he yelled out, "PRAISE ALLAH!" Then he took his right hand and slowly made a cutting motion across his neck as though he was cutting my throat. "You die, you die, infidel, fucking dog, praise Allah," were the last words he yelled. Then he spit on the ground toward me and walked away.

Stunned at the hate, the evil I saw in his eyes, I became even more convinced that this guy's mind-set was similar to a Klansman at a segregation rally. He reminded me of the hate I saw in the eyes of many Klansmen as a young boy in Louisiana. Also, like the Klansman of old, no reason, no logic or amount of information could change this detainee's mind nor clear his heart of the hate and evil he spewed. His rage was foul and almost inhuman.

After many encounters like that, it became clear to me that the new battlefield was not the sands of Iraq or Afghanistan, but the mind of terrorists. *Why?* I asked myself. *Why is the battlefield in these people's minds now, in a way it never was before?* I concluded that this is an enemy like we have never faced before. We have waged wars in sand before, including World War II. The environment in Iraq is the same as the environment in North Africa or plenty of other places we fought in back then—it sucks. Mechanically, for example, the problems are the same. Sand in a tank engine in World War II destroyed it equally as well as it destroys a Humvee engine today. But the mind, language, culture, intent, and will of this enemy is totally different. Destroying the entire Western world is the goal some of them would die for. In wars of the past our enemies wanted to destroy our army, not American women and children walking down the street. They wanted to overtake our military, government, and society, and make us bow to their wills, but they didn't have a fanatical insistence that each and every one of us be killed. This new enemy cannot be swayed to our way of thinking by showing them the finer points of American life. Too many Americans do not understand that this enemy in the global war on terror cannot be won over by tourism and Levi's jeans, by "understanding them" and "respecting their culture." Death to all Americans will be their only victory.

America has never fought an enemy like this, one that has been on this single-minded quest to eliminate all infidels for hundreds of years. Nor do we understand the level of hate and the almost delusional mind-set it takes to maintain a war for centuries. The jihad wars of the Middle East have been fueled by a religious fundamentalism that makes American fundamentalist right-wing anti-abortion hard-liners look like pussycats. As crazy as they might be sometimes, the nuts in the United States have not used suicide bombings as a strategy. No American has walked into a college student union, Madison Square Garden in New York City, or Union Station in Washington, D.C., and blown themselves up for a political cause, killing a hundred innocent other people at the same time. Our terrorist enemies have and will continue to do so on a regular basis in Iraq, Afghanistan, the Middle East, and other parts of the world. I just pray they never employ the same strategy in the United States, that the tragedies of 9/11 will never be repeated in our shopping malls, parks, and schools. Our global war on terrorism is intended to stop exactly that nightmare from unfolding.

I asked myself many times, *Are these guys normal? Is this part of a mental illness or is it a normal part of their culture?* Well, clearly we know that 99.99 percent of all Muslims around the world are peaceful, law-abiding citizens. But that still leaves plenty of others who aren't. After 9/11, when I was attending a conference in Chicago, I caught a ride in a taxi with a driver named Joe. Joe was a Ralph Kramden kind of a guy, with a big, loud, but likable persona. As I approached the cab, I could see Joe's plaid shirt, baseball cap, and a bumper sticker that read, "I love this country." Joe asked me, "Partner, what brings you to Chicago?"

"Man, I'm in town for a conference with some other psychologists," I told him.

Clearly, Joe was one of those taxi drivers who liked to explore the world through impromptu chats with their fares. "Hmmm . . . Doc, I got a question for you," he said. "Why did it take a whole team of you guys to decide if Jeffrey Dahmer was crazy or not?"

"What are you talking about, man?" I asked. "Jeffrey Dahmer, that serial killer who ate his victims?"

"Yeah, that one," he said with a big grin. "Doc, that guy was drugging young guys, tying them up, raping 'em, then the crazy nut would cut up their bodies, stew 'em in a pot, and eat the bodies. Doc, you mean to tell me you really need to have a committee of shrinks to decide if that fucker was crazy? Man, it ain't shit a normal dude would do."

I was stunned to get this question out of the blue, and I just laughed it off without giving Joe a good answer. But it got me to thinking about the same question with some of the Muslim extremists who employ terrorism. Do we need a new mental illness diagnosis for the terrorists? Are they mentally ill?

I had many debates and conversations with other psychologists, often using the American terrorist Timothy McVeigh as an example. He's the former Army soldier who blew up the government center in Oklahoma City in 1995, and was executed in 2001. A colleague of mine by the name of Dr. Harry Jackson told me, "Larry, the guy was perfectly normal."

I responded by saying I didn't see how he could be. "Harry, let me see if I understand your logic," I said. "McVeigh was pissed at the government, so he went out and blew up a building and killed or injured a couple hundred people, correct? Harry, how in the hell is that a normal, rational thought process?"

Dr. Jackson believed that because McVeigh was not hearing voices, seeing little green men, and he knew that his actions were wrong, he was "normal." Of course, I disagreed and told Dr. Jackson that our field needs to rethink what we classify as normal and a mental illness.

Even before I went to Abu Ghraib, I had many conversations with psychologists around the country about the mental state of terrorists. Of course, many loudmouthed, know-it-all PhD "experts" from around the country would say that these terrorists are perfectly normal. Now, mind you, most of these clowns had never sat in a room and looked in the whites of a terrorist's eyes. I have, on many occasions. Major Leso and I, while he was still in Cuba with me, had many long discussions about this. John was of the belief that the desire to kill all "nonbelievers" was cultural and not unique to Muslim extremists. He cited the example of Japanese suicide bombers in World War II and asked if I thought they were mentally ill.

"John, I don't have the answer," I told him. "But it is clear that the mind of the modern-day terrorist is unlike anything we have ever seen before."

Even aside from the question of the terrorist mentality as a new mental illness, I was dealing with plenty of the standard, old-fashioned, unquestionable mental illness among our detainees at Abu Ghraib. No one in the White House ever expected that the rates of true mental illness would be such a problem with this new enemy. We had a significant number of depressed patients and schizophrenic patients, but we did not have the hospitals in place to manage and take care of them. We also had a large proportion of the enemy whose belief structure was so illogical, rigid, and factually incorrect that it appeared to be delusional— the ones who thought the earth was flat or that Iraq was the most advanced nation on earth. Add to this the 10 or 20 percent of their population who were simply dumb as a box of rocks, and we had a real challenge in how to handle these people. Collectively, such an enemy yielded a new battlefield.

Our rates of mental illness such as depression, psychosis, and anxiety at Gitmo and Abu Ghraib actually matched the rates of mental illness in U.S. prisons. So it wasn't that the Iraqi or Afghani population produced more mental illness. It probably produced about the same rate as the United States, but even that was problematic because the prison system back home had some resources, limited as they may be, to deal with those mental illnesses. We had virtually nothing of the sort in Iraq when I arrived. We had to build an inpatient psych unit in Abu Ghraib, just as I had done in Gitmo, and by September we were seeing how much impact those resources could have on these patients. We now know that in future wars we must plan to manage and treat at least 3 to 15 percent of all the prisoners we capture for a psychiatric condition while they are in our custody. Likewise, as this war goes on we will have to plan on fighting an enemy who has many soldiers who are ignorant and cannot read and write and/or may very well be mentally ill.

As a doctor and a soldier, I saw this challenge as a unique opportunity to merge my skills and my professional goals. We have to be ready to treat mental illness in the prisoners we pull off the battlefield, but we also must assess whether we are facing an entirely new mental illness diagnosis in the form of the terrorist whose devotion to jihad is so extreme, so one-dimensional that it may cross a line into a disorder that can be defined and studied. Treating this enemy like any enemy of old would be a mistake.

This new enemy does not want to just go to war with U.S. soldiers, sailors and marines. This new enemy wants to go to war with every American man, woman, and child, to kill them all. As Joe the taxi driver would say, that's not normal.

11

I'm Broken

November–December 2004

Life goes on back home while soldiers are away at wars. Wives and husbands sometimes cheat, teenage daughters get pregnant, sons get arrested, jobs are lost, and thousands of homes are foreclosed on while we're away serving our country. Too often, while we're right in the thick of fighting our nation's wars, death finds the soldier in a combat zone—on the battlefield, by the death of his parents, or perhaps by the death of an innocence he once had.

I left Iraq on October 31, 2004, Halloween night. As I headed to the military air terminal in Baghdad, I mourned the small measure of innocence I still had when I arrived in this place. I was kind of anxious about getting on the plane because of an experience I had two months earlier, when I had to fly into Kuwait to pick up my 9mm pistol that was confiscated when I arrived on a civilian flight without all the right paperwork to bring my weapon into the country. On that flight, the remains of a dead soldier were loaded onto the C-130. As the truck with the coffin approached, the crew chief asked us all to exit the plane and form two lines, one on each side of the huge truck. All activity on the entire runway and military air terminal stopped at that moment. As the coffin was slowly removed from the truck, the order "present arms" was yelled out. We all came to attention and saluted our fallen comrade who had died on the battlefield. An Army chaplain positioned himself in front of the coffin and said prayers as he led the coffin into the C-130.

Most often, planes heading out of a combat zone are filled with chatter, laughter, joy, and fun as troops head home. But not on that day. It was a somber occasion that reminded us all of how lucky and how fortunate we were, and that one soldier on the flight had made the ultimate sacrifice for his country.

The images of that flight kept running through my mind as I boarded the Air Force C-130 cargo plane for the first leg of my flight out of Iraq. Unlike all of my previous flights to and from Baghdad, I was the only passenger this time. Usually there would be dozens of us stuffed in this hot plane like sardines, breathing diesel fumes and each other's stink. Having the plane to myself this time didn't make it much more comfortable, however. I overheard one of the crew members say that it was 145 degrees on the flight line. Once we were squared away and ready to go, we sat in place with the propellers running for forty-five minutes. Why? I have no earthly idea. All I know is that I was soaking wet with sweat down to my underwear. Finally we got the go-ahead for departure and the plane began to roll quickly down the runway. Even though I had done this drill many times, I was still surprised to see how fast this big-ass C-130 could take off, and in such a short distance. I sat up straight, strapped in with a seat belt, and braced myself for the combat takeoff maneuvers that I knew were coming, the departure equivalent of the same wild ride that

I had taken when landing in Iraq the first time. Within an instant it seemed as though we were facing straight up. As the big plane went vertical, twisted, banked, and yanked left and right, I was almost lying down sideways from the force. Then the plane's engines howled, we banked down with a sharp turn to circle the airport, leveled out, and headed south to Kuwait City. I was able to sit up again as the plane flew straight and level. The air became cool as we gained altitude, and my sweating stopped.

After the takeoff-induced adrenaline surge wore off, a sense of calmness fell upon me. As I dozed off to sleep, the loud rumble of the C-130 providing a constant din that helped block out everything but my inner thoughts, I kept wondering who I would be after this experience. *Will I be different when I get back home? Will I get post-traumatic stress syndrome? Am I gonna have nightmares?* For the moment I decided to enjoy the bliss of being at 10,000 feet, safe, out of harm's way, and heading home. I drifted off to sleep.

We landed safely at Camp Doha Air Force Base right outside Kuwait City. A couple of young soldiers were nice enough to help this old colonel carry his gear to the VIP quarters where I would reside for approximately the next two weeks. These VIP quarters were very much different from the VIP tents in Baghdad. The VIP tents in Baghdad were like all the other tents, filled with cots and large air-conditioning units that worked on occasion. The only real upgrade for the Baghdad VIP tents was the sign on the outside of it that said "VIP." The Camp Doha VIP quarters, on the other hand, were significantly better than any accommodations in Baghdad and the standard tents in Doha. These quarters were in a large structure that had tin roofs and tin doors. The rooms had regular beds with linen, a TV, refrigerator, a phone, and, most importantly, regular showers and toilets. After spending time in Baghdad, these quarters looked like a five-star hotel.

I got to my room, put my gear away, took my 9mm pistol from its case, and removed the clip that held the bullets before I locked it away. I headed for the shower and took a hot soak for what seemed to be an eternity. While walking back to my room, it seemed as though the weight of being in a combat zone had been quieted by the hot shower. I got dressed and called my wife to tell her that I had survived the perils of Abu Ghraib and had arrived safely in Kuwait. She cried that night, as did I, thanking the Lord for allowing me to return without the loss of life or limb like so many other brave soldiers. I would soon be in the comfort of her arms again. Afterwards, I called my eighty-one-year-old mother, wanting to assure her that I was all right and also to thank her for steadying me on that first terrible night in Abu Ghraib.

She didn't sound good. Her voice and spirit had been weakened from the forty-year battle of being an insulin-dependent diabetic. Neither I nor my sisters knew it then, but she was dying.

I lay down on my bed to just unwind before I headed to the chow hall for the midnight meal. I was overcome by exhaustion and slept for three hours. At 3 a.m., I heard a loud bang— BAM!—followed by voices in the hallway outside of my room. Groggy and disoriented in the utter darkness of my room, with no lights to help me find my bearings, I responded as I would have in Abu Ghraib. *We're under attack!* With one quick, fluid motion, I rolled out of my bed onto the floor, got to my feet, and managed to find my flashlight. Hurriedly, I found my way to my 9mm pistol, locked and loaded it, and turned the safety off. The voices outside of my room grew louder. Now sweating, a voice in my head was screaming at me. *Hurry, Larry! They're coming for you! They know you're here and they're coming for you! Get ready to engage!* With my loaded pistol in my right hand, I quietly eased my way to the door.

BAM! The loud noise came again in the night, making me flinch and crouch lower to the floor. *Damn, was that another mortar?* My heart was racing as I eased open the doorknob with my left hand while keeping my right index finger on the 9mm pistol trigger. I opened the door, 100 percent ready to engage, and saw two sixty-year-old American women standing outside my room laughing and talking. One of the ladies saw me there, crouched and ready to blow her fucking head off. She either didn't realize what the look in my eyes meant or she was trying to defuse the tension, because she didn't react like someone in the line of fire.

"Shucks, son, sorry we woke you up," she said softly, very gently, and with a bright smile. "Son, just go on back to sleep. You look exhausted."

The look on her face and her gentle tone immediately slowed my racing heart, and after a moment in which I just stared at her, trying to understand what was happening, my thoughts slowed and the fear eased. As I lowered my weapon, I heard another BAM! and turned toward the sound just in time to see a door closing behind someone. Every time someone opened the tin doors at the entryway to the building, they slammed shut with a sound much like that of a mortar's impact into the side of a building at Abu Ghraib.

I got up and hurled myself back into the bed, still clutching my pistol. I lay there trying to understand what had just happened, and at that point it was clear that my psyche had served notice: I was not the same man, nor would I ever be. Even though I was able to quiet my mind again, I knew that the anxiety would reappear. Intellectually, I realized I was safe and out of Iraq, but some part of me still questioned the safety of my surroundings. *It was just a door this time, Larry, but that doesn't mean you're out of harm's way. You're still on the list. They still want to find you.*

I placed the pistol on my nightstand and slid my bayonet within arm's reach under my bed. Assured that I had my weapons within reach, I dozed off back to sleep. Then I had a horrible nightmare. I dreamed that I was on a convoy, hot as hell in the 130-degree heat, soaking wet with sweat, and sitting directly behind the driver, when my Humvee got a flat tire. As we pulled over to the side of the road, my driver got shot in the head. His blood and brain matter splattered my goggles and face as I sat there behind him. In the ensuing frenzy to defend ourselves, my M16 jammed and I dropped my 9mm pistol. I hurriedly found my sidearm, and as I looked up with my 9mm ready to fire, I could clearly see the eyes of a fifteen-year-old Iraqi boy ready to shoot his AK-47 at the soldier standing to my right. Instantly reliving every moment of doubt and moral debate that I had pondered over this moment, I nonetheless pointed my weapon at the boy, pulled the trigger to save the life of a fellow soldier . . . and then I awoke in a panic, chilled in cold sweat, in the quietness, the utter darkness of my room.

My heart raced in a loud *thump, thump, thump* as I struggled to orient myself, to find my way. I only partly realized that I was awaking from a dream. Part of me was still blood-spattered in that convoy, and part of me thought I was waking up but in the midst of a real attack on the base. The voice in my head was screaming, *GET YOUR WEAPON, LARRY! HURRY! HURRY!*

THE FIGHT'S ON! Then, as I frantically struggled in the dark to figure out where I was and what to do, I could hear my wife's voice in the distance.

"Sugar, it's gonna be okay, it's gonna be okay," she whispered, repeating the mantra that always calmed me down when it came from her beautiful lips. "You just had a bad dream, sugar. Settle down. It's gonna be okay."

Finally realizing I wasn't being attacked, I got up and listened for voices outside my door before opening it. I didn't want to bump into anyone and have to chat. Hearing nothing, I opened the door and walked down the hallway to the bathroom. I poured cold water in my hands and splashed the ice-cold water on my face.

Damn, Larry, is this what it's going to be like now? I thought. *Is this what I'm going to face every night?*

Falling back in to my bunk, exhausted all over again from this turmoil and moral haunting, I was able to drift away back to sleep for the rest of the night. I got up around lunchtime and headed for the chow hall. But as I walked to the chow hall I stopped right in the middle of the sidewalk, transfixed by an empty Pepsi can laying in the middle of the sidewalk. *Oh shit, it's an IED.* Slowly, never taking my eyes off the Pepsi can, I took a few steps backward while the young soldiers behind me just kept walking forward, past the can. I crossed the street and continued on for another block, then I stopped again in the middle of the sidewalk. This time it was a brown paper bag that paralyzed my movements and focused my attention. Again I whispered to myself, "An IED, Larry! Hurry! Cross the street! It's gonna blow any minute!"

I hustled across the street, eyes peeled for another IED, ready to dart away at the slightest suspicion. In this way I eventually got to the chow hall as the soldiers around me just strolled casually along.

I soon learned that this cautious process was very common for soldiers on their return home. In Iraq, IEDs were placed in the simplest of life's things, a Pepsi can, a brown paper bag, or even the carcass of a dead cat or dog. Still to this day, although I am not as hypervigilant as in those first days out of Abu Ghraib, an empty bag or a soda can on the sidewalk will get my attention, maybe even spook me if I only see it at the last minute. At night, even though I try to relax and remember that I'm not in a combat zone, I still peek out my window and stare at every car that turns around in my cul-de-sac.

Along the way to the chow hall, as I crossed the street for the umpteenth time, a voice from deep in my soul spoke up. *Larry, turn in your ammo for your 9mm pistol. Turn in your ammo before you shoot somebody, you dumbass.* I realized I was just too damn jittery to be carrying a loaded weapon. So I asked where to find the supply building. "Hey man, where can I turn in my rounds?" I asked one young soldier, as I rested one hand on my 9mm. "I shouldn't be walking around with this."

He smiled and nodded his head like he knew what I meant. "Colonel, I understand, sir," he said. "It wasn't a good idea for me to have my weapon loaded here either, sir."

We both laughed while he gave me directions to the supply building. A few minutes later I turned in two 9mm clips with all of the bullets. However, I kept my KA-BAR bayonet. I just didn't want to be unarmed, even here on this relatively secure base. Although my fear was misguided and irrational, something would not allow me to let go of my hypervigilance. I couldn't help but anxiously think about an intel officer at Abu Ghraib telling me that there was a $25,000 bounty on my head from Al Zarqawi and that I and the other colonels on post were on Al Zarqawi's most wanted list. I never bothered to check "the list" and verify it myself, because I didn't see the point. If my specific name wasn't actually on the list, would that mean I wasn't threatened? No, I'd never assume that. And if my name was on the actual list of most wanted, I didn't see how I would be helped by having that image seared into my mind. I was cautioned to be damn careful and watch my back at all times, no matter where I was—and I did. Each night before I went to bed, I placed my bayonet on the nightstand right next to my bed.

After I ate lunch, I decided to walk over to the food court and visit the Starbucks. Seeing the Starbucks was more of a welcome sight than most people could imagine. I'm a coffee lover who's always walking around with a Starbucks cup in my hand back home, but this time that green-and-white sign meant much more to me than that I would soon get a cup of hot coffee. It was a symbol that said, "Yes, Larry, you really did survive Abu Ghraib and you're back in civilization." It confirmed to me that I was one step closer to going home. Sitting in the Starbucks sipping that warm cup of coffee, I had time to reflect on the difficult night. *Why did you have that nightmare last night?* I asked myself. It was like my psyche, my superego was sitting next to me at Starbucks talking to me, playing the role of therapist. A voice told me, "Larry, perhaps your nightmares are a metaphorical struggle between good and evil. It is actually a good sign. Son, if you did not have nightmares, given the horror of what you saw, you would have normalized these horrible events. Welcome your nightmares, Larry. This is how your soul is telling you that the horror of war is against a decent man's morality."

I took a long time to finish that cup of coffee, thinking through the nightmares and what they meant about how I was handling my experience at Abu Ghraib. I never had that nightmare again. Three years have passed since I returned home and I no longer fear going to sleep.

I stayed at Camp Doha for more than a week waiting to get a seat on a flight home. I was able to power down by getting some sleep in spite of the constant bang of the tin doors. I stopped jumping at the sound, but I often lay there wondering what genius designed the place with doors loud enough to be mistaken for mortars. At the base, I would go to see movies, one of my favorite pastimes, and I called my wife every day. Eventually, along with four hundred other soldiers, I boarded a chartered DC-10 en route to the States. We stopped in Germany, Italy, Nova Scotia, and finally landed at the Baltimore-Washington International Airport's military air terminal. We all cheered as the plane touched down on U.S. soil, some cried, and we all congratulated one another. There was an Army chaplain on board who came on the microphone and said a prayer for the soldiers we lost along the way and asked the Lord to keep them safe. I spent the night at a local hotel in Columbia, Maryland, then boarded a United Airlines plane on to Honolulu two days later.

My wife, Janet, had finally closed on our brand-new home and moved out of the hotel, along with our three-year-old granddaughter, Judy. A rare feat for me was that I slept almost uninterrupted for every leg of my fifteen-hour journey home from the Baltimore airport. Even though I could now get to sleep without nightmares, the inner turmoil that once made its way into my dreams would return in different ways I had not yet envisioned. My arrival at Honolulu International Airport was met with great joy. Being back in the arms of my soul mate of thirty years would always heal and calm me. Along with Janet, my granddaughter, son, and close friends, there were members of my command at the airport to great me. It was a wonderful homecoming.

Settling in quickly at our new home, I slept peacefully in our waterbed. I soon called my mother in New Orleans to tell her I was home safe, but I was dismayed to learn that her health was continuing to fail. Within a matter of days Janet and I were on a plane headed for New Orleans to spend perhaps my last Thanksgiving with my eighty-one-year-old mother. We arrived in New Orleans about three days before Thanksgiving 2004. When my mother saw me, she hugged me as though she knew her time had come, that perhaps it would be the last Thanksgiving with her only son and youngest of six children. I busied myself with chores around the house, enjoying the richness of my Creole culture and spending as much time with my mother as possible. It was indeed a joyous time.

My mother was a night owl like both Janet and me. We enjoyed spending late nights in the French Quarter and bringing my mother home a hot cup of French café au lait and beignets, wonderful French doughnuts, from the legendary Café Du Monde. On this particular night, my mother and I were up late by ourselves, laughing, as she told stories about her youth on a farm in Opelousas and Simmesport, Louisiana. We were enjoying our time together when suddenly she became quiet for a moment. Her expression changed and she said, "Son, I know the Lord has sent the angels for me. I spend more time in the hospital than I spend out of the hospital. I only wanted to live long enough to see you one last time before I go, son." She was looking at me as if this was the moment she had held out for, the time she wanted to just be with me and look into my eyes. Somehow I was able to hold back my tears, but she knew what I was feeling. Realizing my pain and sorrow, she shifted the conversation back to her youth in rural Louisiana, Cajun zydeco music, and how she would dance up a storm as a teenager. We laughed some more, long and hard, then we finished our café au lait and beignets. Reluctantly, but so grateful for the time with her, I went to bed at about 2 a.m.

The morning before Thanksgiving, I loaded my mother in the car and drove her to one of her thrice-weekly kidney dialysis appointments. They had been a consistent burden for her for many years. As I started the car, she placed her left hand on my right arm and said, "Son, I need to talk with you about something. I need your help with it because your sisters will listen to you about this."

"Yes, Ma dear," I said. "What is it, sugar?"

"Son, I don't want to do this any longer. It's my time to go be with your sister Betty, Daddy, and my mother."

I knew what she meant, and I wasn't going to disagree with her. "Ma dear, of course, darling, how can I help you with this?" I asked.

Holding on to my arm, she responded by saying, "I need your blessing to just let go. Is that okay, son?"

I struggled to hold back my tears, but I told her what I really felt in my heart. "Ma dear, you've lived a long, good life, and if you know that it is your time to move on and be with the good Lord, then that is okay by me. And it will be okay for all of my sisters. Sugar, when you're ready to let go and go to be with my sister Betty, just let go. It's okay." My sister Betty died at age fifty-two, due to complications from lupus. My mother, like all parents, felt that no parent should have to outlive one of their children. Perhaps my mother welcomed death so that she could be with her daughter again.

She said, "Thank you, son," and I confirmed that she still wanted to go to the kidney dialysis center today. She did, but along the way we stopped for a café au lait. The next day was a joyous Thanksgiving celebration. My entire family came by my home in New Orleans on Thanksgiving. That night Janet and I went out dancing to zydeco music, and we of course brought my mother back a café au lait and some French doughnuts. My mother laughed with me and told me stories about my Creole ancestors I had not heard before. Again, we stayed up talking together until about 2 a.m. Through this process I was slowly starting to heal. Being with my wife, my mother, and all of my family in the place of my birth was calming for me.

However, our joy was short-lived. The next morning my sister woke my mother up for dialysis. Something was not right. My mother's speech was slurred and her thoughts were kind of disorganized. She had had a massive stroke in the night while asleep. We took her for what would be her last and final visit at Touro Infirmary in New Orleans. Janet and I stayed in New Orleans until Christmas Day and flew back to Honolulu on Christmas night 2004. My mother remained in the hospital and died two days after our plane landed in Honolulu.

Death always has a way of finding a soldier. Death does not stop, nor will life events slow because a soldier is deployed for fifteen months. I was not prepared for this level of loss less than a month after my return from Iraq.

* * *

The rest of December and the remaining holiday season of 2004 flew by with a looming sense of loss and sorrow, while at the same time I struggled to recover from my Abu Ghraib emotional scars. On one Saturday morning in late January, the haunting, the residual effects of the war, found its way to my soul again. It was like most Saturday mornings for Janet and me. We stayed up late on Friday after our granddaughter went to bed and we would rise late on Saturdays. On this one Saturday morning, something was amiss for me. I can't tell you to this day what was at the core of my discomfort on that morning.

I sat in my favorite leather chair upstairs and wore my favorite comfortable pajamas while I watched a movie on HBO. For Larry James, that should be a damn good morning. But something wasn't right deep inside me. I could hear Janet and my three-year-old granddaughter, Judy, downstairs having so much fun. Like most three-year-olds my granddaughter insisted on making her own cereal that morning, slowly pouring milk into the bowl with the cereal. I could hear Janet praising her for doing such a good job, not spilling a drop on the floor. Then Janet grabbed the morning newspaper on the front porch, some coffee for me, and walked up the stairs with our Judy. On the very last step of the stairs, Judy stumbled. Milk and cornflakes went flying on the carpet, the walls, and everywhere. Within the blink of an eye, a demon was unleashed in me that I had not ever seen before. "WHAT'S THE MATTER WITH YOU, JUDY? ARE YOU STUPID?" I yelled at the top of my voice. "GODDAMN IT, I'M SO TIRED OF THIS SHIT! SIT YOUR ASS DOWN AND CLEAN UP THIS CRAP!"

Neither Janet nor Judy had ever seen me rage like this before. This was totally unlike me. My world went into slow motion as my three-year-old granddaughter became afraid of me. I saw it in her eyes. She screamed, cried, and begged for forgiveness as loud as her lungs would allow. I yelled again, "SHUT UP, GOD-DAMN IT!" I grabbed her by the right arm as I yelled louder and louder. I was out of control.

Thankfully, Janet gently placed her right hand on my left arm and whispered softly, "Larry, it's gonna be okay. Now, just settle down. I'll clean this mess up. Why don't you go in the bedroom and relax? I'll take care of this." She picked up little Judy and hugged her. As I walked away, I turned and looked at my wife. Her eyes told me that she wondered if her once calm, gentle, fun-loving husband would ever be the same. For the first time, it was not only clear to me, but to Janet as well, that I was not well and not that same man who left for Abu Ghraib. As usual, the gentle touch of my wife served as my elixir. I calmed down. Janet kept Judy quiet and away from me for a couple of hours. Later in the day, Janet asked, "What was that all about this morning?" I shrugged my shoulders, walked away to the upstairs bathroom, locked the door, and cried my eyes out, thinking about the terrified, hurt look on that innocent child's face as I was screaming at her like a madman. I got down on my knees and asked God to help me. I begged for his forgiveness. Part of the problem was that I didn't know the full answer as to *why* I had unleashed such anger and rage at my three-year-old granddaughter the way I did. She was a child and didn't deserve it. Or perhaps I was now able to see that I had become emotionally impaired like so many other veterans. I had heard of veterans tearing their houses apart in an unstoppable rage after returning from Iraq, but even as a psychologist I never really understood what prompted such outbursts. Was I just like them?

No! I said to myself, *I'm better and stronger than them, and plus, I'm a psychologist. This PTSD stuff can't happen to me.* I gathered myself, went downstairs, and hugged my granddaughter and told her I was sorry. Almost within an instant she smiled and asked me if we were going to go to the beach. Children are so wonderfully forgiving.

Over time, either in person or by phone I would have several conversations with an old friend and senior psychologist from Walter Reed, Dr. Hal Wain. Talking with Hal was always enlightening but it was also healing for me. He helped me work through many of these issues and he never made me feel as though I were mentally ill. He framed what I was going through as a perfectly normal response to abnormal events. I shared my experience at the Starbucks in Kuwait with Dr. Wain. Hal, in his usual brilliant way, helped me to realize that it was the classic psyche struggle.

"Larry, your psyche has figured out a way to reframe the nightmares for you in a healthy way," he said. "Don't run from this, Larry. Embrace it."

He was right. Slowly, over time, I began to return to normal, or so I thought. I busied myself again with teaching, getting back to doing research, and seeing patients. The symptoms of our nation's new PTSD was in many cases, like mine, very subtle and unlike the old Vietnam veteran stereotypes. Many of us did not disappear from society or turn to alcohol or drugs like the PTSD vet of earlier eras. Janet was the first to see the subtleties of my condition. One evening I was walking downstairs at our home with a cup of coffee in my right hand. Our downstairs is flat with level carpet. Suddenly the coffee cup fell from my hand. A few days later, a bowl of cereal just fell out of my hands. This became common and would occur at least once or twice a week. Whatever I had in my hands would just fall to the floor.

While I was struggling with the lack of muscle coordination in my hands, I started to have trouble with tripping while walking on a level, flat surface without any obstructions. I would be walking down the hallway at my department and I would stumble or trip. The problem would also occur at home. One day Janet and I were loading up in our car, and I went back in the house to get a cup of coffee. While walking across the living room, I stumbled and the coffee cup hit the wall and carpet. Janet came to my rescue, never complaining or patronizing. Again her patience had a curative effect on me.

We loaded in the car and needed to stop by my office on our way to downtown Honolulu for a meeting. By the time we arrived at my office it was after hours and I had left my keys and wallet at home. This was a significant event for Janet. Even though I tried to downplay it, she knew it was a sign of something terribly wrong with her husband. In our thirty years together, I had neither misplaced my keys nor ever lost my wallet. That just wasn't something I ever did. She said, "No problem, sugar, we can just go back home and get your keys." Forty-five minutes later we arrived back at our home, but for a long while I couldn't find my keys or my wallet. On the drive back downtown, Janet spoke up.

"Sugar, I'm really worried about you. You can't find your keys, your wallet, and you're stumbling and falling all the time. Larry, what's going on? You're yelling and screaming at Judy in a way like I've never seen you yell at anybody. I think you ought to go and see our doctor." Her voice trembled with worry and fear for me as she continued. "You look like shit and you can't walk around the block once without taking a nap. You used to be able to run four miles a day, do 150 push-ups and 300 crunches without taking a break. Now you're fatigued all the time. You need to see our doctor because I'm really worried about you."

I promised her that when I went in to work on Monday I would schedule an appointment with our physician. I never did.

I think I meant to follow through with what I promised Janet, but my worsening symptoms only made me more fearful of admitting to someone else that I had a problem. I got up early on Monday morning as usual for my four-mile run, but I couldn't finish the run. I was so fatigued after fifteen minutes of running that I had to just stop and walk. Somehow I never found time to go and see my physician. I thought I'd just tighten up my bootstraps and soldier through it, whatever it was. The level of fatigue I was experiencing was like carrying an extra fifty-pound backpack around all day long. I didn't care. I just drove on. *Larry, there're soldiers coming back from Iraq with one leg who run marathons*, I told myself. *Don't be a pussy, Larry. Just soldier through this. Hang on. It will get better.*

Either my staff at Tripler Army Medical Center was very patient with me or I was damn good at bluffing my way right through my mental confusion and cognitive lapses. I had worked with many of my staff members for years, but for some strange reason I would lose their names right in the middle of conversations. It was like my mental hard disk drive was crashing. Sometimes it would work and other times it didn't. Novel information from patients I had very little difficulty handling. But trying to recall old information was troubling, as when I was having a conversation with Dr. Jim Kamona, who had been a psychologist at Tripler for years. Jim came in my office one morning to seek my advice about a research project. Right in the middle of our conversation, I couldn't recall his name nor could I figure out what in the hell we were talking about. Within an instant, my brain was engulfed in a mental fog. It was as though he had called me at 3 a.m. and asked me to say my Social Security number backwards. I didn't panic; I just smiled a lot, nodded my head often, and after about fifteen minutes or so, it all came back to me. That became my strategy when I found myself lost in the wilderness like that, and I think most of the time the other person didn't catch on. They didn't know, but I was terrified! I thought I was losing my mind.

Janet saw this more and more at home, first by me losing my wallet and keys ten times the first week I was back home. She would just remain calm, never showing her frustration, and wait until the fog lifted. I was horrified by the episodes and scared, for the first time in many years, that the once articulate senior Army psychologist would be lost forever.

Then a weekend would go by without me dropping anything or losing my memory. My symptoms would come and go. The more I thought about it, the more I realized that this was consistent with early-onset Alzheimer's disease. I was perplexed by all of this. I was not myself at all. But what seemed strange was that I didn't fit the typical PTSD Vietnam veteran stereotype. I wasn't having nightmares anymore, I didn't drink much alcohol at all, and I wasn't beating my wife. Yet I was clearly feeling the effects of the war. I just wasn't right, as my wife said more than once.

One Monday morning I turned the TV in my office to CNN. Amazingly, an old colleague of mine from Walter Reed Army Medical Center was doing an interview. Dr. Deb Warden, a noted neurologist and psychiatrist, was talking about how researchers had discovered that some soldiers who had been exposed to blast injuries or extreme stress had abnormal brain scans. Dr. Warden lifted the whole world off my shoulders by explaining my symptoms to me through her CNN interview. I sat there dumbfounded but increasingly relieved as she described every symptom that plagued me: mental confusion, memory loss, rage episodes, and spontaneous stumbling while walking were now commonly seen in some veterans returning from the war. We also now know that the symptoms of soldiers who lose consciousness during a blast explosion get worse, and some never return to who they were before the war. I was lucky—I never lost consciousness. But still, I was one of those veterans who was struggling. I couldn't hide it anymore.

I went home that night and had a long talk with Janet. She and I were relieved now, glad that at least we knew what was wrong. Dr. Warden's interview vividly illustrated what happened to a soldier's brain when he was blown off his feet by a bomb blast—as happened to me several times in Iraq. Dr. Warden explained that the tricky thing is that, like me, even though the soldier doesn't crack his skull or get shot, the force from the blast still damages the brain. Put this together with the stress placed on the central nervous system from constant psychological strain of being in a combat zone, sleep deprivation, food deprivation, and the 120-degree heat, and the result can be an adverse impact on a soldier's brain functioning and central nervous system—the *new* PTSD.

What was happening was that these soldiers were slipping through the cracks of the medical system, just like I did. Why? Well, soldiers like myself were never shot, never hit our heads, nor had any shrapnel from a roadside IED in us. We had two eyes, two ears, a nose, walked okay, and didn't report any nightmares. The medical system had no reason to pay attention to us.

We seemed normal when we returned home and didn't request any assistance. The only saving grace was that, even when we didn't seek help, for most of us the prognosis was good. Dr. Warden went on to say that most of these soldiers would return to their predeployment condition. Others—no one knew why—would never be the same.

My struggles grew less as time went on. Just when I thought I had it bad, a new patient, a new soldier walked into my world. I was in my office one day, as usual sipping on a cup of hot coffee and working on an article. My phone rang. It was my secretary. She said, "Colonel, I need your help up front, sir. There is a guy up here who needs some help." She sounded a little odd. I said yes, that'd I'd come up front, but I didn't understand why she was calling me with this. "Shouldn't you be sending him to the psychiatry outpatient clinic or the emergency room?"

"Well sir, yes, I should but this soldier insists on only talking to somebody who is a combat veteran. Sir, most of our providers are civilians."

I told her I would be right there.

Sergeant Jose Gomez was one horse of a soldier. This twenty-four-year-old specifically requested to see a psychologist who had been deployed to Iraq. Sergeant Gomez was a hard-charging, dedicated career medic. He loved being a soldier. He had a handsome Latin tan that seemed to accentuate his coal black hair and deep brown eyes. From his frame one could clearly see that this soldier dedicated at least two hours per day to the gym, with a purpose.

"What brings you in to see me, soldier?" I asked.

He responded with two words. Two words that symbolized

the life, spirit, mind, and body of many soldiers upon their return home. He said, "I'm broken."

"Son, I'm not sure I completely understand all of what you mean. What's broken on you?" I asked.

"Sir, it's not on me," he said, obviously struggling to explain something that he didn't fully understand himself. "It's *in* me, Colonel. My heart . . . something . . . Sir, my mind, sir . . . My mind ain't right, Colonel."

Sergeant Gomez and I spent three hours together that day. He told me about how he had witnessed the carnage in Sadr City, Iraq, the worst ghetto and most dangerous place in that country. He was assigned to an armored cavalry unit. As a medic he was required to go wherever his unit went. The fighting was intense and almost daily for his unit. He saw old men, children, and his buddies get blown apart. And as a medic, he never had the option of turning away and trying to put it out of his mind. His job was to go into the worst of the carnage and try to help.

"Sir, I had to just put all my emotions in a box and not deal with this shit until I got back home," he explained. "Colonel, I can't sleep. I hear my dead buddies' voices all the time. I have to drink three beers just to get to sleep at night, sir. I'm scared."

Gomez had the more common PTSD-type symptoms. But what brought him in to see me right now?

"Sir, I threatened to choke my wife if she didn't stop talking. Man, I was out of it this morning, Colonel. I never, ever thought about hitting my wife before." As he told me this, Sergeant Gomez wept like a child whose mother had just died. I got his family physician to prescribe him medication for sleep and I would work with him in therapy twice a week for the next month and then each week for about six months. Sergeant Gomez got better, stayed with his wife, and rotated on to his next Army duty assignment. There were thousands of soldiers just like him.

My experience with Sergeant Gomez made me think back to a good friend, Colonel Charles Hoge, who had taken a team of researchers from Walter Reed to Iraq to conduct intensive study on the extent of mental health problems among our soldiers deployed to Iraq. I realized that Colonel Hoge and his colleagues had predicted exactly the symptoms that troubled Sergeant Gomez. The colonel and I shared a tent at Camp Victory every Saturday in August and September 2004. Charles and I would doze off to sleep at night while debating. I thought that his numbers overstated the levels of PTSD, depression, and anxiety among the troops. He, in his usually eloquent way, would disagree and say that they most likely underreported the seriousness of the problem. I had to agree now that Sergeant Gomez was neither rare nor unusual. We now know that at least 3 to 15 percent of soldiers and marines have some problems with PTSD, depression, or anxiety when they come home. We also now know that at about ninety days after a guy gets back from Iraq the numbers increase to at least 30 percent. Back at home, the loss of a job, family problems, and grief frequently combine to push many soldiers over the edge. I can't imagine what it would have been like for me upon my return if I had learned that my wife had left me and/or my home was being foreclosed on.

On many occasions the system gets in our way of helping a soldier get the help that he needs. A reporter by the name of Lisa Chedekel published an article in the *Hartford Courant* on October 3, 2007, about how many soldiers who committed suicide on their return home from the war had previously been seen by an Army mental health provider. She reported that 43 percent of the soldiers who committed suicide had been prescribed psych medications before and 60 percent were seen by mental health providers before the suicide. A shocking 36 percent had been seen by an Army mental health provider within just thirty days of committing suicide.

Death always finds a soldier, either on the battlefield or at home. That thought kept going through my mind over and over as I reviewed this newspaper article. Chedekel didn't know that the system gets in the way. Usually these soldiers get lost in the system and commit suicide not because they receive poor treatment by the psychologist or psychiatrist, but because the soldier's commander won't listen to them. I wish I had a nickel for every time I said to a commander, "Captain, this guy is not doing well. You need to leave him home," but then they made my patient deploy anyway. Well, usually they had to send the soldier back early from the deployment. This was a common battle between the mental health department and the manpower demands of the commander's mission.

On October 19, 2007, *USA Today* published an article saying that mental illness was the number two complaint among soldiers when they returned home. The numbers are simply staggering. Since 2006 they increased by 20,000, which was about a 70 percent increase over the twelve previous months. According to this article, one out of every seven returning veterans reports a problem with PTSD, depression, or alcohol. Most of the reports just don't know that these numbers are a gross underestimate. Like me when I returned back from the war, I was not going to say "yes" or "true" to any questions on any medical/mental health screening form. Why? Well, the answer was simple. If I said yes to any questions, that meant that I would be kept at a regional hospital for another month or two, perhaps maybe five or ten months until everything was diagnosed and treated. Soldiers want to go home to their wives, just like I did.

Also, I felt the screening questions to be a violation of my privacy. I did not ask to be evaluated and I wanted to deal with my PTSD symptoms in my own way. As a result of these dynamics, we missed a lot of soldiers like myself. I honestly felt emotionally harmed by the screening process. Just when I would neatly tuck the emotional pain away, some medical general would get an idea to have us screened again. The nightmares returned every time after they forced me to dredge up those memories. Or we would be forced to attend some bullshit seminar on combat battle fatigue taught by an officer who had never deployed anywhere. That was usually an immediate turnoff. Soldiers who have deployed a lot, including myself, find it difficult to take advice or orders from those who have never deployed. On one occasion I was ordered to attend a seminar at Tripler Army Medical Center with two hundred of my closest friends who had all deployed. At Tripler, an Army psychologist who thought he knew it all told us, "You *will* have nightmares, get drunk a lot, have PTSD, beat your wife, and threaten people." This enraged me. How dare this ignoramus tell me I'm going to do all those things just because I was in combat?

Given the staggering amount of data documenting the prevalence of mental health problems among the troops, I reflected on my fight with Colonel Kerry Matson when I was down range at Abu Ghraib, trying to convince her that the soldiers at Abu Ghraib needed mental health care on site, not a dangerous convoy trip away. The fact that I even needed to make that argument to her was amazing and awful. I also thought of the warrant officer and interrogator Betty Patterson, who often talked with me about how she had seen two interrogators blown apart by a mortar attack. Her words rang in my ears as I wondered how she was doing, probably home from Iraq by now: "Sir, they died right there in front of my eyes . . . One of their body parts were laying on the ground. I stood there dazed when the medics picked them up and put them in a body bag. After a while, I couldn't do my work and I just cried a lot. Sir, we didn't have no psychologists, no chaplains or anybody to help us deal with this. Colonel, sir, it was shameful how they just left us there with no help."

No human being should have to see that amount of death and feel that amount of pain. *I was sent into hell and asked to fix it*, I said to myself. *Did I? God, I hope I really made a difference.*

The global war on terrorism will go on for many years to come. But I was coming to realize that, yes, I had survived, psychologically and physically. And I was beginning to realize that I had made a difference. Many of the positive changes I recommended are still in place at Army detention facilities around the world, and that is one of my proudest achievements.

Another morning found me in my favorite Old Navy pajamas, hot coffee in hand, kicked back in my favorite chair upstairs with the TV tuned to a movie on HBO. I could hear Janet and Judy downstairs, happily making breakfast. Unlike the recent, shameful episode in which I lashed out at my sweet grandchild, this time I was truly relaxed and felt whole again. But still, as I sipped my coffee and enjoyed the quiet of the morning, my thoughts drifted away for a few moments, back to the death ceremony when we loaded the soldier's flag-draped coffin onto the C-130 cargo plane on the flight line in Kuwait. I could see myself standing there in 130-degree heat, saluting as the honor guard marched by with my fellow soldier's coffin. I did not know that soldier's name. All I knew was that this soldier had given his or her life in service to our country, fighting evil on a foreign soil. And this soldier was somebody's brother, sister, mother, father, son, husband, and America was a better place because of him, his deeds, his dedication to duty for us.

As I heard my granddaughter's laugh again, I snapped back into the present. I smiled to myself and took comfort in knowing that my rage had faded away, as well as my many hauntings in the night. But then again, the image of the soldier's coffin being carried on board the C-130 I would always hold on to. I decided to never allow myself to forget this image, my sense of gratitude for those who volunteer for the fight and pay the ultimate price. This image over the years would serve to provide me with a sense of comfort knowing that America has many great men and women willing to make the ultimate sacrifice for its safety, and the fight against evil, tyranny, and terror.

My granddaughter came up the stairs, jumped on my lap, and took a big swig from my coffee cup. I hugged Judy tight and felt a warm satisfaction in this quiet moment with one of God's sweetest creations.

I look forward to the day when I can sit at Café Du Monde in New Orleans, have a café au lait with Judy, and tell her the story of the great men and women I served with in Iraq, Cuba, and Afghanistan. I want to tell her how I was a part of the fight to help save our humanity.

12

Go to the Basement

May 2005

Even though I felt that I was getting back to normal, smiling and laughing like my old self, my brain and my psychomotor skills still sometimes showed some of the aftermath of my time in Abu Ghraib. With no warning, my brain would involuntarily go on pause. To cope, I busied myself with administrative matters of the department while my colleagues, staff, friends, and students attempted on many occasions to get me to talk about what happened at Abu Ghraib. It wasn't until May 2005, while I was teaching a psychology workshop to a group of young Army captains in our training program, that I seemed to come out of the mental fog. In my time away from classroom instruction, I started organizing my thoughts on Abu Ghraib, trying to bring some order to my memories and to find the lessons that might help other soldiers and psychologists. I was reluctant to talk with anyone about those experiences and what I had learned, but I knew that it was important to document them.

One day I was about halfway through my planned classroom discussion when I asked if anyone had any questions. A young

Army captain by the name of Jessica Schuster from Minnesota surprised me and spoke up. Captain Schuster was like many young female Army officers. She was a former goalie on a girls' hockey team, frequently lifted weights, and she had a get-down-to-business approach and style.

"Sir, I got an e-mail from one of my professors back at Minnesota and he told me that you were the guy sent to Abu Ghraib to put procedures in place to fix that horrible tragedy," she said. "Colonel James, our year here is winding down. Sir . . . so, even though you haven't talked about this much, my question is . . . sir, what leadership principles did you take away from Abu Ghraib?"

It wasn't the first time I had been asked this question, of course, and I was used to just brushing it off. I could have easily demurred and returned to the day's lesson, but for some reason my mind was receptive when the query came from Captain Schuster. At that moment, my brain and my memory seemed to start working again and in a very fluid way I was able to organize my thoughts. I felt like I was finally ready to tell someone about Abu Ghraib. I felt I finally understood it enough that I could offer some useful lessons. I don't know why it happened at that moment, but it did, and I decided to answer the captain's question.

I thought for a moment about the notes I had been making on lessons from Abu Ghraib, and then I turned, looked Captain Schuster right in the eyes, and whispered, "Schuster, *you got to be there.*"

She responded in a kind of a confused way. "Sir, what did you say? I didn't hear you, sir."

I repeated myself, louder, so the whole group could hear. "You have to be there. Captain Schuster, as a leader you need to always remember to be there. Never allow yourself to be a vacant, distant, and emotionally detached leader."

I explained that there were many reports of the brigade commander, the post commander, and the task force commanding general of Abu Ghraib as simply being vacant leaders. They weren't there.

"Sir, forgive me for asking something stupid and dumb, but Colonel, I really need to get in the weeds of it because when I graduate from here, I may never have another chance to talk with you about this again, sir," she continued, speaking with an intensity I had not heard from her before. "Sir, why is this so important?"

"Well, Schuster, if I'm not there as a leader that will leave a message to my subordinates that I'm gone, not only physically but most importantly it sends the message that I left the mission, and I don't care about the mission," I told her. "When that happens we may as well pack up our shit and go home."

She looked stunned, like she didn't expect such a strong answer from me.

"Captain Schuster, you and your student colleagues need to hear what I'm about to say next," I said, glancing around to the other attendees, who were now paying attention. "*You gotta go to the basement.*"

I heard one of the other students, Captain Jones, whisper, "Huh?" as she looked to the person next to her. "Go to the basement? What's he talking about? Did he get hit on the head in Iraq?"

She didn't think I had heard her and was a bit embarrassed when I looked directly at her and said, "Yes, I did get hit in the head. But nevertheless, Captain, you still need to look in the basement every chance you get."

Nobody in the room seem to get my meaning yet, and Jones spoke up for the confused but intrigued. "Sir, what do you mean by 'going to the basement'?"

"Well, gang, here's the deal," I said. "As a leader, you need to learn the value of getting up off your asses and looking under every rock when people least expect it, and going down into the basement and checking under every rock of every building. Then and only then will you be able to figure out what the hell is going on in an organization. More importantly, your troops will respect you for it. One of the problems in most organizations is that rarely will you find its senior leaders getting down and dirty to the lowest level and looking in every closet and every basement of every building."

"Sir, what's that going to tell you?" Captain Schuster asked.

"Easy answer, Captain," I said. "Number one, it will tell you where the skeletons are, and number two, it will tell you where all the broken crap is hidden. Number three is most important. It will tell your subordinate troops that you have a vested interest in their organization and let them know that they can't hide anything from you. Remember, Captain, your troops will judge you by your deeds, not your bullshit words."

"But sir," Schuster responded, "would it be better to have this as a planned inspection schedule?"

"Hell no," I told her. "Good leaders are available twenty-four seven. On many occasions at Abu Ghraib, I would simply go walking around the compound and just see what I could find. I would find doors and gates unsecured and guards sleeping on duty. They'd see me walking around and act like they'd never seen a colonel before, because in that place, many of them hadn't. No wonder we had so many goddamn escapes every month. Sometimes the best way to figure out how well an organization runs may very well be to show up at 0200 and ask a bunch of questions to the first private or young officer you come across. And while you're there, it would be a good idea to just sit down and have a cup of coffee with a bunch of the soldiers and let them ask *you* questions about the mission, your goals, and the Army. And guess what, you'd be amazed at how much you can learn about what works and what's broken. The added benefit would be that these young troops will love the hell out of you and respect you no end for taking the time to reach down, talk with them, and ask them how they feel about something."

I paused for a breath and realized that the young officers were intensely interested in what I was saying. *Damn, I think they're getting it,* I thought.

"Captain Schuster, I need to also add that, as a leader, you need to have a very, very clear set of behaviors that are the dos and don'ts for your organization. In other words, they should be posted everywhere, what behaviors will be accepted in our organization and what is clearly, flat-out not to be tolerated."

I talked with them about the quote from Colonel Banks as I was leaving Fort Bragg, North Carolina, for Abu Ghraib. Banks had told me, "Larry, remember people will do what their leaders allow them to do." I explained that Morgan told me on many occasions that the rules had to be clear at all times. Unlike most psychologists, the colonel had served as a company commander of a forward-deployed unit in the first Gulf War back in 1990–91. He knew that a good leader has to set clear boundaries and that when any soldier crossed the line, it had to be dealt with immediately.

"This meant that if the infraction was not dealt with by the leaders, soldiers would continue to do it because it was allowed by the leaders in charge. And as a result, behavior would begin to slowly drift away from the SOP," I said. "That's a lot of what I found when I got to Abu Ghraib."

"Sir," Captain Schuster said, "isn't that the same as a vision statement?"

"Heck no," I said. "Look on the wall in our conference room and you'll see the general's vision for this hospital, but in that vision statement nothing is said about what important behaviors will and will not be tolerated. That's the message that needs to get out to soldiers through meetings, handouts, small cards, e-mail postings, whatever you can think of to get it in front of them. More importantly for the soldiers, everyone in the command needs to know what's not going to be tolerated—things like DUIs, sexual assault, and spouse abuse. Early on in Abu Ghraib, all the soldiers I have talked to who were there when the abuses happened told me that there were no rules. It was like the Wild, Wild West."

I was pleased to see the captains were tracking with me. They were getting it, and that encouraged me to open up more.

"The tragedy of this was that while Abu Ghraib was morally falling apart, the leadership was not there to take the necessary corrective action," I said. "Captain Schuster, it will be critical to your operation to have active attorneys lay out the rules of engagement. These attorneys will help these young soldiers and officers interpret the Uniform Code of Military Justice and how to interpret the rules of engagement and what conduct is appropriate. Captain, I want to come back to something I said earlier, and that is how important it is to *be there*. By this I mean living, eating, sleeping, and praying with your soldiers. One of the problems I saw in Iraq was that there were approximately thirty-five generals living in the lap of luxury at Camp Victory. These generals were living in actual palaces that Saddam Hussein and his sons once owned. Now, as for myself, whenever I went to Camp Victory, I slept in a tent with privates and I rode around post on the same public buses that all the other privates and sergeants rolled around post on. Keep in mind that if you want to know what in the hell is really going on at a command, talk to the privates and sergeants. I never learned a damn thing by hanging out with colonels.

"The generals, on the other hand, were chauffeured from point A to point B in air-conditioned vehicles and would return home at night to the air-conditioned palaces that were built and owned by Saddam. The average soldier, on the other hand, slept in hot-ass tents and went to sleep every night worrying if a mortar would come through the top of the tent. I went to sleep many nights in Iraq in tents, saying my prayers, and, as I dozed off, would ask the Lord to take care of my wife if I got blown up in the night. Captain, I heard a famous saying once but I don't remember who said it. It goes like this: 'A leader who stays in the rear will take it in the rear.'"

The captains chuckled a bit at that line, but they were still paying attention.

"Most of these young soldiers literally slept in their underwear because they either did not live in an air-conditioned tent or the air-conditioning was usually broken. Dehydration was a very, very common problem on convoys for many junior soldiers because the vehicles were not air-conditioned. Now, yeah, war is hell and all that, and you can't whine about not having air-conditioning, right? But you know, the generals' dehydration was never a problem because they always drove around in air-conditioned Humvees.

"Eat where your soldiers eat. Sleep where your soldiers sleep. Pray where your soldiers pray. And drive in the same crappy vehicles your soldiers drive. Be out front and do whatever you ask your soldiers to do. This will garner their respect, and most importantly, it will always position you to know what the hell is going on in your organization."

I was going through my Abu Ghraib notes in my head and for a minute I wished I had brought them with me. But then I realized I didn't need them, that I knew these lessons as well as I knew anything.

"Now, listen to what I'm about to say. You need to write this down. I'm going to give you eight rules to lead by. These are the big lessons I brought home from Abu Ghraib, and you can use them no matter what type of an organization you're in. Here you go: Rule #1 is 'You got to be there.' Don't hide like a chickenshit bastard. Be available at all times. The leaders at Abu Ghraib hid and allowed rogue soldiers to commit atrocities. I can't tell you enough times how important it is for you to be there with your soldiers. Eat at their tables in the chow hall, sleep where they sleep, everything. You got to be with them and they will love you for it.

"Rule #2 is 'Be seen.' When leaders are not seen by their subordinates, they will begin to drift away from following the rules. You'll have to show up unannounced at all hours of the day and night.

"Rule #3 is 'You must be involved.' Captain, as I said a few minutes ago, you must be everywhere in the organization. Along the way there, talk with and have fun with the lowest-ranking people you meet. The privates, the secretaries, the janitors, those who feel as though they're the nobodies of society. That's where you will really build morale and turn a failed mission into a successful one.

One of the young captains asked, "Sir, why do I ever need to talk to a janitor?"

"Captain," I said, "you're not tracking with me yet. An old aunt of mine told me a long time ago, 'Take care of those who take care of you.' If you just be kind to that janitor and ask him every day how he's doing, your office will be spotless all the time. And even better, Captain, he'll tell you when some shit is really screwed up. That guy will cover your flank all the time.

"Rule #4 is 'Be bold.' Make the right, hard moral calls. Your troops will love you and respect you for it. We all love being around a leader who has a big set of balls. That's the person we all want to follow. Be bold and lead.

"Folks, Rule #5 for me is 'Be passionate' in everything you do. Your soldiers who work for you will see it in your eyes, and more importantly, Captain Schuster, they will feel it in you. Your passion will spread to the rest of your unit like a wildfire. Some of the officers I met at Abu Ghraib seemed to operate with a management style like that of a guy who owned a funeral home. They had a job to do, but they did it with very little passion and they would move about the post in a very emotionally detached way. A blind man could see that these type of leaders didn't want to be there.

"Rule #6 is 'Be fun.' You guys know how I am. I'm always cutting up with folks, telling stories, having a good time. That's the kind of colonel I am."

"Sir, we always know when you're in your office," one captain offered. "I can always hear your laugh all the way down by my office."

I looked Captain Johnson in the eyes with a wide grin on my face and said, "Son, you got it. Nobody likes being around a mean, nasty boss. Not only is it not fun, but it drains your energy and you just don't want to come to work. It ain't fun. You need to have a blast at work, and it will inspire those around you to have fun as well. As a leader, *you* set the tone. If you're miserable, they're miserable. If you're motivated and passionate, they will be too.

"So Rule #7, gang, is 'Be energetic,'" I continued. "Do whatever you do with energy and people will want to be around you. It will be infectious.

"Rule #8 is 'Be clear.' Everyone who works for you must at all times know the rules of engagement. This has to be over-trained. Remember, soldiers will do what their leaders allow them to do. If you allow it, a soldier will do it. Thus, you better be clear on what are the appropriate and inappropriate standards of conduct.

"Ladies and gentlemen, now you got it. That's what I learned at Abu Ghraib and these are the things I live by. Our time for this morning is up. I'll meet with y'all next week."

As I got up from the table, Captain Schuster said, "Colonel, would you mind if I ask one last question, sir?" I told her it would have to be quick.

"Sir, are you the same person now that you were back before the war?"

A quietness fell upon the room as the group stopped getting their belongings together to leave and waited to hear my answer. It was as though they all took in a deep breath and held it. I didn't answer immediately, and I began to see faces and images of the past, to reflect on the death of my mother, the loss of my soldier buddies, and I could almost hear the sound of incoming mortars all over again. I didn't realize that about thirty seconds went by in total silence as the group waited for me to respond. Finally, I took a sip from my coffee cup and said, "Captain, we'll have to talk about that one next week."

Then I walked away before they could say anything more.

13
Facing My Critics

October 2005–August 2007

I was still having periods of restless sleep as I debated the doctor versus soldier conflict deep within my psyche each night. When I was a young child, my mother would always tell me, "Don't worry 'bout nothin', son. Just when you can't find your way, the good Lord will always send an angel to help you along the way. All you gotta do is just be patient with it." I tried to follow her advice on those nights when I couldn't sleep because of the images and concerns racing through my mind.

On one bright and sunny day in October 2005, I was sitting by myself in the hospital cafeteria and must have looked like ten miles of bad road. My old fried Chaplain Peter Boudreaux from Opelousas, Louisiana, just came and sat with me. Pete was an Army colonel as well as the head chaplain at our hospital. After being a minister for over thirty years, Pete could sense when things were amiss in anyone. Plus, Pete and I had a special bond because years earlier we had served together in the 25th Infantry Division. He and I crafted a program to reduce the incredibly high suicide rate at the division post. His grace, peacefulness, and

240

calmness had often soothed my disquiet. Chaplain Pete in many ways reminded me of Father Francis Mulcahy, the chaplain on the TV show *M*A*S*H*—a gentle, kind, peaceful, and pleasant human being.

Pete sat down and said, "Larry, how was it in Iraq? I have been thinking and worrying about you, son."

I didn't really answer his question. Instead, I asked him about something I had been wondering about. "Pete, why don't chaplains carry weapons in combat?"

"Well, we can't, not ever. How can I serve God and kill another? Us chaplains have to choose, Larry—be a minister or not," he said, immediately sensing why I had asked the question. "Larry, you're a doctor. You guys take an oath to 'do no harm,' and I never understood how a doctor, a healer, could take such an oath and carry a gun at the same time."

My world stopped in time at that instant. Chaplain Pete had reached into my soul and placed his right index finger on pause, stop, just hold right here for a moment. My eyes began to tear up right there in the chow hall. Chaplain Pete knew what he was doing when he asked me that question. He already knew I was having a hard time resolving how to be a doctor and a soldier, and he helped me bring it out into the open.

"Larry, that's a real burden for you to carry, trying to be faithful to both roles," he said. "I know you have to be struggling."

He reached over the table, gently placed both of his hands on top of mine, and began to pray. If was as though the hundred other people in the chow hall were motionless, silent, and part of a distant background. He said in his gentle voice, "Heavenly Father, please place your arms around your son as he struggles to find the right road, the right path on his difficult journey. Keep him safe in either a combat zone or at home. Oh Lord, guide him to always have a good heart and a clear mind. In Jesus's name, amen."

The chaplain stood up, patted me on the shoulder, and walked away. I never saw him again. He retired shortly after that but his words are still with me to this day. It was a simple gesture that told me he knew the pain I was hiding, and praying with my friend helped me take another major step forward in resolving this debate deep within me.

The debate raging within me was bad enough, but the evolution of the doctor's role on the battlefield became a hotly debated public issue during the global war on terror, and I became a primary target for the critics. Sometimes hateful attacks upon my character began to heat up in the latter part of 2005. By the time I returned to the States from my Abu Ghraib deployment, many journalists from around the country, in an effort to sell newspapers rather than present the truth, began to attack the notion of a psychologist working to help interrogators in any way. Several misguided psychologists and psychiatrists from around the country jumped into the melee and accused Department of Defense psychologists like myself of being diabolical devils, basing their charges on no data whatsoever. The facts were clear for me: I was not even in Cuba when the abuses occurred in 2002. I arrived there in January 2003. Likewise, I didn't get to Abu Ghraib until June 2004, six to eight months *after* the dirty pictures of the abuses showed up on TV. Moreover, there were no psychologists at Abu Ghraib during the abuses. But for some reason the attacks raged on.

At the beginning, it was difficult for me to understand this criticism and remain silent. My orders had been clear: help these young interrogators gather intelligence in a safe, ethical, legal, and effective manner without any abuse whatsoever. Sadly, while in Cuba and Abu Ghraib I had done many media interviews and very few got any traction at all in the general media. Apparently having me explain all the good things we were doing and all the improvements that had been made already just wasn't interesting enough to be publicized. What did get all the traction and attention was this notion, without any clear data, that Army psychologists were torturing people. On June 20, 2005, *Time* magazine had published an article that some interpreted as accusing Major John Leso of torture. The article soon took on a life of its own, with antiwar activists and torture opponents claiming it as evidence that Army psychologists were assisting in the torture of detainees.

The *Time* article didn't even say that. The closest it came was in reprinting an excerpt of an interrogation log—an interrogator's record of multiple sessions with Detainee 063—that the magazine obtained. The detainee was Mohammed al-Qahtani, a follower of Osama bin Laden's and the man believed to be the twentieth hijacker on September 11, 2001. That excerpt starts with this entry:

23 November 2002

0225: The detainee arrives at the interrogation booth at Camp X-Ray. His hood is removed and he is bolted to the floor. SGT A and SGT R are the interrogators. A DOD linguist and MAJ L (BSCT) are present.

0235: Session begins. The detainee refuses to look at SGT A "due to his religion." This is a rapport building session.

The full session log covers interrogations conducted with the same detainee between November 23 and December 21, 2002.

"MAJ L" was Major Leso, but *Time*'s excerpt from the session log only contains one reference to him, indicating that he was present on November 23, 2002, for what was called "a rapport building session." He is mentioned only in the excerpt from the interrogation log. The main *Time* article made no mention of Major Leso or BSCT, and the anti-Gitmo tone of the article suggests that they would have gladly mentioned any other evidence that Major Leso was participating in the abuse of detainees. The actual interrogation log for Detainee 063 (once classified secret but now widely available on the Internet) contains these five other references to "MAJ L" or "BSCT":

Control puts detainee in swivel chair at MAJ L's suggestion to keep him awake and stop him from fixing his eyes on one spot in booth.

BSCT observation indicated that detainee was lying during entire exchange.

The BSCT observed that the detainee was only trying to run an approach on the control and gain sympathy.

Interrogator began to play cards with MP to ignore the detainee due to a BSCT assessment that the interrogators may be becoming the family figures of the detainee, and the interrogator wanted to see if the detainee would try to seek attention.

BSCT observed that detainee does not like it when the interrogator points out his nonverbal responses.

That hardly amounts to evidence that Major Leso was torturing detainees. Not even close. Nevertheless, many members of the Divisions for Social Justice and Peace Psychology of the

American Psychological Association took the *Time* article as conclusive evidence that Leso had tortured people. Most of his accusers had never read the article, much less the actual interrogation notes, and they just blindly accepted the claims of anti-war activists that Major Leso had violated his duty as a psychologist by helping to torture a detainee. Because his name was in the record of an interrogation, and because he was an Army psychologist, critics of our work at Gitmo seized on those facts as a way to score points. He was demonized for abusing detainees, instead of the two CIA contract psychologists who actually conducted abusive interrogations prior to Major Leso's arrival on the island.

I sincerely believe that the allegations against Major Leso are not only false, they are also in direct opposition to what he did at Gitmo. I never saw any data and never received any information to document that he, a doctor, was teaching interrogators how to torture detainees at Gitmo, and I just can't imagine Major Leso in that role. Unlike me and how I welcome taking charge all the time, Major Leso was uncomfortable telling others what to do. He felt that his role was only an advisory one. And as such, he had no legal authority to tell other soldiers what to do. Despite being uncomfortable with his new role at Gitmo, Major Leso made a positive impact on the Intelligence Control Element and the Joint Task Force and it is a damn shame that anyone thought otherwise.

Because of the debate and attention on this subject, the American Psychological Association put together what is now known as the PENS (Psychological Ethics and National Security) Task Force, of which I was a member. This task force was directed to come up with special guidelines for psychologists working within the intel community. The results of this blue-ribbon panel were controversial. The panel issued twelve statements concerning psychologists' ethical obligation in national security–related work, making it clear that torture was wrong and also that all psychologists, regardless of the setting, have an obligation to protect the welfare of those who cannot protect themselves. These were the twelve statements of the PENS Task Force:

1. Psychologists do not engage in, direct, support, facilitate, or offer training in torture or other cruel, inhuman, or degrading treatment.
2. Psychologists are alert to acts of torture and other cruel, inhuman, or degrading treatment and have an ethical responsibility to report these acts to the appropriate authorities.
3. Psychologists who serve in the role of supporting an interrogation do not use health care related information from an individual's medical record to the detriment of the individual's safety and well-being.
4. Psychologists do not engage in behaviors that violate the laws of the United States, although psychologists may refuse for ethical reasons to follow laws or orders that are unjust or that violate basic principles of human rights.
5. Psychologists are aware of and clarify their role in situations where the nature of their professional identity and professional function may be ambiguous.
6. Psychologists are sensitive to the problems inherent in mixing potentially inconsistent roles such as health care provider and consultant to an interrogation, and refrain from engaging in such multiple relationships.

7. Psychologists may serve in various national security–related roles, such as a consultant to an interrogation, in a manner that is consistent with the Ethics Code, and when doing so psychologists are mindful of factors unique to these roles and contexts that require special ethical consideration.

8. Psychologists who consult on interrogation techniques are mindful that the individual being interrogated may not have engaged in untoward behavior and may not have information of interest to the interrogator.

9. Psychologists make clear the limits of confidentiality.

10. Psychologists are aware of and do not act beyond their competencies, except in unusual circumstances, such as set forth in the Ethics Code.

11. Psychologists clarify for themselves the identity of their client and retain ethical obligations to individuals who are not their clients.

12. Psychologists consult when they are facing difficult ethical dilemmas.

I thought the panel's conclusions were all no brainers. What decent, moral psychologist could disagree? The blue-ribbon task force was also asked to answer, "Is it okay for a psychologist to conduct an interrogation?" and "Is it proper for a doctor psychologist to aid and consult with interrogators?" The panel concluded that a psychologist should not conduct interrogations but that it was okay to consult with interrogators. Well, I knew that very often these interrogators were nineteen- to twenty-five-year-olds who had not yet fully developed their own interpersonal skills. We had lots to offer as psychologists.

But this was not enough for many of the radical left-wing members of the American Psychological Association and other human rights and physician societies around the country. Somehow these organizations saw the PENS Task Force report as an endorsement for DOD psychologists to torture people. They disregarded the facts and created their own. In June 2007, a group of forty psychologists crafted a letter attacking myself and other members of the blue-ribbon task force. In essence, they accused me and the other DOD members of the panel of "reverse engineering" the principals of behavioral science for interrogators so they could torture detainees in a better way. The physicians at Gitmo faced similar challenges from some medical groups around the country. We had about twenty detainees who were on starvation diets in 2006 and 2007. Our choice was simple: we would not allow anyone to die by starving themselves to death. It was no different from a psych patient telling me, "Dr. James, I'm going to hang myself tonight." My response would not be, "Okay, that's your choice." Under no circumstances would any reasonable doctor do such a thing. So I could not understand why some physicians wanted us to just stand by and watch detainees starve themselves to death.

The psychologists' "evidence" was drawn from an August 2006 DOD inspector general report that had some inaccurate information in it. This August 2006 report said that Colonel Morgan Banks conspired to teach psychologists and interrogators from Cuba how to reverse engineer SERE school to torture detainees. SERE stands for "Survival, Evasion, Resistance, and Escape" and it is a special school designed to teach U.S. soldiers how to survive being a POW. In addition to teaching various survival and escape skills, the school puts trainees through some of the more common forms of abuse they are likely to suffer at the hands of their captors. The idea is that the captured soldier will be better able to withstand the real thing if he has been exposed to the abuse in a controlled way during training. The training that Colonel Banks developed for Leso was to teach him how to perform the biscuit role safely, ethically, and humanely. For the first time in my military career, I read a report where the DOD inspector had gotten the story about the SERE psychology training at Fort Bragg all wrong. Morgan Banks did not teach torture. The big problem is that the DOD inspector who did this investigation never, ever talked to Colonel Banks, his staff, or me about any of this. Thus Colonel Banks would be falsely attacked in the press by other psychologists as a doctor who teaches torture. It was either one hell of a lie, flat-out bullshit, or a factual error—it didn't happen the way the August 2006 DOD inspector said it happened.

In July 2007, Katherine Eban published an article in *Vanity Fair* titled "Rorschach and Awe." In this article, Eban chronicled how the leadership in Cuba in 2002 brought in two contract CIA psychologist operatives to reverse engineer SERE tactics. She got the story and the facts right. I was happy to see this article, frankly, because in a way it vindicated my colleagues and me on the PENS Task Force, and it put the blame on the CIA, where it belonged. In particular, the story cleared the name of Colonel Morgan Banks. He had nothing to do with the abuse of detainees at either Gitmo or Abu Ghraib. But in a way, it was too late. My character and his had already been attacked, tarnished, and I could hear the quiet whispers behind my back that Colonel James was torturing people. I had put so much of myself into fixing the hell I found in Gitmo and Abu Ghraib, and here I was accused of torturing people, of using my skills as a psychologist to harm the people I was supposed to protect. That hurt.

Other articles got some of the information correct but not enough. For example, the *New Yorker* published a story about how psychologists from Fort Bragg's SERE school were reverse engineering SERE and teaching interrogators how to torture people. Well, my colleagues at Fort Bragg had nothing to do with this. As the *Vanity Fair* article correctly explained, it was contract psychologists from the CIA. Army psychologists and I got blamed for this and the damage was already done by the time the *Vanity Fair* article had been published. The facts were irrelevant to our critics; people just passed on the "truth" they heard about how my colleagues and I were torturing prisoners.

This was especially painful and hurtful when people who called themselves doctors and health care professionals crafted a letter and published it on the Web, attacking my integrity, my person, and most importantly my sense of humanity without any hard evidence that I had ever done anything wrong. Their plan was to discredit all of the military officers who served on the PENS Task Force and use this to pressure the American Psychological Association to withdraw its support of military psychologists.

The amazing thing was that the people who wrote the slanderous letter about me tried to indict me without any evidence that I had ever been at Gitmo or Abu Ghraib during the abuses. Their plan backfired. Their attacks pissed off psychologists from across the country. Anyone who knew me or had ever worked with me knew that I could never strip and sodomize a prisoner. And after being through hell in Abu Ghraib, this soldier wasn't going to stand by and let people accuse him of such atrocities. At a meeting of the American Psychological Association in 2006, I confronted one of my critics and threatened to shut his mouth for him if he didn't do it himself. I'm told it was the most excitement at an APA meeting in about twenty years.

I also responded publicly to the assault on my character with a letter to the APA president:

> The authors of this letter—who do not know me, my values or my work—have seen fit to besmirch my reputation by associating me with the perpetration of torture. Let me provide just a few facts for the authors' information. I have never been through "SERE" training. I do not teach "SERE" techniques. I do not use nor have I ever used "SERE" techniques in any aspect of my work related to interrogations. Dr. Morgan Banks has emphasized repeatedly that in addition to being unethical, using a "SERE" approach in an interrogation would be counterproductive to obtaining useful information. I strongly suspect that using a "SERE" approach to an interrogation would yield data worthless for investigative and destructive for adjudicatory purposes.
>
> I will be as clear as I possibly can: I strongly object to, have never used, and will never use torture, cruel, or abusive treatment or punishment of any kind, for any reason, in any setting. They are antithetical to who I am as a person and as an officer in the United States military. Had any of the individuals who signed the open letter saw fit to ask me, I would have provided this information to them directly. Apparently none believed it worthwhile to give

me that opportunity before using my name in a letter that they then distributed widely, including to the media.

Throughout my career, in all my work, I have done my best to adhere to the highest standards of ethical conduct. For me, that has meant treating every individual whom I have encountered—from generals in the United States Army, to custodians at military bases around the globe, to detainees in United States custody—with dignity and with respect. Never has anyone in my chain of command ordered me to do anything inconsistent with this code of behavior. Having custody and control over an individual is an awesome responsibility. When I was sent to Abu Ghraib, following the well-publicized abuses, I relied upon psychology and well-known psychologists to help me fulfill my mission—to develop training and implement systems designed to prevent further acts of abuse. The support of these colleagues, whose research and materials I took with me to Iraq, was invaluable—not only in terms of their expertise, but also because of the values that imbue their approach to psychology. I will be forever grateful to them for being with me in spirit on that difficult mission.

I will likewise be grateful to other colleagues, such as Dr. Mike Gelles, who took concrete action that has been made public, to stop detainee abuses. It is my understanding that a United States Senate committee will hold hearings on the issue of interrogation practices. I welcome this development.

Please let me be clear: Letters such as the one sent to you do harm. APA's continuing work has given psychologists an invaluable resource to fight against ill-informed and misguided promoters of harsh and abusive interrogation techniques. We are making excellent progress in that fight. Letters that name and that associate individuals with torture through innuendo have no place in an informed and responsible discussion. They are deeply painful. They are also extremely discouraging to psychologists in the military seeking to do the right thing, many of whom are early in their careers and often in dangerous settings far from family and from loved ones.

A groundswell of support began for military psychologists around late June 2007. A group of over one hundred nationally recognized psychologists wrote a letter in support of my character and the work of military psychologists to the president of the American Psychological Association. People got downright pissed that I, a decorated military officer and psychologist, was ever attacked in this way. Fifty-five psychologists signed a letter sent to the APA president in my defense:

> We want to respond to your open letter to APA President Sharon Brehm, in which you strongly object to the implication that you have ever, in any setting, been involved in the use of torture, cruel and abusive treatment or punishment. We appreciate the need for you to speak out in honor of your dignity and integrity.
>
> We want you to know that we believe that this unfortunate portrayal is antithetical to who you are as a person and as an officer in the United States military. The portrayal is certainly antithetical to what we know about you.

We believe that throughout your career you have done your best to adhere to the highest standards of ethical conduct. We are pleased to hear that no one in your chain of command ordered you to do anything inconsistent with this code of behavior.

We are aware that you are a person of color who has taken a unique leadership role among psychologists in the military. We perceive you to be a hero in your work at Abu Ghraib to develop training and to implement systems to prevent further acts of abuse. We are proud of your application of psychological research, materials and principles in doing so.

We are very pleased to hear that you perceive that APA's continuing work has given psychologists an invaluable resource to fight against promoters of harsh and abusive interrogation techniques, and that we are making progress in that arena.

We regret that well-meaning psychologists have engaged in the listing of your and others' names associated with torture, directly and through innuendo. We can only imagine the demoralizing impact on you and others. We strongly regret this, and want you to know that many others of us see things differently.

In August 2007, the American Psychological Association held its national convention in San Francisco. The more extreme anti-Bush, antiwar APA members made a motion to have all military psychologists withdrawn from DOD detention facilities around the world. They had no data that I, nor any military psychologists, had ever done anything wrong. It became clear to me that their misguided efforts were really an attempt to express their hate and outrage over the Republican Party, President Bush, and their opposition to the war. The motion failed miserably. One colleague said, "Larry, now let me get this straight. Twenty prisoners at Gitmo are on a hunger strike, three or four of them committed suicide, there was a massive riot at the prison at Camp Bucca, Iraq . . . and somehow pulling out all the psychologists will improve the situation. That's what they want us to believe? This does not make any sense whatsoever."

The motion that passed was a strong statement saying that the organization was firmly against torture. *Fine with me*, I thought at the time. *So am I.* It also listed a set of harsh techniques that psychologists were prohibited from ever advising in a consultation with interrogators. I had no hesitation about supporting that statement. Those techniques were not used under my watch at Gitmo or Abu Ghraib and I would never recommend them as an ethical, moral way to obtain intel.

The debate did help answer some of the questions raised about the role of the psychologist in this war. Psychologists should not do interrogations. They should stay out of the interrogation booth. I always knew that if I were ever to be court-martialed while at Gitmo or Abu Ghraib, it would have been because I lost my objectivity and did something stupid while trying to be an interrogator. I knew that I had to stay out of that room and not be an active participant in the interrogation. My job was to help interrogators avoid behavioral drift. In other words, I helped them stay within the boundaries of the SOP and stay away from abusive behaviors.

Throughout all of this debate I had many conversations with well-respected military psychologists from around the country. I remember talking with Colonel Tim Watson from the Army's Intel Command at Fort Meade, Maryland. Tom was a senior, highly regarded Army psychologist. I debated the issue of combatant versus doctor with him and Colonel Banks on many occasions. The question that I had struggled with for so long—*How can I be a psychologist and a combatant at the same time?*—kept coming up over and over as we talked.

"You can't, Larry," Colonel Watson told me during one of these talks. "You have to keep your role as a psychologist and as a doctor separate and never shall the two cross. It would be like being someone's defense attorney while also serving as their prosecuting attorney at the same time. It ain't gonna work."

From these many conversations with Colonel Banks, Lieutenant Colonel Dobson—my deputy in the Department of Psychology when we were at Walter Reed who was involved with Major Leso's assignment to Gitmo—and I began to shape the national DOD policy for the biscuit. Now, what has evolved is that the biscuit psychologist provides no actual medical care and serves as a military officer in intel units. Others provide mental health care, but the biscuit psychologist stays firmly in the role of soldier, not doctor.

14
Conclusions

September 2007–January 2008

I spent much of my time after my stint in Abu Ghraib analyzing what I learned as Biscuit 1 and what can be done to prevent a repeat of the hell we faced there. The worst outcome of our experience in Abu Ghraib would be to learn nothing from what happened there, to blindly stumble into the next detainee operation without bringing with us the lessons we learned from fixing that hellhole. As I told those young captains at Tripler, the mess at Abu Ghraib happened because no one was in charge, no one knew what had to be done, and no one led the way.

So what can—and needs—to be done as we move into the future? Where are our shortfalls and our vulnerabilities in this war on terrorism? How can the United States fight a "new" enemy effectively, while remaining within the humane boundaries of the Geneva Conventions and presenting a good role model of democracy to the rest of the world? Are there very distinct things that need to be done immediately in order to achieve success, and prevent a future Abu Ghraib from occurring?

We have come a long way since the 9/11 attacks. At that time our nation was totally unprepared to deal with the rates of mental illness, behavioral problems, the number of juvenile terrorists, and the myriad cultural issues of our enemy, as well as the asymmetrical battlefield tactics, such as IEDs and urban warfare. We went to war without enough mental health staff in place to treat the soldiers at Abu Ghraib and the detainees—a moral tragedy of sorts. The shame of it all was that the leaders failed to plan for it or denied that it was a real need. Along the way, out of revenge, pathology, or just plain old stupidity, some few American soldiers chose to torture detainees at Abu Ghraib. Clearly, these acts were a combination of failed leadership, moral disengagement by the soldiers who committed the acts, and unchecked behavioral drift.

We now know that most of the abuses at Abu Ghraib had nothing to do with interrogations. Rather, the abuse was done by a few soldiers who had become combat ineffective under the cloak of darkness, abusing the detainees for their own pleasure and twisted needs. It is a fact that out of any large number of human beings, soldiers or otherwise, there will be some small percentage who will take advantage of others, particularly the weak and powerless, to indulge their own worst, most craven desires. Unfortunately, at Abu Ghraib their leaders were not there to ensure proper adherence to standards.

I was brought to Abu Ghraib to put procedures in place to prevent these atrocities from ever happening again. I'm proud to say I successfully completed that mission. I did it. I trained a biscuit staff and monitored the behavior, training, and job performance of interrogators. We did this not to teach abuse but rather to prevent it. By the time I left Abu Ghraib in October 2004, major milestones had been reached. We had videotaping

capability for all interrogations and one-way mirrors in all interrogation rooms. We became important consultants to the intel
commander as well as the military police who guarded the detainees. Slowly but surely, a hospital was built with inpatient
psychiatric capabilities. Colonel Robert Thomas, Abu Ghraib's
post commander, spent $300 million improving the infrastruc-
ture there, building a hospital, upgrading the living facilities for
the soldiers, and improving the quality of life for the detainees.
Abu Ghraib had three colonels, Colonel Thomas, the new hospital commander, and the new intel center director, who were
dedicated to humanity and always doing the right moral things
at all times. This is a secret that America never knew. The mass
media frenzy forced us all to be mentally stuck on those horrible
pictures, the abuses, the torture. Mention "Abu Ghraib" and
those images immediately come to my mind. Most people assume that little has been done to improve the situation in Abu
Ghraib, that perhaps the outright abuse has been stopped but
probably little else has changed. Those people are seriously
mistaken. Somehow, the nation was never told that the United
States spent over $300 million to do the right moral thing at Abu
Ghraib after the abuses were uncovered.

What must we do to prevent abuses in the future? First and
foremost, we need well-trained interrogators and military police
who have responsibility for the humane care and custody of the
detainees. When I arrived at Guantanamo in 2003 the interrogation regulations were so broad they allowed almost anything to
happen, except the death of a detainee—that would have been
considered bad. Now the regulations that govern interrogations

and the rulebook for the military police have outlawed abusive tactics for interrogations and for the military police.

Second, unlike at the beginning of the war, we have a training course for psychologists who work in the detention arena. They are incredibly well trained. Unlike Major John Leso, these young officers have a detailed set of guidelines that lay out what a BSCT psychologist can and cannot do. Leso was flying blind, doing his best to figure out the rules on his own. We know now that well-trained psychologists should remain a major part of the detention and interrogation team. Why? Because they can provide oversight on when behaviors are starting to drift and identify the early signs of abuse. These are the critical things the Department of Defense can do to prevent the occurrence of abuses or torture in prisons, whether in a U.S. prison or a POW facility.

Lieutenant Colonel Frantz once told me, "Sir, I have no problem with torturing these guys to get information if it will save American lives. Heck, Colonel, I don't see what the big deal is about using information out of a detainee's medical record. If that's going to help us save a soldier's life, well, what's the problem with it?" I suspect many civilians would take the same position, but my experience in working at Gitmo and Abu Ghraib reaffirmed the position I previously held on these issues. I now know, more surely than ever before, that I am against torture.

When Lieutenant Colonel Frantz brought the issue up, I explained my position by saying, "Frantz, is America going to be a moral leader in the world? When you torture a prisoner, the information you get is not reliable. We cannot allow our anger and need for revenge to serve as a compass in the global war on terrorism. It's really about morality, and Frantz, we must treat every human being with decency and respect. I was taught as a child to always take the high road, and as an officer, I was taught to never violate the Geneva Conventions. It will only fuel the enemy."

As an American soldier who believes wholeheartedly that we must fight the Muslim extremists who want to see us all dead, and fight them aggressively, I support the American military's effort to extract valuable intel from detainees. But I do not support torture, because it is simply wrong from a moral perspective, it violates my duties as a psychologist, and—this is an important point that can negate the need to debate the first two—it is not as effective as the other methods of interrogation that I put in place at Gitmo and Abu Ghraib.

Much has been written about Major General Geoffrey D. Miller, the commander at Abu Ghraib and earlier at Guantanamo Bay. He never ordered me to teach torture. It was the direct opposite: he told me to teach the interrogators how to work with detainees without any abuse whatsoever. His gruff appearance and style got in his way at times. In terms of how he was presented in the media, he sometimes did himself no favors with the way he interacted with people. But it was General Miller's desire to do the right thing that led to the humane treatment of the juveniles at Guantanamo and the large field hospital being built at Abu Ghraib. Likewise, I have no data to show that Major Leso ever tortured anyone. Leso's efforts to change the way prisoners were interrogated at Gitmo was like watching an aircraft carrier do a 360-degree turn in a harbor. It was going to change course and head in a new direction, but everybody watching knew that it was going to take some time. Major Leso got that carrier started in the turn, and eventually it did head in a new direction.

The BSCT and all medical services are now separate from one another and there is no sharing of medical information. Moreover, we now have the American Psychological Association's guidelines for psychologists who work in the intel and detention arenas to serve as a guide.

From the day I arrived at Abu Ghraib in June 2004 there were no more incidents of abuse reported by an interrogator or a psychologist, and we handed the prison back to the Iraqis on September 6, 2006, in better condition than we found it. There also have been no incidents of abuse at Guantanamo Bay by either an interrogator or psychologist reported since my arrival in Cuba in January 2003. Clearly, the role of the psychologist on the battlefield in the global war on terrorism has made a difference.

The procedures that were put into place have served to prevent abuses and help ensure that all under our care and custody are treated with humanity and respect.

Epilogue

April 2008

It is very fitting that I have been deployed to Guantanamo Bay, Cuba, once again. The place where I first deployed in support of the global war on terrorism is the place where my twenty-two-year military career ends. Many things have changed since I left Gitmo in May 2003. It is now under the command leadership of the U.S. Navy rather than the Army. When I departed here in 2003, there were over 600 detainees. We now have fewer than 275, with plans for the numbers to decrease even more over time.

The harsh tactics are gone and the overall experience has improved for detainees. The minimal living conditions have been replaced with a meal menu that has six choices, state-of-the-art facilities, a cultural adviser, a detainee hospital, and rigid adherence to the Geneva Conventions guidelines. The International Committee of the Red Cross has open access to interview any detainee. Guantanamo Bay Naval Station no longer mirrors an overseas remote-duty station with few amenities. It has matured into a sophisticated military complex with a Starbucks, wireless LAN systems, cell phones, nightly movies at an outdoor theater, rock concerts, regular appearances by celebrities, and frequent visits by family members of those deployed here. The Gitmo detention facility is now state-of-the-art. It has a thirty-bed hospital, with five to ten physicians and fifteen nurses on duty. The inpatient psych unit has a psychologist, psychiatrist, nurses, and psych techs dedicated to treating the mental health needs of the detainees. Many of the detainees have attorneys and there have been over a thousand legal visits in 2007 alone.

Admiral Mark "Buz" Buzby is the commander of Joint Task Force Guantanamo Bay, Cuba. He is a far cry from the early leaders at this facility. A Merchant Marine Academy graduate and polished gentleman, he is indeed a career military officer. He and his deputy commander, Brigadier General Cam Cameron, dispel the notion that you have to be a foulmouthed jerk to be a great military leader. They have set a tone of decency and respect for all of Gitmo. They simply would not tolerate abuse, hate, torture, or anything that resembles indecency. The chief of staff, Navy captain Pete Husta, was brought in to organize and carry out the admiral's intent of "humane care and custody" for the detainees. Captain Husta is a brilliant organizer and motivator and has a way of getting the task force to move in the right direction at all times.

Navy captain Pat McCarthy is the senior attorney at Gitmo. He and his deputy commander, Dan Jones, are two of the finest legal minds I have come to know. They, together with their large legal team, keep us on the right side of the Geneva Conventions and common sense. They are hypervigilant at making sure Gitmo does its very best to always take the correct moral and legal road.

Paul Rester is the director of the Joint Intelligence Group at

Gitmo. He brings to the job four decades of skill, experience, and most important, humanity. Paul would simply not tolerate any of his interrogators abusing any one—I admire and respect him. Also, the FBI has a large detachment there and works hand-in-hand with the DOD intel community. One complements the other and as a result, the level of skill, expertise, and professionalism is increased tenfold.

The biggest change is that the guard force is under the command of a career Army military police officer by the name of Colonel Bruce Vargo. He was command-selected for this position rather than being a reservist who was randomly assigned here with his reserve unit. Back in 2002 and 2003, many of the leaders here were reserve officers, and although they had good intentions, many of them simply didn't know what they were doing. That has changed. The reserve and guard force today have come a long way. The soldiers, sailors, and marines who make up the task force here are well trained and represent the best America has to offer. Colonel Vargo is a graduate of the Army War College and brings to Gitmo and the Joint Task Force a level of competence that was lacking in 2002 and 2003 among the guard force leadership. His leadership has made a difference. Now the guard force is incredibly well trained and is far superior to the untrained guards of the early Abu Ghraib and Gitmo abuse era. Clearly, abuse and torture will not be tolerated, from the youngest private to the senior officer. We are one another's keeper and are always hypervigilant against abuse and torture. I am fully confident about what would happen if I walked into the detainee camp late one night, found a young guard on duty, and suggested we take one of the prisoners out of his cell so we could rough him up and try to get some intel, maybe even have some fun along the way.

That young sergeant would look at this colonel and say, "No sir. That is against my orders," and then he'd be on the phone immediately, within minutes, reporting the incident to his superiors. And I'd be in a shitload of trouble. That's exactly what *should* happen, and I sleep easy at night knowing that this culture is now the norm at Gitmo.

The biscuit at Gitmo is alive and well, established as a major and important part of the mission. All biscuit officers at Gitmo and around the world receive intense training prior to serving in a biscuit capacity. Unlike Major Leso, these young officers come to the fight well trained and incredibly prepared. They will have read all that has been written on their roles, duties, and functions in detention facilities. Moreover, there is now a network of biscuits available for consultation 24/7. We did not have this when I arrived here in 2003.

Many have moved on to the next phase in their life. General Miller retired from the Army. Major Leso resigned his Army commission and no longer resides in this country. I think of John often and hope that he is well. Lieutenant Colonel Denise Dobson is now the chief of Walter Reed's psychology department. On November 1, 2007, she was selected for full colonel. Denise has excelled at helping the Army and the Department of Defense develop policy that serves as the law for those health professionals working in the intel community. She, along with Colonel Banks, myself, and others, developed a course to train all new biscuit psychologists, who now undergo a three-week intensive course coupled with a six-month Web-based portion.

Colonel Banks remains as the command psychologist for the Special Operations Command at Fort Bragg. He has made a real difference in the fight against evil and terrorism. Colonel Banks is the finest operational psychologist I have ever known. Our nation owes him greatly. Lieutenant Colonel Frantz completed his deployment at Abu Ghraib and returned home to chewing tobacco, hunting, and the beauty of rural America. I often think of him and many of the other soldiers I served with in Abu Ghraib and at Gitmo. Almost daily, when I'm fatigued, in pain, and wanting to stop, I think back to the coffin of the young soldier we loaded on that C-130 in Kuwait. Those images have served to fuel me in ways I never could have imagined.

I will retire from the Army at the end of this deployment. I hope to be back in Janet's arms and never leave her side. I cannot put into words how much I owe her. Her heart, touch, brilliant mind, and humanity have kept me balanced and have allowed me to fight evil in foreign lands around the world. As I write these words, my mind is flipping through a scrapbook in my head and I see clear images of the faces we have lost along the way—fine men and women who fought for their nation and what our nation stands for. Indeed, it has been an honor to walk among America's best for a little while. I am them, they are me, we are one, in this global war on terrorism. I am a better person, human being, father, soldier, and psychologist for having served. Most importantly, I am a better American and citizen because of my experience with the U.S. military. With pride in my heart, I rest easy knowing that we have such great Americans in the fight, at the tip of the spear, keeping us safe, keeping us strong, fighting for freedom around the world. Indeed it was a privilege to stand between good and evil and be a part of the fight to help save humanity.

This is Biscuit 1 signing out.

Sequence of Events Regarding U.S. Military Prisons in Guantanamo Bay, Cuba, and Abu Ghraib, Iraq

2002

JANUARY 11, 2002: U.S. forces transport twenty men seized as enemy combatants in Afghanistan to the U.S. military base in Guantanamo Bay, Cuba, which previously had been used mainly for Navy support and refugee operations.

FEBRUARY 19, 2002: Civil rights advocates challenge the detainment of the Afghani prisoners at Guantanamo Bay, filing a brief in federal court claiming three of the men are being held illegally. A federal judge soon dismisses the case.

APRIL 25, 2002: Construction crews in Guantanamo Bay complete Camp Delta, the more permanent, long-term housing for detainees. The creation of Camp Delta is seen as a signal that the military expects a long-term detainee operation.

JUNE 2002: Army Major John Leso arrives in Guantanamo Bay to provide psychiatric services to detainees and military personnel.

SEPTEMBER 20, 2002: The Army assigns Major General Geoffrey D. Miller as commander of Joint Task Force Guantanamo. In this position, Miller is responsible for the entire operation of the military base in Cuba, but by this point the detainee operation has grown large enough and important enough to become his primary focus.

2003

JANUARY 2003: Colonel Larry James arrives in Guantanamo Bay to replace Leso and improve the treatment of the detainees.

MARCH 19, 2003: Coalition forces begin striking military targets in Iraq. President Bush addresses the nation and says the strikes are "the opening stages of what will be a broad and concerted campaign."

MAY 5, 2003: Colonel Larry James leaves Guantanamo Bay after instituting policies intended to prevent prisoner abuse at all military prisons.

AUGUST 2003: The U.S. military takes over the existing prison facilities at Abu Ghraib in Iraq. The ramshackle buildings had been used for years by the Iraqi government for detaining criminals, the mentally ill, and political prisoners. Most recently, Iraqi dictator Saddam Hussein had used Abu Ghraib to detain and torture his own citizens.

OCTOBER 2003: The number of prisoners at Abu Ghraib has already reached seven thousand, guarded by ninety-two MPs. The International Committee of the Red Cross (ICRC), a humanitarian group that monitors the conditions of prisons and other situations in which people are held against their will, sends a delegation to the prison. The ICRC inspectors report that the U.S. military is abusing prisoners.

OCTOBER 9, 2003: The ICRC, which also has been monitoring conditions at the detainee camps in Guantanamo Bay, issues a "statement of concern." The statement calls attention to what the ICRC calls the "deterioration in the psychological health" of detainees at Guantanamo Bay.

OCTOBER TO DECEMBER 2003: The photos that will become the focus of the investigation into the abuse of detainees at Abu Ghraib are taken during this time period.

2004

JANUARY 4–8, 2004: Another report from the ICRC states that conditions and treatment of prisoners at Abu Ghraib are improving.

JANUARY 13, 2004: The abuse of prisoners at Abu Ghraib comes to light when a military policeman with the 800th Military Police Brigade, in charge of security at the prison, gives a computer disk with digital photographs to a military investigator. The photos depict nude detainees at Abu Ghraib piled on top of one another, wearing hoods and electrodes, being taunted by guard dogs, and similar scenes. The photos also depict several identifiable soldiers posing for the camera.

JANUARY 14, 2004: One day after the photos are given to the military investigator, the Army launches a criminal investigation into possible abuse of prisoners at Abu Ghraib.

JANUARY 18, 2004: Four days into the investigation, military leaders are certain that some prisoners at Abu Ghraib have been abused. The senior commander in Iraq, Lieutenant General

Ricardo Sanchez, responds by reprimanding Brigadier General Janis Karpinski, the commander of the 800th MP Brigade who was responsible for preventing the abuse. Sanchez also suspends a National Guard officer and a company commander at Abu Ghraib.

JANUARY 19, 2004: Six days after the photos are given to the investigator and five days into the criminal investigation, Sanchez orders an additional investigation of the 800th MP Brigade's performance at Abu Ghraib.

JANUARY 31, 2004: Major General Antonio M. Taguba is appointed to head the investigation into the 800th MP Brigade.

FEBRUARY 26, 2004: Sanchez confirms in a press conference that seventeen military personnel have been "suspended from their duties" while the investigation continues. He declines to give any further information about allegations against them.

MARCH 12, 2004: Taguba delivers his report on the allegations of prisoners at Abu Ghraib to his commanders. The report's conclusion states that Taguba found evidence of widespread abuse of prisoners, not just isolated incidents.

MARCH 20, 2004: The Department of Defense announces that six soldiers will be court martialed on charges that they abused prisoners at Abu Ghraib.

MARCH 22, 2004: The Department of Defense announces that Miller, the commander at Guantanamo Bay, whom James worked under while rectifying abusive conditions at that military base, will become deputy commander for detainee operations, Combined Joint Task Force 7/Multi-National Force—Iraq. This position puts Miller in charge of the prison at Abu Ghraib.

APRIL 4, 2004: The Army confirms that investigators have recommended administrative discipline against several commanders responsible for managing prisons in Iraq. The Army does not release the names of the commanders to be disciplined.

APRIL 12, 2004: Producers with the CBS television news program *60 Minutes II* contact the Department of Defense and state that the network has some of the photos showing prisoner abuse at Abu Ghraib and will broadcast them. Military officials ask the network not to broadcast the photos, saying the images will incite violence in Iraq.

APRIL 28, 2004: After delaying the broadcast several times while the Department of Defense and the Bush administration made their case for why the images could harm the U.S. military, CBS shows the photos to the public. President Bush and Secretary of Defense Donald Rumsfeld say that, though they had been briefed on the allegations of abuse, they had not seen the images before CBS aired them.

MAY 1, 2004: The Department of Defense updates the progress of the ongoing investigation at Abu Ghraib: two soldiers are relieved of their duties, four more receive an administrative reprimand, and another receives a milder reprimand.

MAY 6, 2004: In a Rose Garden speech, President Bush says he apologized to the Arab world for the abuse at Abu Ghraib while meeting with Jordan's King Abdullah. "I told him I was sorry for the humiliation suffered by the Iraqi prisoners and the humiliation suffered by their families," he said.

MAY 7, 2004: Rumsfeld testifies before the Senate Armed Services Committee. "I feel terrible about what happened to these Iraqi detainees. They are human beings. They were in

U.S. custody. Our country had an obligation to treat them right. We didn't, and that was wrong. So to those Iraqis who were mistreated by members of the U.S. armed forces, I offer my deepest apology. It was inconsistent with the values of our nation. It was inconsistent with the teachings of the military, to the men and women of the armed forces. And it was certainly fundamentally un-American." He also says he failed to promptly inform the president and Congress when he first learned of the abuse.

MAY 10, 2004: A report by Seymour Hersh in the *New Yorker* magazine provides further detail and photos of the prisoner abuse.

MAY 19, 2004: Responding to queries about how prisoner abuse could have happened on his watch, Sanchez tells U.S. senators that he has repeatedly issued orders to treat detainees in Iraq humanely. He tells the senators that in September and October 2003, and again in May 2004, he "issued interrogation policies that reiterated the application of the Geneva Conventions and required that all interrogations be conducted in the lawful and humane manner with command oversight."

MAY 24, 2004: President Bush delivers a speech in which he outlines five steps for improving security in Iraq and helping the nation move toward democracy. In the course of that speech, Bush proposes demolishing the prison at Abu Ghraib.

JUNE 2004, the first week: Colonel Larry James arrives in Abu Ghraib to address the problem of prisoner abuse and provide psychiatric services.

OCTOBER 20, 2004: One of the soldiers accused of some of the worst abuse, Staff Sergeant Ivan Frederick, pleads guilty to charges of conspiracy, dereliction of duty, maltreatment of detainees, assault, and committing an indecent act. In return for his guilty plea, prosecutors agree to drop other charges. Among other abuses, Frederick was accused of making three prisoners masturbate. He also admitted to punching one prisoner in the chest so hard that his heart stopped and he had to be resuscitated. Frederick is sentenced to eight years in prison.

2005

JANUARY 14–15, 2005: Army Specialist Charles Graner, considered by most to be the ringleader of those participating in the abuse at Abu Ghraib, is found guilty of conspiracy to maltreat detainees, and failing to protect detainees from abuse, cruelty, and maltreatment. Graner also is found guilty on charges of assault, indecency, adultery, and obstruction of justice. He is sentenced to ten years in prison.

MAY 5, 2005: The Department of Defense announces that, as a result of the investigation into the abuse at Abu Ghraib and her failure to properly run the prison, Brigadier General Janis Karpinski, commander of the 800th MP Brigade, has been demoted to colonel.

SEPTEMBER 26–27, 2005: Private First Class Lynndie England, featured prominently in the abuse photos while posing with detainees and perhaps the most widely recognized of the accused soldiers, is convicted of conspiracy, four counts of maltreating detainees, and one count of committing an indecent act. England receives a three-year prison sentence. The lead prosecutor said England had admitted to humiliating and degrading prisoners to entertain other MPs. Referring to the notorious photographs of England, the prosecutor told the court, "The accused knew what she was doing. She was laughing and joking. She is enjoying, she is participating, all for her own sick humor." During the early portion of the investigations, England was pregnant with a child fathered by co-defendant Graner. She gave birth to his son in October 2004, before her conviction.

A total of twelve soldiers have been convicted of charges related to the abuse at Abu Ghraib, including those who received minor sentences.

2006

SEPTEMBER 6, 2006: The U.S. government hands over control of Abu Ghraib to the Iraqi government. The prison has not been demolished.

Acknowledgments

There are many I would like to thank for their support, guidance, and assistance in preparing this book. First I need to thank my wife, Janet, for her support, counsel, and advice. It was a three-year journey to prepare this book, and without Janet I would not have had the constant resolve to complete it. She helped me bring out the humane and moral issues I struggled with along the way.

I will always owe a great deal to Colonel Morgan Banks. Morgan is respected by many four-star Army generals around the country, and without his support and advice I never would have been successful at Gitmo and Abu Ghraib.

Dr. Phil Zimbardo, the author of the famous Stanford Prison Experiment, has been an immense resource, friend, and supporter. Phil and I have many political differences but what we have in common is a desire to see that all in our custody are treated humanely and with respect.

My agent, Gillian Mackenzie, was a true godsend. Gillian had poise, brilliance, and the respect of many in the book publishing industry, and the calmness to navigate me through this journey. Most of all, she became a trusted confidante and friend.

I would like to thank Mitch Hoffman and his staff at Grand Central Publishing. Mitch had a vision for my book that was ideal, and his intellect and style made it an easier task for me.

I faced many bitter, diabolical, unfounded, and misguided threats upon my person by fellow psychologists. Without the support of Drs. Steve Behnke, Melba Vasquez, Jennifer Kelly, Nadine Kaslow, Gerry Koocher, Rosie Phillips Bingham, John Robinson, and Ray Folen it would have been easier to just resign my membership in the American Psychological Association and move on. Thanks to all who signed the letter supporting my character and work in the global war on terror. Their support made a difference in my life at a very difficult time. Thank you!

Index

Indianapolis
Marion County
Public Library

Renew by Phone
269-5222

Renew on the Web
www.imcpl.org

For General Library Information
please call 269-1700